Advance Praise for
My Mother's Money

"Losing someone is never easy. Like Beth Pinsker, I know what it's like to navigate loss and the financial aftermath. *My Mother's Money* can help make one of the hardest times in your life easier."

—Tiffany "The Budgetnista" Aliche,
New York Times bestselling author

"Drawing on her training as a CERTIFIED FINANCIAL PLANNER® and decades as a personal finance journalist, Beth Pinsker details her journey as her mother's financial caregiver to create a template for those who follow in her footsteps. *My Mother's Money* is a heartfelt guide for family caregivers to ease their journey, supply resources, and provide hope."

—Mary Beth Franklin, CFP®,
Social Security expert, and founder of RetirePro, LLC

"MarketWatch columnist Beth Pinsker has written a vital and relatable book for anyone and everyone dealing with the financial issues that come with aging, whether their own or those of a family member. Based in part on her own experiences as her mother aged and needed assistance, *My Mother's Money* provides practical tools and advice that will help any financial caregiver avoid pitfalls. Among the tips I especially liked were her mother's medical cheat sheet that listed her vital information that any healthcare provider would need. In addition, Pinsker describes the hurdles banks and other financial institutions place on the use of durable powers of attorney and the advantages of having a joint account. This very approachable book will help family caregivers avoid hours of frustration and wasted time."

—Harry Margolis,
elder law attorney and author of *Get Your Ducks in a Row:
The Baby Boomers Guide to Estate Planning*

MY
MOTHER'S
MONEY

MY MOTHER'S MONEY

· · · · · · ·

A Guide to Financial Caregiving

Beth Pinsker, CFP®

CROWN CURRENCY
New York

CROWN CURRENCY
An imprint of the Crown Publishing Group
A division of Penguin Random House LLC
1745 Broadway
New York, NY 10019
crownpublishing.com
penguinrandomhouse.com

Library of Congress Cataloging-in-Publication Data
Names: Pinsker, Beth [author]
Title: My mother's money: a guide to financial caregiving / by Beth Pinsker, CFP.
Description: First paperback edition. | New York, NY: Crown Currency, [2025] | Includes bibliographical references and index.
Identifiers: LCCN 2025008365 (print) | LCCN 2025008366 (ebook) | ISBN 9780593800577 trade paperback | ISBN 9780593800584 ebook
Subjects: LCSH: Aging parents—Finance, Personal | Aging parents—Care | Terminally ill—Finance, Personal | Adult children of aging parents
Classification: LCC HG179 .P5535 2025 (print) | LCC HG179 (ebook) | DDC 332.0240085—dc23/eng/20250731
LC record available at https://lccn.loc.gov/2025008365
LC ebook record available at https://lccn.loc.gov/2025008366

ISBN: 978-0-593-80057-7
Ebook ISBN: 978-0-593-80058-4

Editors: Leah Trouwborst and Madhulika Sikka
Associate editor: Amy Li
Production editor: Liana Faughnan
Text designer: Aubrey Khan
Production: Chris Andrus
Copy editor: Lynn Anderson
Proofreaders: Kevin Clift, Miriam Taveras, Chris Fortunato, and Tess Rossi
Indexer: Jay Kreider
Marketer: Tara Gilbride

Manufactured in the United States of America

1st Printing

First Paperback Edition

The authorized representative in the EU for product safety and compliance is Penguin Random House Ireland, Morrison Chambers, 32 Nassau Street, Dublin D02 YH68, Ireland, https://eu -contact.penguin.ie.

Simply, and always, for Ann.

Contents

Introduction

The happiest day I had taking care of my mother's money was when she called me enraged a few months into her illness to ask me to dispute a credit card charge. She was in bed at a rehab facility in Florida and I was sitting in my car in Brooklyn, running an errand. Her aide had stopped by her apartment to bring her mail. "What's this $12.99 charge from the cable company?" my mom demanded. "Can you tell them it's wrong?"

I burst into tears, then started laughing. Ann Pinsker was back, for the moment. After many months of her being seriously ill and not paying any attention to the world around her, I was ecstatic that she was on the ball and ordering me around. I had never wanted to be in charge of her finances, and the whole time I managed her affairs I felt certain she was going to be mad at me for messing up her very precise system. I deposited her checks with a bank app on my phone, for goodness sake, and that was just not the way she did things.

It was not easy to step into her shoes. I did the best I could, but even though I'm a financial planning columnist and CERTIFIED FINANCIAL PLANNER® professional, I stumbled at every turn as my mom's financial caregiver. I had book knowledge in a situation that demanded street smarts, and that made me feel helpless against the giant financial and legal machine that governs how everything gets done in the United States.

I got through it with the help of a lot of experts, other caregivers, family, friends, and some righteous indignation. My day job at that point was writing a financial planning column for the retirement section of MarketWatch. Plus, I had thirty years of journalism experience prior to that—as a columnist at Reuters for nearly a decade and as the editor in chief at the website WalletPop—as well as what I learned from my studies for the CFP® exam. I started writing articles about the biggest issues that flummoxed me in the financial caregiving process, almost in real time as I went through them. I set about tracking down answers and figuring out solutions. Baffled by Medicare? I was able to invite the head of the government agency for a taped Q&A. When I was stuck on tax questions, a whole community of specialists offered me aid. Over my years as a personal finance writer, I interviewed hundreds of regular people and experts about estate planning and money management topics, and for this book I interviewed a hundred or so more.

I wrote this guide to pull together all that information in a way that people could easily understand, which always comes down to storytelling for me. To really get what's involved, you have to feel it. Details matter, and I knew my story best and could be as open about it as possible. So this book is primarily a description of my own journey through the morass and all the things I learned along the way. It's meant to be educational and inspirational and not to be comprehensive or to offer direct financial advice. If you have more complicated circumstances that you need help with, you'll need to consult a professional, but I hope this book will at least give you a good start.

Being a financial caregiver means that you jump into somebody else's world with little notice, take over their affairs, and stick with it to the end. Most people are dragged into this process sideways, and many do it out of a sense of family service. If you get an emergency call about a parent or an older relative—or whoever else you're responsible for—there's no telling how that person might have been handling their money. You've got to pick up the pieces the best you can.

No matter how well somebody has planned, little things get lost. Even the most on-the-ball people I talked to had their breaking point over something they couldn't figure out: Social Security problems, filing taxes, transferring money with an authorized medallion stamp. My breaking point was a lost home equity line of credit that I knew nothing about (more on that on page 211).

All the work you need to do to take care of these things is a huge slog. You might even be called upon to put your own funds on the table if you're dealing with a family member who can't afford the care they need. Know this: However impossible it seems at times, there's always some solution.

My time taking care of my mother's money encompassed a complete life cycle of events, from getting that emergency phone call to filing her final tax return after she died. For me, the intense part included handling all her bills, managing caregivers, dealing with Medicare, making sure her money would last, closing accounts, transferring assets, selling her apartment, and divvying up all her stuff. That all happened over the course of a little more than a year, which you may consider unusually short or endless, depending on your own situation. I wrote this guide in the order in which I came upon things and what I found useful to know at each point along the way to keep it from becoming too overwhelming. I imagine that readers will come to this story in a number of different ways.

If you're going through this now and need a step-by-step guide to how to get through it, you'll have my insider tips on how to manage the process, from what to say to banks to tips for recordkeeping.

If you're afraid you're going to go through this soon and want to do what you can now to make it less bad, this book will help you forestall some of the worst outcomes. Maybe you can prevent a major family fight or save some money by making decisions sooner instead of later.

If you're concerned about your own affairs, you'll get a good window into what somebody would have to go through to walk in your financial shoes. I had that feeling a lot going through this with my mom, and I changed the way I handle my own affairs to spare my kids, especially the amount of useless paperwork I stack up.

If you've already gone through this with loved ones, maybe my story will help you with your grief or at least make you feel seen for all the hard stuff you went through. Writing about my mother certainly helped me through my loss.

As you follow along, each chapter will have some action items at the end that would be helpful to do at that stage of the process, and there are more detailed resources at the end for those ready to dive in deeper.

I know it's a hard sell. Most people in the history of time have gotten sick and died without the protections they could have had with smart planning. You can go all the way back to the Bible or look at most of William Shakespeare's work for stories of inheritance fights. Today, even after a global pandemic and the constant political and economic uncertainty that started in 2020, most surveys still show that 60 to 70 percent of American adults don't have wills. That's somewhere north of 150 million people.[1]

Only a small subsection of those who do have an estate plan take the further step of setting up a trust of some kind. Depending on the study, between 50 and 60 percent have some kind of life insurance, generally through an employer.[2] Consistently less than 10 percent have long-term care insurance, with the number usually pegged at closer to 3 percent.[3]

More pet owners have some kind of continuing care plan for their pets in an emergency than name a formal legal guardian for their minor children in a will—more on that in chapter 23.

All this is happening while more than ten thousand people each day are turning 65 as the baby boom generation crests into retirement.[4] Nearly 40 percent of these folks have nothing saved for retirement and will have only Social Security to count on.[5] That could be an enormous problem in the future, as the program is forecast to start lowering benefits by 2034 or 2035 if Congress doesn't act to fix its trust fund.[6]

The rest will leave something behind, somehow. Around $84 trillion will change hands over the next twenty years in what's being called "the Great Wealth Transfer," according to a much quoted report by Cerulli Associates.[7] But how will that happen if they haven't made plans? It'll be a huge mess.

My goal is to help you understand that there are things you can do to make this process easier on both yourself and your loved ones. Most people assume that estate planning is too hard—that it's complicated, expensive, and onerous. After a year of dealing with the paperwork of sickness and death, I ask: Compared to what?

I want to chase down every random person on the street who knows they should have a will but hasn't gotten around to it yet and explain to them how much harder and more expensive it is for everyone involved *not* to do estate planning.

Luckily for my readers, you don't need to live through a bad experience to figure this out, as my story and those of the people I interviewed can be your cautionary tales.

I'll let you in right away on the biggest thing I learned in this process: It all comes down to love. You can try to scare people by showing them the math or trying logic, but those usually don't work. Ask the generations of estate attorneys and financial planners who have tried and failed. The only reason that these difficult topics are worth confronting is because we have people in our lives whom we love and who love us.

I felt that most when I was talking to hands-on caregivers for this book. I asked them all why they did the hard things they were doing. That was when they paused, their voices cracked, and they got to the heart of the matter.

Andre Morrow teared up when he told me why he retired from his job and moved in with his dad, even though they never got along. "It's just love, huge love," he said. Danielle Miura said her grandmother was the light of her life and even though she was twenty-five when she started as a caregiver, it was worth it to her to do it right. Jeanne Wiener said she had taken care of her mother for more than a decade. Her voice breaking, she said, "When things get really sucky, like they are now, and my mom is not really my mom anymore, I remember that my dad would have wanted me to."

When it was my turn to be a caregiver, I did it out of love, but maybe even more out of respect. My mom was the most competent person I have ever encountered, and she used her powers for good. She was a public school teacher and helped generations of students. She launched her high school's International Baccalaureate program, long before it became trendy, and even though the school, J. P. McCaskey in Lancaster, Pennsylvania, had always been considered something of a failing institution. She never wrote off any kids, and if that meant dropping off homework packets at the juvenile detention center on her way home for absent students in custody, that was what she did. She baked thousands of brownies, designed interactive lesson plans that would drive discussion, and sourced professional clothing for kids who didn't own sport coats to go to debate and mock trial competitions.

I'm always tempted to use the cliche and call my mom "selfless," but that denies the fact that she was her own person, with her own thoughts and dreams. My mom had lots of opinions, was well read, and had an uncanny ability to remember trivia. She was a fabulous cook who grew up in a family-owned catering business—the legendary Savadove & Getson in Philadelphia—and ran her own catering company for a time. At one point, she started a side business selling cookie telegrams—"Get Well Soon" spelled out in chocolate-dipped cookie letters and the like. She was even a published author; she co-authored a book with my English-professor father that was a teacher's guide to *The Catcher in the Rye*.[8] She had boundless energy and would cook for parties and catering jobs long into the night while the rest of us slept. She could not be contained if she got mad about something, but she didn't yell as my father did. If she was disappointed in you, it stung so much that I still remember each time I failed her. I wanted to make her proud of me by showing I could handle things right with her finances.

Pretty much all of my mom's advanced planning, in turn, was because she loved her family. She didn't want me to have to do any of the things she had to do for her parents. Even the surgery that precipitated her health crisis was about righting past wrongs. She didn't like the way her mother suffered physically at the end of her life and was dependent on her children to pay for her care. My mom didn't want to go out like that.

She did the best she could to line up everything for me, but there were still so many things I didn't understand. If you're going through this, too, I hope this book helps you to cope better—or, even more important, I hope it helps you avoid any big messes with smart planning. That will mean less time spent doing to-do lists on a pressured deadline and more time spent enjoying your loved ones.

Part 1

· · · · · ·

Getting Started

1

That Phone Call

My mother was excellent at handling her own affairs—until she wasn't. Even though her health had been bad for a while, it still seemed to happen all at once that she could no longer manage running her household. The call finally came—the one with bad news that changes everything—in the fall of 2022. My mom had a date for a major back operation, and it was sink or swim.

My mom was seventy-six at the time and not old in any way except physically. She was the treasurer of her condo building, which had more than three hundred units and a staff of dozens. She followed politics and pop culture and could keep up with all the drama of four grandchildren on the phone without missing a beat. She texted memes. She never forgot a birthday and could still recite from memory her childhood best friend's phone number; she had me call Rozanne one day from the car to prove her point. She was that quintessential Jewish grandmother, the *Bubbe* to everyone, who made amazing chicken soup and brisket and was the keeper of all the old family stories.

She clocked in at about four feet, ten inches tall by that point, down three inches over the years as her spine collapsed. The grandkids liked to take pictures with her in the middle as they towered over her. She kept her silver hair cropped short—she stopped coloring it because she couldn't lean back to have it washed at the salon. She had kidney issues, congestive heart failure, diabetes, arthritis, and puffy eyelids and then developed some kind of undiagnosed swelling issue after a car accident at the start of the Covid pandemic (which was not her fault, she always pointed out). She used a walker, and even that was hard. She could barely get out of a chair and teetered dangerously once she was up. The summer before the surgery, she ramped up her household help to full-time, which by that time involved a regular daytime caregiver, one at night, and a patchwork of their friends to cover weekends.

Surgery was risky because of all those health problems, but my mom was prepared for a potentially bad outcome. Unlike me, she was never a person who seemed plagued by doubt or anxiety or second-guessing. I preworried, worried as I went, and then hashed over things endlessly after they happened. I wasn't sure about surgery at all, but I wasn't in charge yet. My mom said repeatedly that she felt that surgery was worth the risk because it could keep her walking, and that was everything to her. She said she didn't want to live out the rest of her life in a wheelchair, which sounded defeated and depressed to me—couldn't she have enough of a life and be with us still?—but it was clear for her: She had lived with pain for so long that she knew what she could tolerate and what she couldn't.

For years, surgeons had refused to touch her complicated spine, which was like a line of dominoes that kept falling. She already had three back and neck fusion surgeries. That wasn't because of an accident, but rather some congenital weakness in her discs that toppled them one after another. My grandmother suffered a similar condition and spent the last years of her life wheelchair bound. I had my own first back surgery ten years prior, when I was in my early forties, with my mom sitting by my side. I was fighting against having a second operation while going through the process with my mom.

If my mom could no longer walk at all, she would have to change her living and caregiving situation. She loved her condo in Fort Lauderdale, which had a balcony overlooking the ocean. The building was full of older people, what's called a naturally occurring retirement community, or NORC. She had a lot of friends, even if some of them had lately turned on each other like a senior citizen version of *Mean Girls*. If she left, she'd likely have to move to a facility of some sort. Maybe that would entail moving near me in Brooklyn or near my brother in Pennsylvania, and she was unsure if she wanted to do that. She also knew that being immobile would exacerbate the rest of her medical conditions. That simply wasn't the life she wanted.

Not many people knew how much she struggled behind the scenes. Even the close friends she updated honestly about her health didn't really know how bad it was to live inside her body all those years. She wasn't a complainer. You could see pain flash across her face at times, though. And if you were in the house with her, it was hard to miss how much she struggled and yet still pressed forward.

So my brother and I gave our blessing for surgery—reluctantly—because it was her decision. I made plane reservations, shifted my custody time with my two teenage children to my ex-husband, and got my boyfriend to stay at my house with the dog. I braced for whatever would come, but I hated everything about the situation. This time was different from past visits I'd made over the years for medical emergencies. When my dad fell ill eight years prior, I showed up for moral support and to help in whatever way I could. My mom was firmly in charge, and everything functioned normally in the household. In the four years since my dad died, my mom had been ill, but none of her hospital stays were long or serious. It was always a day or two here and there. Things always went quickly back to normal, and we put aside our worry.

This time, I was taking charge. Or at least taking half charge. My mom named my brother and me co-trustees and co-proxies on everything. But I had the financial training as a CFP® professional and my day job as a personal finance columnist, so I took the lead on the paperwork and the details. She asked me to come there a few days early before the surgery to hand over control of her bills and whatever else needed to be done around the house, both of us hoping that it would be a temporary assignment. It wasn't easy on either side, because she was proud and had never needed that kind of help before, and I thought she was superhuman and that I could never live up to handling anything as well as she could.

This call happens differently in every family, but eventually everyone can see that something is wrong. In my case, we had a distinct moment when my mom needed a risky surgery. She had all her faculties at that point, but she needed significant help. My father's moment came when he had a fall in the summer of 2014 at a pool in New Jersey. What seemed like a scraped knee suddenly turned into a serious heart infection called endocarditis, which in turn caused a stroke. My mom called me from the hospital to come quickly for what we thought were his last moments, and I jumped into the car and drove for two hours. That was the beginning of four years of ups and downs, which fell mostly on my mom to manage as his full-time caregiver, with some help from private aides in the end.

My mom's father, on the other hand, slipped slowly into dementia, with my grandmother caring for him at home with an aide until finally he went to a nursing home. When my grandmother was on her own, she moved into an assisted living facility and stayed there for the next twelve years, with a full-time aide and my mom and uncle handling her finances, including paying for everything. My father's parents both died when I was little from illnesses that took them quickly.

Any illness can lead to the need for help from a caregiver, but some of them come with specific known challenges. Cognitive decline and memory issues usually require constant supervision, while with Parkinson's disease and other neurological disorders you might focus more on safety in the house to prevent falls, at first.[1] Other conditions that often lead to long-term care include cancer, diabetes, heart disease, stroke, arthritis, other musculoskeletal issues, multiple sclerosis, mental illness, and intellectual disabilities.[2] Many of these overlap. My mom didn't have any of those big ones, but she was still very ill and needed full-time assistance.

Warning Signs by Condition That Help Is Needed

Condition	Warning Sign
Dementia	Wandering off
Parkinson's	Tremors or stiff walking
Heart disease	Unusual swelling of legs
Cancer	Fatigue or weight loss
Stroke	Sudden weakness or numbness; loss of vision
Diabetes	Weight loss, frequent urination
Multiple sclerosis	Balance and eyesight issues
Mental illness	Changes in appetite and sleep
Musculoskeletal issues	Falls

Source: National Council on Aging[3]

These conditions also do not affect only seniors or just your parents. Health issues cross all gender and economic lines. The person you may end up being responsible for could be an extended family member, neighbor, friend, or sibling. They may have long been disabled but outlived their primary caregiver, so you're next on the list. About 28 percent of older adults are solo agers, according to the United States Census Bureau in 2024, which amounts to about 22 million people.[4] These are people who were never married, previously married, or widowed but who have no other living relatives, and they have to form a community of care around themselves. The LGBTQ+ community, whether married or unmarried, faces some unique challenges, because there may be family estrangements and because laws that protect the right to marriage are constantly in jeopardy.

Sometimes, parents in particular may assume that their children will take care of them, and this is their entire aging financial plan. It was what they did for their parents and what everyone in their community does and so on down the line. This can apply equally to all their children or fall on the eldest daughter—or any daughter. Some may expect not only to be taken care of financially but also to live with their children.

Whatever the case, at some point it's likely to be your turn to care for somebody, and then it may come to be your turn to need to be cared for, so you have to be prepared. Joy Loverde, an eldercare expert who is the author of the books *The Complete Eldercare Planner, Revised and Updated 4th Edition: Where to Start, Which Questions to Ask, and How to Find Help*[5] and *Who Will Take Care of Me When I'm Old?: Plan Now to Safeguard Your Health and Happiness in Old Age*,[6] is the first choice for nearly everyone she knows to administer their power of attorney or be their trustee or caregiver. She managed the care of her mom, her stepfather, and her father, then an aunt, before they died. With her sister, she was the executor of her father's will. She's also executor for a friend who died, and she's on somebody else's list for executor when they pass. Her brother named her as guardian for his daughters if anything happened to him. When we spoke, she was in the midst of assisting multiple family members. She is also a seasoned speaker and "mature-market consultant," helping clients and readers of her books, many of whom are solo agers, with aging plans.

There's a range of duties for her financial caregiving. "For my sister, who is recently widowed, she's very sad and I have my eye on her," Loverde said, while for others it involves more paperwork. "People know I'm a planner and I'm organized. I know how to manage the costs associated with aging. I get things done. There's not a lot of emotions when you're in the executor role. I see it as a job."

Who will take care of Loverde when she's the one who needs care? She has already made decisions about her possessions and property. Her legal documents are in order. She exercises every day, so she hopes she won't need much physical care and won't have to lean too much on her daughter or grandchildren. "I will not be aging alone, but I'm also not planning on living with any of them," Loverde told me. "I see how busy my daughter is; she's running her own company and raising kids."

In my family, nobody thought about declining any of the caregiving tasks that presented themselves. We all loved one another, and caregiving was the obligation of whoever was closest in the family hierarchy, with everyone else pitching in as they could. The fact that my mom was a nice person and deserving of care really didn't have much to do with it. My father was a difficult person and not cooperative, and I still hung in there and did my share.

When I spoke to Andre Morrow about his caregiving experience with his dad, Sam, who was ninety-two and failing, it took until the end of the conversation before he told me how bad his relationship with his dad had been while he was growing up. "My dad did two tours in Vietnam and was a mess," Morrow said. In return, he wasn't much of a bargain as a teen, constantly getting into trouble. There was yelling. There were beatings.

But things change. Morrow got his life together, married, had kids, and worked for the city of San Jose, California. He became a mentor to young teens in his neighborhood. After his mother, Odette, died of breast cancer in 2013, somebody had to step up and look after his father. At first, he and his siblings hired caregivers, but the experience was not good. Morrow walked in one day unannounced to find an aide screaming at his father abusively, so he had to fire her. He decided he wanted to take over the caregiving himself. That meant having a family discussion with his wife and siblings. For Morrow, what made sense was for him to retire early from his job, at age 58, and move in with his dad. It would work if he could also get some sort of stipend to cover his lost pension income. Everyone agreed. Then he, his wife, and one of his children handled caregiving and the house: fixing fences, cooking, helping his dad bathe even when he didn't want to.

"I wasn't my parents' favorite child, for sure," said Morrow, who was 65 when I spoke to him and had been caregiving for seven years. "I never had a father-son relationship growing up. I was running the streets. When I told my dad I'd be the one taking care of him, he was shocked. He said, 'Out of all the children, I would never have expected you to do it.' But it's been awesome. I don't even remind him of what happened fifty years ago. I tell my dad every day, 'I love you,' I hug him, and I kiss him. No regrets ever."

DO NOW

Set up a written emergency plan, complete with contact numbers, that can be followed if there's an emergency. See the template on page 232.

2

Financial Red Flags

Not everyone needs a full takeover. Most of the time, financial caregiving ramps up slowly, maybe some help with taxes or dealing with a complicated insurance bill. People generally don't like to give up control, and they tend to keep a tight rein on their financial information. It can also seem like too much for the caregiver, who doesn't have the time or patience to step in proactively.

But you will see cracks if you look for them. Financial warning signs actually double as signs of overall decline, because research consistently shows that financial acumen is one of the first cognitive functions to slip.[1] This is one of the reasons elder fraud is rampant and seniors so often fall prey to scams that seem obvious to other people.

Top Senior Scams

1. Social Security imposter scam: Robocall to reactivate number
2. Tech support scam: Gains access to computer
3. Lottery scam: Costs money to claim
4. IRS imposter scam: Claims you owe money
5. Romance scam: Preys on the lonely and then asks for money

Source: Elder Justice Initiative, U.S. Department of Justice[2]

The financial warning signs will vary depending on the ailment. Cognitive decline will look very different from a balance problem, where falls are a main concern. A cancer diagnosis or the need for dialysis for a diabetes-related condition might present more as scheduling issues, especially if the ill person needs to travel to appointments.

Physical mail is the key for most older people, but you may have to extend that to email and texts if a person has gone fully online. You can see so much about how a person is doing by looking at their incoming communications. You'll see if things are getting too overwhelming for the person to care for themselves. This shows up with dementia, physical ailments, and even caregiver fatigue. My mom had all her marbles but often couldn't make it to the mailbox in the lobby of her building when she was on her own. That was when we both knew that she needed to hire some home help.

When you visit in person, take a peek and see what's in the correspondence. Are there bills stacked up or past due notices in the current mail pile? Autopay can be your friend if this is the situation. Almost all bills can be paid electronically in some way, and you can monitor the accounts from wherever you are. You can also hire a bill-paying service or what's known as a geriatric care manager, who can help with the day-to-day mechanics of the finances.

You can't outsource all of it, though, because there are things that only a close family member or friend with proper legal authority can do. And there are some things that only those closest will notice. At some point, you need to dig even deeper and glance at a bank statement and a credit card bill to look for unusual recurring charges or large distributions. There could be outsized payments to caregivers or people you don't know or excessive giving to charity.

Short of having all the mail forwarded directly to the financial caregiver—which is a good option when it's time—another way to forestall lapses in important policies is to be added as an authorized user on everyday bills such as utilities and as a "trusted" person on key accounts with regular premiums, such as life insurance and long-term care policies.[3] Being an authorized user will allow you to pay bills and get account information. Being a trusted person on a brokerage account or life insurance will not allow you access to make changes to the account, but it means you'll be alerted if your loved one misses a payment, is in danger of losing a policy, or is trying to make unusual transactions. You're basically on call in case the financial representative senses something amiss cognitively or behaviorally, such as an older person calling to arrange a large wire transfer to a foreign country or trying to buy thousands of dollars worth of gift cards.[4]

"There are a growing number of scams and frauds out there, and even the most well-meaning person can be influenced by these," said Rob Williams, who is the managing director of financial planning for Charles Schwab's Center for Financial Research. "If you have a trusted contact, a broker can reach out to them and get a second opinion or help."

The second biggest warning sign is how a person is getting around. Are they falling often? Can they drive? Should they drive? You can look for dings on the car or see if they are parked haphazardly.

I spoke to Annalee Kruger late on a day when she was struggling to deal with her 85-year-old father, who crashed his car on the way to an appointment. Kruger is a family caregiving and dementia consultant who runs a company devoted to helping families set up plans in advance of possible disaster. This goes further than making a phone tree for an emergency; this involves setting up a full aging plan until the end of life.

Because of her father's accident, Kruger had to scrap her morning commitments to make sure her dad was okay, deal with the insurance company, then cover what was needed if he wasn't going to be driving for the time being—or ever again. Kruger is a well-prepared person, so of course she had a plan in place for her dad—and for herself—to roll with changes as they came, such as the pacemaker and hip replacement that quickly followed the accident. She had already contemplated a day coming when he could no longer drive, which would be her indicator that a different level of care was needed.

She takes the same care with her own affairs, mind you, and carries her healthcare proxy and Do Not Resuscitate (DNR) authorization with her wherever she goes. "You never know," she said. "I am a disaster specialist; I'm just living what I preach."

And you do never know. Years ago, she was just back from a trip to China giving a presentation about crisis planning, when she was crossing the street in a small town in Wisconsin and was hit by a school bus. She was sent through the air and landed fifteen feet away, shattering her face along with other injuries, and she spent the next year on her family's farm because she needed help. She wrote about her experiences in the book *The Invisible Patient: The Emotional, Financial, and Physical Toll on Family Caregivers.*[5]

For over thirty years, Kruger has helped families so they aren't caught short when trouble like this starts. The all-important first talk—most often a video call to pull together far-flung families—is meant to keep things simple and lay the cards on the table. You assess where everyone is in the process and what they need and want, as well as who is available and capable of making things happen. It can be crucial to be joined by a facilitator such as Kruger or a social worker or other professional, to help keep the discussion on track and not get derailed by old family resentments, but family members can certainly do this on their own.

"The goals are always the same: Mom and Dad want to age at home but worry they will be a burden on the kids. The kids say, 'We love our parents, but taking care of them like this isn't sustainable,'" Kruger said.

Not everyone is ready to listen at the same time. Kruger, who also trains financial professionals to be Elder Planning Specialists, a program she created with financial planner and author Bob Mauterstock (and of which I am now a graduate),[6] told me about a family that she had been working with for months, with a mom and dad in their eighties and three adult children scattered across the country. That first video call was a bit of a disaster.

The mom looked terrible, Kruger noticed, which is the third red flag: Watch for signs of fatigue, lack of personal hygiene, and pallor. Kruger kept remarking about it as an obvious sign that the mom was not managing well. "I asked three times about her looking tired, and she said that her husband, who had dementia, wasn't sleeping and she was exhausted," Kruger said.

It can sometimes be hard to judge how somebody looks if you don't see them all the time, but you should be able to observe general signs of exhaustion and stress during a video call. If you know the person well enough, you should even be able to hear a shift in tone of voice and heed the warning just from a phone call. I always knew that something was wrong with my mom when she cut conversations short and didn't seem to want to talk.

Fatigue can cause all sorts of ancillary problems, and it means, generally, that the person isn't coping well. Kruger said you also need to check with the neighbors and see what they have to say. If you aren't on-site, they're the ones who may notice things before you do and can call if, say, a person with dementia starts wandering off regularly or it looks as though the lawn isn't mowed. When I visited my mom in Florida, old ladies used to take me aside in the pool when my mom was out of earshot and tell me that my mom didn't seem to be doing so well. I wrote them off as being catty, but I should have listened more.

After that family call, Kruger told the adult children that their mom needed more help and that she was neglecting her own health; she had a hip problem that needed to be addressed, and she was losing weight quickly because of all the stress. Kruger pointed to a dire statistic from the National Institutes of Health that primary caregivers over the age of 60 have a higher mortality rate than their peers who are not caregivers.[7] The kids weren't ready to hear it. They decided to call more often for the moment.

"That's not a plan," Kruger said. "It's not going to help their dad sleep at night. But I don't chase families. I know they'll call me back when they are in crisis."

And of course they did call back, and it wasn't a happy ending.

Kruger tells the kinds of cautionary tales that jog people into action. The way she looks at it, if you understand what could happen, it will become crystal clear that you need to put plans into place. This goes for everyone over the age of 18; at the very least, you should have a healthcare proxy and power of attorney (see chapters 4 and 8). After all, she was literally hit by the proverbial bus out of nowhere. Anyone with an involved family life needs to discuss their end-of-life wishes, where they want to be buried, what should happen to their assets, and how to access their financial accounts. "It's just part of being a grown-up," Kruger said.

It's possible for loved ones to push through without these things, but it's much harder. The financial and legal systems in the modern world require a certain level of attention, and none of it is cheap or easy. You might think you or your loved one doesn't have enough money to worry about trusts and wills and other paperwork, but even if a person has a negative bank balance, they are still connected to the grid of civil society. That's what makes putting plans in place for when you are incapacitated or you die an act of love, rather than one of control. It's about sparing the people you love from the painful paperwork our financial and legal systems put us through at the absolutely most stressful times.

That call Kruger got from the adult children was because they had trouble reaching their mom for a couple of days, and the daughter who lived closest was dispatched to drive five hours to see what was going on. Her dad answered the door confused, dirty, and not recognizing her. She spent twenty minutes talking her way into the house, which was chaotic and smelly.

The mother, as you might have guessed, was dead, lying on the kitchen floor, and the father had been too confused to know what to do. "So then they saw the value of an aging plan," Kruger said. "But by then it was a crisis plan."

DO NOW

Call your loved ones who you think might need care and really listen to them. Try to have a first conversation about how things are going and what they might need to do to set up a care plan. There is a template for an agenda on page 237.

Start with a Final Resting Place

I 'm not sure this is where I would have started for myself, but my mom's main concern before her surgery was making sure I knew where she was to be buried. Once I thought about it, that made sense, because she was dealing with the worst-case scenario and getting it out of the way.

That first afternoon I was in Florida before her surgery, we dismissed the daytime caregiver early. My mom sat in the reclining chair in her room, where she slept because she was too uncomfortable to lie in bed. I took things to her and scurried around her apartment at her command. She wanted to start divvying up her jewelry. The good stuff was still in the safe deposit box at the bank, but that was a task for another day. My job was to be helpful. Supportive. Cheerful. The situation was a little grim, but I went with it. I needed to keep her mind occupied, so I put on a happy face and ate everything I could find to help me get through it all. My mom was down on her physical luck, but she had still made sure to get the caregiver to stock the house with all my favorite snacks and a special treat from back home in Lancaster, dark chocolate Wilbur Buds. I agreed to take whatever family heirlooms she wanted home for my kids even though they weren't ready to appreciate them yet. My mom and daughter share the same first initial, so I put aside everything with an "A" charm. There was a tie clip of my father's for my son and some things for my nephews.

Then she had me pull out a folder marked "Cemetery" that she had stashed under her computer keyboard in her home office. I thought she was being dramatic, but she was serious.

The "Cemetery" folder marked out her rectangle in yellow highlighter on the map of the family plot, which was in a cemetery near Philadelphia. Working out the details of her burial was something of an obsession of hers for the past five years. The last time we were there was for my father's funeral. When we walked up to our family's area of graves, which is in the middle of a grassy row, she realized that the hole that was dug for my father's grave was in the wrong spot. He was going where a still-living family member was supposed to go eventually, and that person was standing right there looking down into the open earth. It was like the worst party seating chart disaster ever. What to do? Stop the funeral and get the digging crew back? There ended up being some hushed discussions among the grown-ups, and we proceeded.

My mom wasn't going to let that sort of mix-up happen to anyone else in the family, so afterward she put in a lot of effort coordinating with all her still-living cousins to shore up the plot map with the cemetery liaison. That involved renegotiating burial contracts and buying out a few of the cousins. My mom documented it all in the folder, so all I had to do if something happened was call the number and tell them her name.

Many people die without any sort of plan for their burial, leaving their relatives to scramble. Others have it all planned out and paid for years ahead, even picking out the music. My mom was somewhere in between, and we got to the details of how to pay for all of it further down the road. But her motivation was the same as that of most people in this situation: She wanted to spare others the fuss she had to go through when it was her responsibility to bury somebody.

She was lucky to have a family plot. The next generations in our family will have to figure it out for themselves because the spots are now all accounted for. In that situation, you basically make a real estate deal because you're buying a small plot of land. That land is only going to appreciate, and burial space is always running short, so the sooner you buy, the better.

Not everyone wants to talk about these things. When Warren Kozak's wife, Lisa, was dying from cancer, he tried every way to get her to talk about where she wanted to be buried. She was a doctor and knew all too well the seriousness of her situation, but talking about her death was the last thing she wanted to do. To spur the conversation, he tried to talk to her about what he wanted, and little things started to come out. He told her that he planned to be buried in Wisconsin, near his family's summer lake house that they both loved, rather than at her family's plot in Pennsylvania, which they both thought was depressing. Later, she started to chime in. "She'd be looking at her iPad, and she'd say, offhand, 'I suppose I'll be buried in Wisconsin,'" said Kozak, a journalist and speechwriter, who wrote about his journey through grief in *Waving Goodbye: Life After Loss.*[1] When the conversation dropped off again, he took action and bought eight plots in a new field near the rest of his family's graves because their section was filled.

"You don't want to deal with this when somebody dies. You have a million and one things on your plate. This is a big decision. Get it done early. Be the adult. Deal with it," he said. "On that horrible day that she died, there was at least one big decision that was already made . . . and that was kind of a relief."

To look for a plot, the best place to start is with a local cemetery or a religious group, if you're affiliated with one. The average plot in the United States runs over $3,000, but costs can vary depending on demand in the area.[2] The Neptune Society or a local funeral home can also direct you to cremation options, which is generally cheaper, or you can look online for more creative ideas, such as being launched into space or turned into a brick.

Last Resting Place Options

- Burial in a cemetery
- Cremation
- Ashes turned into biodegradable planter or other material
- Aqua cremation, or alkaline hydrolysis (uses water instead of heat)
- Infinity burial suit, a biodegradable shroud made popular by actor Luke Perry
- Recompose—human composting, available in only some states
- Burial at sea (rules apply)
- Ashes sent into space, as done by *Star Trek* creator Gene Roddenberry
- Donate body to science

Sources: *Los Angeles Times,*[3] Funeralocity[4]

If you need help with this process, there are free social services and paid professional services that can direct you (see page 245 for more references). Nicole Daigle, who helps coach people through these hard times as a certified death doula with the Chicago Death Doula Collective, worked with a woman who was facing the death of her wife and needed help with the details. Daigle got in touch with a funeral home for her and made sure all the details were prepared. When the wife died, Daigle became the point person for logistics. "When you have a loss like that, your brain is not functioning, so I was there to take notes. I gave her some reminders of things she wanted to ask. So just kind of that quiet support," she said.

My mom pulled out the folder that night because she wanted me to know what to do if things went wrong. I think she was also trying to prepare me for the realization that you can try to avoid this issue, but somebody, some-day, is going to have to think about these things for you if you don't do it yourself. My mom did it for herself so I wouldn't have to. I realized that I wanted to do the same for my kids, but I definitely did not want to be buried in that family plot—the thought of a "permanent resting place" is as old-fashioned to me as putting punctuation in phone texts is to my children. And so, in my will, I have asked to be cremated and turned into a garden planter.

DO NOW

Ask if your loved one has a burial plan in place; if not, see if they're open to conversations about what they'd want you to do if they died. See page 246 for conversation prompts.

4

Get Medical Access

In Florida, I was soon scaling a mountain of paperwork: Medicare documentation, long-term care insurance reimbursement forms, checking account statements, and bills. Textbooks do not teach you how to manage these things.

First I needed to learn about my mom. She had a cheat sheet for that. After many, many doctor and emergency room visits over the last ten years for my father and herself, my mom had developed a system.[1] She had all her pertinent information on a single sheet of paper, front and back, that she gave to every caregiver and carried in her wallet. It listed all her demographic information—name, address, birthday, and so on—and all her doctors, primary ailments, medications with dosages, and surgical procedures. I had no idea she'd had so many surgeries. Her list went all the way back to her tonsillectomy in 1951 and appendectomy in 1955. She had a specialist for virtually every body part and had issues of some type in every major system. And she was allergic to azithromycin, an antibiotic. I would hear her repeat that at every new stage of the process over the next nine months and would repeat it for her when she couldn't speak for herself.

I felt guilty when I looked at that long list because I had protected myself from it for so long. My mom had her condo board duties and the family, but most of her time was spent managing her health conditions. And before paying attention to herself, she was taking care of my dad. It had been nearly ten years altogether of constant health crises. The only thing I knew before was her blood type, because it was the same as my own and my two kids', and that she was completely deaf in her left ear, because that was a practical issue we lived with for years. But why didn't I know that she was allergic to azithromycin? She would know something such as that about me. It seemed like a key personal detail that I was missing, as though I didn't really know her or wasn't paying enough attention to her.

The cheat sheet, especially the medications, meant I didn't have to be one of those people who show up at the ER with a bag of pills they grabbed in a rush from the medicine cabinet. I snapped a picture of the paper on my phone so I'd have all the information whenever I needed it.

The next item on the agenda was readying the healthcare proxy, which designates who will make medical decisions if the person can't, and the HIPAA authorization, which says who has access to the person's medical information.[2] These are two separate, simple documents that designate the person or people to make decisions.

Paperwork You Will Need in a Medical Emergency

- Healthcare proxy
- HIPAA authorization
- Medical information sheet
- Living will
- Durable power of attorney

Sources: Centers for Disease Control and Prevention,[3] U.S. Department of Health and Human Services[4]

Usually, you want legal forms to be drawn up by a lawyer, but healthcare proxies and HIPAA authorizations are easily downloaded and filled out on your own. Many workplaces include access to such services as a voluntary benefit for a small charge or for free. Some hospitals will help with this, or you can use a self-help online legal service.

A living will is a bit more complicated, and this is a step that most people skip unless they're doing a full estate plan with a lawyer. This is the document that states what your wishes are if you become incapacitated: what lifesaving measures you want employed and for how long, if you want extreme measures to be taken, and if you want to be an organ donor (but there are other ways to opt for the last, such as on a driver's license). You can get as detailed as you want on these documents or keep it simple. Putting it down on paper makes it much clearer than merely having a conversation about it. My mom had a living will when she was going into surgery, but we didn't dwell on it. She repeatedly said throughout her life that she didn't want to be kept alive artificially. When my grandmother would annoy her, she'd say, "Just shoot me if I turn out like that," and cock her hand like a pistol to her head. Of course, we were going to be more reasoned than that, but our discussions about it came much later in the process.

On the other hand, we used the healthcare proxy at the hospital the first minute we checked in. I had a printout in my backpack, along with my snacks, water bottle, phone charger, neck pillow, headphones, laptop, and eye mask. I was prepared for the long haul, as we had to be up at 3:00 A.M. to get there. The surgery was expected to last eight hours, and then who knew what. I was prepared to stay overnight if needed.

The healthcare proxy merely said in the event my mom should become incapacitated, my brother and I could make decisions for her. Of course, it takes five pages of legalese to say it. A spouse has the immediate legal right to healthcare information and to make decisions, but when you are helping a solo ager, a surviving spouse, or an LGBTQ+ partner or friend in an unfriendly environment, you need documents. One man I interviewed was helping care for a friend whose family had cut him off years earlier because he was gay, and the only way he could help him was to have proper healthcare proxy forms, or else the hospital would go looking for a next of kin who wouldn't be respectful.

If you forget about this, you can usually get it done at the hospital if you need to, but that doesn't always give you time to think it through or prepare for all the nuances. Michelle Buonincontri Petrowski found that out the hard way after she and her sisters had conflicts with her mother's new husband. The senior couple had moved to Florida in 2022, away from the rest of the family in Arizona, and it was the stepfather who took Petrowski's mother to the emergency room when she got sick three months after arriving, at 75 years of age. Petrowski, who is a financial adviser, helped her mother do basic estate planning to make a will and draw up a postnuptial agreement years prior, but the new husband was on tap for healthcare decisions. Petrowski found him mostly concerned with what money he could control if her mother died, given Florida's spousal homestead protections, instead of dealing with setting her up for cancer treatments.

"Every time she got sick, we went two at a time to deal with everything. We'd get her chemo set up and deal with Medicare, and then her husband would undo whatever we did," Petrowski said, still angry years later. After a few months of that, she got her mother to agree to make her sisters, who are both nurses, the healthcare proxies. "We had to do it in secret," Petrowski said. "Her husband was telling doctors not to talk to us and not even to her. But really, he shouldn't have been making decisions unless she couldn't."

Even when things aren't that bad, it's still confusing at the hospital for most people. When we took my mom for surgery, the hospital scanned her documents and we put them to use right away because my mom sort of went blank from fear. She was uncomfortable lying on the gurney in the prep room and already a little out of it. She was cold and wanted to keep her arms under the blanket. Nurses kept asking my mom to sign papers and then wanted proof that I could sign for her, even though it was in the system. But I had the printout and my cheat sheet with her medical information, and I knew to say by then to everyone that she was allergic to azithromycin. My mom dozed on and off. Time crept on toward 7:00 A.M., then 8:00 A.M.

My brother and I traded off sitting with her, and then we were both eventually allowed to stay. Finally, she was taken to surgery. I sat in the waiting room the rest of the day, clutching my sheaf of papers and wondering what would happen. The air-conditioning didn't work well and by about 4:00 P.M., it got sweaty. Toward dinnertime, the crowd dwindled. At 8:00 P.M., the volunteer attendant at the desk on the surgical floor left. And still we waited for information.

Eventually, we were able to track our mom down in the ICU and the surgeon came out to talk to us. The procedure had gone fine, he said, but one warning sign was that the team had "lost her electrical conductivity" in the midst of it and taken some measures to get it back. That sounded to me like doctor talk for saying her heart stopped beating momentarily and they revived her. Had she died? Was she okay? It was my first clue that things were not going to be easy, but I was so shaken at that point and glad she was done with the operation that I pushed aside that little detail for the moment.

We went in to see her, hooked up to machines and still in pretty rough shape from being face down for the long surgery, and then we went home for a couple of hours of sleep.

Very quickly, I discovered something valuable: The HIPAA authorization allowed me to log in to the hospital's electronic records system. It used a version of MyChart, which was available as an app on my phone, and most facilities use something comparable. That gave me access to my mom's medical records to see things happening in real time. That was my touchstone for the next few months. When I didn't know what room she was in because I wasn't there in person or was on edge waiting for blood test results, I could track her on MyChart. Sometimes I could see blood test results before the doctors got them. My phone would ping at all hours. I always knew her nurse's name, what doctor was assigned to her that day, and when she was given certain medications. I knew, for instance, that first day in the ICU, that her blood sugar was not being tracked, even though she was listed as diabetic on her chart. That kind of little thing slipped through the cracks easily, especially because I was not yet an expert on her medical situation.

There were already decisions to make because she couldn't, such as how to manage her pain medications and how much breathing support she would need and for how long. I had to get up to speed pretty quick on medical terminology. I typed gobbledygook frantically into search engines. The negotiations over how long she'd stay and in what part of the hospital also started immediately. I'd have originally put that into the category of medical caregiving, but I later realized that every medical decision we made was truly a financial decision, and that goes not only for those over 65 and on Medicare.

At first I didn't consider the cost of my mom's care at all. I assumed that she was covered by Medicare, and that was that. I knew that she had some money put aside and the whole purpose of it was to pay for times like this. I hadn't yet dived into the nuances of hospital days versus rehab days, what kind of Medicare supplement plan she had and what it covered, and how we were paying for the private aides we layered on top of the hospital staff. I knew a lot about Medicare in theory, but not much in practice, it turned out. But at the start of that medical crisis, that was not my main concern. There would come a time soon enough when I would learn the ins and outs of those things (see chapter 13). My mom could not even talk in the ICU, and somebody had to be with her 24/7. At that moment, we were doing whatever was needed on autopilot. When you're functioning like

that, you have to hope that any advance preparation you've done will protect you.

DO NOW

Ask for your loved one's health history and make your own cheat sheet, down to the
dosages and frequency of the medicines they take regularly. A template is on page
234. Also, make sure they are signed up for whatever electronic chart system their
doctors use. You might need a code from a physician to get started.

Title Bank Accounts
Ahead of an Emergency

I'd been able to forge my mom's signature confidently since middle school and never had any qualms about doing so, but writing out checks that first week when my mom was in the hospital made me queasy. I knew better by now.

Still, people needed to be paid. My mom's surgery was on a Tuesday, and her caregivers were due checks on Friday. After coming out of anesthesia and getting settled, my mom wasn't ready to add up their hours, which the main caregiver kept track of on little slips of paper. Her hands and arms were so swollen that she couldn't lift a pen. She couldn't even manage to press the call button for the nurse or hold her water bottle.

I had the power of attorney paperwork, which legally allowed me to have access to my mom's accounts and to make financial decisions for her, but I had not yet gone to the bank to execute it. Without that step, it was just pieces of paper. I was sitting there next to her in the hospital, acting with her complete permission, but I was living in a bit of a gray area because we had not paid enough attention to how her financial accounts were titled.

Choices for Accessing Bank Accounts

1. Joint ownership: Allows open access
2. Power of attorney: Allows open access but is accountable to other heirs and the principal
3. Transfer-on-death beneficiary: Is available only after death with documentation
4. Trusted contact: Is for information purposes only

There are all sorts of ways to handle this basic banking situation, but a lot of people do it wrong. By wrong, that means they violate the letter of the law—something akin to speeding or jaywalking in my book, but still wrong.

The way you are supposed to do it is to go to each financial institution with the principal person when times are good and either add a person they trust as a joint signer or give that person the power of attorney and enact it with the bank.

Experts and people who have gone through this disagree on the best way to handle it. There are those who swear by having a joint signer on bank accounts, especially for an older person who is still functioning independently but is starting to slip cognitively. Others feel that adding a joint signer creates more problems than it's worth and it's better instead to execute a power of attorney and name a pay-on-death or transfer-on-death beneficiary to receive the funds when the time comes.[1]

"It's always good toward the end of life to make sure a financial surrogate is also a check-writer on an account, but it has to be very individualized," said Carolyn McClanahan, a physician who became a CFP® professional and now specializes in helping people where money and health cross paths.

One answer might be to have a mix of both, which is what my family did. You're going to need the power of attorney anyway if somebody gets ill; it's the only way to have the broad financial powers you need beyond writing a check. And you could have at least one account where there is a joint signer, so you have continued access even after the person dies.

The reason this is complicated is that the moment a person dies, the power of attorney ceases. Suddenly the bank, the mortgage company, and the credit card people won't talk to you anymore. Even if you don't notify these companies yourself, they're likely to lock the accounts within days. As soon as a death is registered, word goes out to Social Security, Medicare, and financial institutions to freeze the deceased person's accounts so there's no fraud.[2]

If you're counting on bills, such as rent or utilities, being paid from an account that didn't have a joint signer, you might end up stuck. That happened to a client of McClanahan's who died from a brain tumor and thought she had put her children as joint signers on her account when she was first diagnosed. Instead, the bank had them listed as transfer-on-death (TOD) beneficiaries, which is not as immediate as it sounds.

"All the automatic bill paying stopped when they froze that account. Everything was digitized, so we didn't know what bills went out and when," said McClanahan.

After a death, the bank will transfer the funds to the designated heirs, but usually not any of the other account information such as account statements or lists of payees. And it will take some time. First, you'll need to wait for a death certificate to be issued, which could take two or more weeks, depending on where you are located. A bank may also want you to go in person to a branch to take care of the transaction—it might even want you to go to a local branch where the person lived—and that might not be feasible.

The arguments against having a joint signer revolve mostly around the assets' counting toward the extra person signed up. The most important reason I didn't want to be joint signer on my mother's accounts was that I had teenagers by the time we were talking about it, and I didn't want to have to claim my mother's funds on future financial aid forms for college. Even if the accounts belonged to her, they'd legally be my assets, too. Joint signing could also have affected my mother's eventual Medicaid eligibility, should she have needed it, if there were sums going into and out of the account that would push her over the thresholds to qualify.

Another consideration was that I'm divorced, and even though my financial settlement was long ago, you never know when you might need to step back in and fill out income disclosure forms that would include those funds as assets. I didn't feel as though I was in much danger of having other creditors, but if I did, joint accounts could also get tangled up in collection efforts.

Then there's the issue of inheritance if there's more than one heir. If you're a joint owner of a parent's account, the account transfers over to your ownership after death, which supersedes any beneficiary designations or stipulations in a will or trust. So if you have one child who is joint signer on the account of an aging parent and that parent dies, the one who is joint signer inherits the balance. It's up to that person's goodwill to split it with any other siblings. That may work out fine, or there can be hard feelings.

I didn't foresee that happening with my management of my mom's money, but I asked Karyn Stiles, a certified public accountant (CPA) who specializes in administering estates, if she had ever come across such a scenario, and she laughed and said she couldn't think of a specific case because it happened so often.

"They think they deserve the funds because they took care of Mom or Dad, and maybe they do, but that may not be what the parents intended in their will," said Stiles, who is also the director of operations for Alix, an estate settlement company.

The joint-signer scenario is also a conduit for potential fraud. Since joint co-signers have full rights on the account, they can transfer funds out of the account anytime they want.

Whatever way you do it, this is a decision you want to make when the person is healthy and alert. Once someone gets sick, it's usually too late to change things. If your loved one can't travel to the bank or sign legal papers, it's a mess to get access any other way. Banks and financial institutions are particularly stubborn on this point, and for good reason: They're trying to prevent elder fraud, and they're serious about it.

What we set up for my mom was not in any way ideal, and we knew it all along and still never corrected it. We did our best, though. We did go to the bank during the good times to look into it. We made an appointment at her branch, which was down the street from her apartment building, during one of my visits with my kids after my father died. What we found out then was that my father's name was still on the main checking account and the safe deposit box, and to put me on it or name beneficiaries, we'd have to come back with his death certificate and have him taken off first.

That required too much back-and-forth to the bank for my mom right then, so we shelved that plan for a later time and instead added me to her linked savings account, which was in her name only. She didn't keep much money in the savings account generally, so she promised that it wouldn't affect my finances. Instead, she opened a different savings account with high-yield interest where my brother and I were each named as a 50 percent beneficiary. Then Covid hit, and we couldn't get down to where she lived for a while. When we finally could travel again, we were busy on our visits and she never felt up to it. We found ourselves in the hospital for that big surgery without having solved the problem. Her main bank account didn't have proper beneficiaries named, nor was anyone a joint signer on the account with her.

Sitting there that first week with the checkbook, the best thing for me to do would have been to write checks from my own account and eventually transfer money to myself from her savings account, of which I was the joint owner. The problem with that was that I thought it might affect her reimbursement from the long-term care insurance. So I simply signed her name on the caregiver checks and vowed to figure out how to do it properly by the next time I had to write checks.

DO NOW

Check the beneficiary designations on all of your loved ones' financial accounts and figure out who has access (and do this for yourself, while you're at it). Make a list and keep track, using the template on page 246.

Set Up a Care Schedule

After the surgery, I thought my mom would be up and running her own affairs by the following week. I was so optimistic that I flew home a few days afterward. I assumed that she would have a short postoperative stay in the hospital ward, then transition to the hospital's rehab floor as we had planned and then home.

There's a difference between being there and being a thousand miles away and hearing only a few scattered details. That was when we had to establish a care system to figure out what time and resources everyone involved could devote. It was mostly me, my brother, and the paid caregivers, but my mom also had her cousin in town, friends who lived nearby, and a faraway sister-in-law and nieces and nephews who offered to help. If we had looked for more help, it would have been there. My mom was still in the hospital, so she didn't need Meals on Wheels or any other community social services, but those are available for people at home who need a little extra assistance. This is another circumstance in which a geriatric care manager can help, especially a local one if you are far away.

It's a big step to set up a formal long-term plan because it requires more than just an emergency mentality, but I knew it was time because as soon as I got home, I could hear that my mom didn't sound right. When I called, she said she was fine but shooed me off the line after a few seconds. I texted the caregivers and got scraps of updates in misspelled half sentences about catheters coming out and going back in, about attempts to get my mom out of bed and walking down the hall and her blood pressure getting worry-ingly low.

My brother and I checked in after each contact to compare notes and we realized that she was giving us both the same brush-off. To make sure we were there enough to keep track of everything, we planned a back-and-forth schedule, hopscotching each other, working around our kids and jobs and major holidays.

At home, I juggled Thanksgiving meal prep, cramming in a dentist appointment, my mammogram, and handling the kids' needs. And I worked. I was two months into a new job at that point and still trying to make a good impression. But I was scattered, and I felt as though I wasn't getting anywhere on anything. "It's a lot," became my mantra.

I was only two weeks into a caregiving experience, and already I was burned out. Weakling? Or was it just that hard? Evidence supports the idea of it being just that hard. Caregivers suffer severe economic consequences. They lose wages. They deplete their savings. They don't advance in their careers. An AARP study found that 70 percent of the 63 million caregivers in the United States were working at the same time, and nearly all of them felt pinched. More than a quarter of them said they had to shift from full-time work to part-time work or stop working to handle all their responsibilities.[1]

Annalee Kruger had one client at Care Right who asked her to help with an aging plan because he was spending thousands of dollars on flights and losing work while he was dealing with his parents. "He was flying every two weeks and said he was missing out on, like, seven thousand dollars of billable time already. He was an only child. His wife was supportive for, like, four minutes, then the resentment started. Even the most supportive spouse will get angry," Kruger said. "It's a big web of ickiness if people don't have their affairs in order."

Caregivers at a Glance

- The typical annual out-of-pocket spending by a caregiver is $7,242.
- 61 percent of caregivers are women.
- 45 percent have suffered at least one financial impact.
- 21 percent of caregivers say that their own health is poor.
- 14 percent of the U.S. population—37 million people—provide unpaid eldercare.
- 61 percent of caregivers are employed.

- 41 percent of caregivers are aged 45 to 64; 15 percent are age 65 plus.
- 4.5 million caregivers are "sandwich generation" with kids under age 18 and caring for a parent.
- 24 percent provide daily care, averaging 3.6 hours a day.
- 15 percent have been providing care for 10-plus years.

Sources: AARP, National Alliance for Caregiving,[2] U.S. Bureau of Labor Statistics[3]

Dr. Erika Rasure, a financial therapist and transformational coach, reassured me that the task felt hard because it is hard. "This is a huge emotional and financial burden; it's not for the weak. It can make you feel powerless," she said.

Her two biggest suggestions to get through it were these: Set healthy boundaries and don't listen to the chatter. Her own mother did that when serving as a caregiver to Rasure's grandmother. She set expectations right up front: I will not support you financially, but I will make sure the lights are on; and I will not get sucked into emotional drama, but I will make sure you get to every medical appointment. "You have to make it very specific," Rasure said. "People have this all-or-nothing mentality and think they have to do everything themselves and maybe even pay for it, but it's a tenuous space to navigate."

She said that the caregiving burden is especially hard for only children, but the flip side is that when there's a lot of siblings and other relatives and friends involved, you can get derailed by second-guessers. "You get all these other opinions that can make you feel wobbly. It can get you off your game," she said. "The only thing you have to think about is to honor the person's wishes."

All of this affects women disproportionately, typically right during what should be their highest-earning career years. When I started to talk to people about this, I was shocked by how easy I actually had it. Jeanne Wiener started going back and forth between her home and her mother's in Washington State about twelve years earlier, after her father died and her mother was diagnosed first with breast cancer and then with dementia. In that time period, she also took care of an autistic son now in his thirties. Wiener, who is a certified public accountant in northern California who specializes in tax issues for trusts and estates, eventually ratcheted up to making the trip to

Washington about one week a month, every time more difficult than the last as her mother's illnesses progressed.

"She's declining, and we're hoping to keep her at home. She doesn't sleep, she won't take her medications, and sometimes she steals them from the aides and hides them. She struck one of the aides," Wiener said, weary of the machinations of trying to stay one step ahead. "Every visit has its challenges."

No two care situations will be alike, as no two families are alike, and no care situation will stay static as you are dealing with it. The care plan starts by dipping a toe in to see what needs to be done right away. Lean on whatever resources you can, and take things as they come. If you live nearby, that might mean taking the person dinner and groceries once a week, then chauffeuring them to medical appointments or arranging ride shares— some cities might have assistance programs if money is tight—if the person can't drive. If you live farther away, it might mean a daily phone call or several. Your loved one might need a day program at a local senior center. You might need to make monthly visits or go a couple of times a year if you have other help. You might be able to share these shifts with other family members or friends. It could take some coordination for a while, and then, when the situation changes, you'll have to make harder decisions about the person's living situation. When the person can't make it on their own, you'll have to discuss if there's money for help or if they need to move elsewhere.

At the beginning of my caregiver journey, I didn't see how the kind of sustained energy Jeanne Wiener had drawn upon for taking care of her mother for so long could be possible. I was tired after one trip to Florida from New York. But then I did what I had to do: I ended up taking eight trips in eight months, each for at least a week and the last for about three weeks. My brother had a similar itinerary on opposite weeks. Our overall caregiving journey was short, but it was intense.

My first trip back was originally scheduled to be when my mom was heading home from rehab. When I got there, though, it was clear that she was in no shape to be going anywhere anytime soon. She was not even able to attend most of the rehab sessions because she was dizzy and fatigued from low blood pressure. She was barely eating.

The good news was that when the hospital staff could get her out of bed, she walked better than she had in years. It was amazing to see her toddle down the hall, standing straight, holding on to the walker, but not hunched over, and picking up speed. I followed behind her with a wheelchair in case, and it made me feel as though it might have all been worth it and she could be okay.

There were bad signs, too. Moving from side to side was torture, and getting into and out of bed was worse. Her arms were even more swollen than they had been after surgery, and she was not herself. But there was really nothing to do. She needed time to recover, and it was going to take whatever it took. I stayed that first night until visiting hours were over and then took a cab to her apartment, where it was quiet and spooky and cold.

DO NOW

Discuss a care schedule with all those involved in a person's care to divide up tasks to minimize the chance of anyone's burning out. Use the list on page 241 for reference.

Reverse Engineer a Budget

When I was back in my mom's apartment on that second visit, I went to the lobby for the mail and then sat down at her desk in the office/ guest room to try to get a bead on things. Enough time had gone by that I knew that bills needed to be paid—electric, cable, insurances, credit cards, condo fees, whatever else there was. I had no idea what was automated and what she still paid by check. I had no idea how much money was available in her checking account nor her general cash flow.

I needed to reverse engineer a budget to see how those bills were to be paid and what day of the month they went out. I usually use spreadsheets for things like that, not software or apps or other tools. But to get started with my mother's money, I needed to keep things simple, so I used the notes app on my phone to jot the information down. Her desk was a jumble of papers, so I made stacks. I didn't yet have access to her bank account online, but I realized I would need to be able to do so soon. I did what I could that night to track everything by looking at the statements.

This kind of budgeting is no different from what you'd do for any household budget, except that you're not trying to change anything at first, just get a basic list that has income at the top and the regular expenses at the bottom, then tally it all up to see if you have money left over or are running a deficit (see worksheet on page 36). Then you need to keep paying the current bills as they come due to keep the household running.

My mother's regular monthly inflows were simple: Social Security and a pension from the state of Pennsylvania—for a surprisingly small amount given that she was a teacher almost all of her adult life. I added the two numbers together, and I knew immediately that it was nowhere near enough to cover what I assumed her monthly expenses were. She also had money that she pulled in from her retirement accounts, but I didn't know yet when or how that happened.

She had her car payment, mortgage, and power bill taken from her checking account, and her prescription drug plan, cell phone, home warranty service, and various other charges billed to her main credit card. My eyes caught what looked like some scammy monthly subscription fees for what we call "gray charges" in my personal finance advice world. That's when you get hooked into small recurring bills for things you don't notice and can't figure out how to cancel. Yes, of course, she was paying AOL $13.07 a month for who knows what. But there was no time to bother with small change now.

My Mom's Notepad Budget	
Income	
Incoming	Social Security $2,450
Pension	$833
Expenses	
Car payment	$507
Condo maintenance	$400
Mortgage	$1,952
Medicare supplement	$346
Life insurance	$13
Florida Power & Light	$145 (variable)
American Express credit card	$1,000 (current balance, with autobills, such as cell phone and Part D drug plan)
Caregivers	~$13,500
Shortfall	$12,628 before reimbursement from insurance

I found that her savings account, on which I was a joint signer and was promised not to have much money in it, was stocked with a large amount. I presumed that it was her annual required minimum distribution (RMD) from her retirement account that probably dropped in there in early December while she was in the hospital. The account was at a major national bank and was earning less than 1 percent interest at a time when rates at online banks were climbing to 5 percent.

I fought the urge to move the money immediately, because it wasn't mine. I felt voyeuristic enough looking at her spending. I was seeing things such as how much she spent on food delivery, how many of the caregiver checks were going as gifts rather than wages, and what was going toward political donations. She was sending out money to what seemed like every politician in the country. I knew from reading research that seniors are particularly prone to scams asking for money, such as a tally from the FBI showing that scams cost people over age 60 more than $3.1 billion in 2022 alone.[1]

I was surprised that my mom's mail showed those top warning signs I knew so well: past due bills, unusual spending, and excessive giving. Cracks don't always show outwardly. The long-term care insurance company seemed particularly upset with her for owing thousands of dollars for a late premium, which worried me immensely. If you don't pay the premium on an insurance policy, the company boots you fast. However, it didn't seem right that she would have to pay and be making claims at the same time. Something had to be up with that, so I put it at the top of the list to solve the next day. Right under it, I put an overdue notice for what looked like a life insurance policy, and then the rest of the bills that needed to be paid manually.

One of the elder fraud experts I spoke to, Pamela Teaster, comforted me that these red flags are easy to miss and that it's not a sign of neglect but merely something you have to jump on when you see it. Teaster, who is the director of the Virginia Tech Center for Gerontology, has done a lot of work on elder abuse, in terms of both scams and caregiver exploitation.[2] But even she missed some of the signs as her father aged. It wasn't until she was visiting him from across the country that she noticed a stack of more than twenty calendars—free gifts for making donations to various organizations. There was nothing necessarily nefarious going on, but it got Teaster's attention that he was writing out a lot of checks on a whim. "That's only something I saw because I was there visiting," she said. "You can't Zoom this in. You need boots on the ground."

The situation became even more worrying when her dad, a former banker, asked her to help balance his checkbook. "I just can't get it to add up right," he told her. After looking at it for a few hours, she couldn't, either, which she found even more scary. That was when she knew it was time to take over. "So I said to my dad, 'How about I help you with this from now on?' And he said yes."

My mom must have been in a similar place as Teaster's dad because her incoming cash didn't even cover the basics, let alone touch the caregiver checks going out weekly, though I figured that some portion of that would eventually be reimbursed. I was worried that she was about to overdraft, if she hadn't already, and it seemed like something that needed to be solved right away with a money transfer.

It would have been soothing if I'd known I could pack up all the bills, go over to the hospital the next day, and ask her about them, but she didn't really seem in the mood, and there would have been no privacy to discuss numbers. My mom had a roommate in rehab who was always talking aimlessly through the curtain, plus the caregivers lurked nearby and the nurses were in and out constantly.

My mom had asked me to step in and take care of things, and I wanted to do right by her. My brother was a smart and responsible person, but this wasn't really his thing. It was supposed to be mine. Just as every family needs a doctor and a lawyer, it also needs somebody who's good at getting stuff done. My mom was always that person for everyone. Now it was going to be me. I could string along for a while, but at some point, I would need to enact a power of attorney.

DO NOW

Look at your loved one's mail, even if it seems like an invasion of privacy, and try to sit with them to sketch out a budget of what they have incoming and outgoing, using the template on page 249.

8

It's Hard to Use Power of Attorney

In the middle of the chaos, I went off to the bank with my printouts of the power of attorney forms so I could get access to my mom's checking account, thinking that going to her neighborhood branch would make life easier. I went up to the glass partition and said to the clerk, "I have these power of attorney forms, and I need access to my mother's accounts."

The clerk shook her head no.

I held up the papers and said, "But I have these forms."

"You need a court order to get access to another person's accounts," she said.

"But I have these valid power of attorney forms," I insisted.

She motioned to give her a minute, and she scurried into the back office. A manager in a suit emerged in front of the glass.

"You need a probate court order to access an account that's not yours," he said.

"But I have these valid power of attorney forms," I insisted again.

I knew my forms were good, and I knew the bank would eventually have to accept them, so I was starting to get frustrated that standing my ground seemed so obstinate to them, even if my voice was level and my tone was as patient as I could make it. It was humid in the office already at 10:00 A.M., and of course I had places to be. Technically, I was on the clock at work, and I was missing rounds at the hospital to wait for the bank to open and get this done.

The manager asked me to slide the forms through the slot and then disappeared again for a few minutes. He came back and said I could talk to the bank's customer service representative if I could wait for her to finish an appointment. So I retreated to the lounge chairs. When the rep was ready for me, she had a much better bedside manner as she looked over the forms, but she still couldn't help me.

Types of Power of Attorney

- Durable: Most common; is used to give general powers if a person is incapacitated but can also be used if the person is unavailable, for instance, if they are overseas
- Springing: Can be used only when certain specified conditions are met and can be verified
- Nondurable: Can be used for specific circumstances, such as a broker making trades for the person
- Financial: Gives specific powers to an agent to do things such as pay bills, make deposits, or file taxes
- Medical: Also known as a healthcare proxy; gives the power to make medical decisions for a person

Sources: American Bankers Association,[1] American Bar Association,[2] FreeWill[3]

"It would be a lot easier if your mom could come in with you and fill out our bank forms," she said.

"I'm sorry, but that isn't possible," I replied. I offered to get my mom on the phone or a video call, or have the bank's special forms certified by an online notary, but none of that was any good. The woman even remembered my mom—the value of a local branch—but still no dice.

"These are valid forms," I insisted again.

The representative said she would try to work it out if I could come back for a two-hour appointment another day, with the forms, my father's death certificate, and my mom's trust documents. So we set it up for a few days later, while I went home to try to put my hands on my dad's papers—which turned out to be the easiest part of the process, because my mom had them in a labeled folder on top of her desk.

When I went back, it did indeed take two hours for the customer service rep to make her calls to the corporate office for them to approve the request. There was a lot of photocopying and scanning, much hemming and hawing. I had to go back a third time for a scheduled appointment to finish the job and get access to the safe deposit box. But I got it done. After that was all wrapped up, I had online access to her checking and savings account at that bank and could sign my name as power of attorney on her checks, the proper and legal way.

I was lucky I knew enough about the process to stand my ground, but that's not always successful. I reached out to an Indiana-based elder law attorney, Jenny Rozelle, because she had posted a reminiscence about suing a bank to make it accept her client's power of attorney form to access his mother's bank account.[4]

"I knew the document was good because I drafted it," she said. "So I told them, 'You should be able to accept this. It's not something from the internet.' It was fine."

When the bank still said no, she threatened to sue under an Indiana statute that requires financial institutions to accept such documents, which Rozelle said most states have. Still no. So she did it. "A lot of people don't have the means to file suit for something like that, but I filed suit. Things settled pretty darn quickly after that. The moral of the story that I tell people is that I knew we would win, but what drives me nutty is that we had to do what we did to get to that point," she said.

Fortunately, my mother and that particular client of Rozelle's had not kept the needed power of attorney documents in their safe deposit boxes, which many people do, along with their wills and other important papers. When this is the case, the people helping can't even get started, because they can't get into the box. This happens so often that Rozelle can't even keep track of how many times she has had to go to court to request access for a family as a first step in the process.

That first experience enacting a power of attorney wasn't one I wanted to repeat, but there was a list of other banks to deal with, plus credit cards, insurance accounts, and utility bills for which I had to go through the same sort of back-and-forth process where everyone said no at first and I had to keep calling to make it work. Everyone says you need these documents— and you do—but nobody ever tells you how hard they are to use.

"There's the legal world and the real world" was how the New York estate attorney Eric Einhart explained it to me when I asked for a MarketWatch story why it was so difficult.[5] One thing I did right was to go directly to my mother's branch, where they knew her in person. Doing it all on the phone or online, if the institution is web-only, is even harder.

"During Covid it was challenging. And it's difficult to do it from a different state. You can email or upload documents to a secure website, but all of that is easier said than done. It's exponentially easier to walk into a brick-and-mortar branch and talk to a person," said Einhart.

Another issue that many people run into when trying to use power of attorney forms is that they get stale quickly. If the principal person puts one of these into their estate plan and years go by, state law could change by the time they are needed. The person might also have moved. Power of attorney requirements are much different in Florida than they are in New York, as an example. You can find out your state's rules through the comptroller's office or other state agency that governs banks.

Another impossible situation that many people face at banks, particularly when transferring ownership of accounts, is paperwork that needs a medallion stamp. A medallion stamp is akin to a notary certification, but you can't just go somewhere and pay $4 to have a clerk check your ID and physically stamp your paper. The medallion stamp certifies the financial institution's high level of confidence that it has positively verified a customer's identity, and not every branch has somebody who is qualified to execute the stamp. Even if it does, it typically provides the stamp only for customers and only for documents it deems valid, because it is wary of taking on liability.[6]

The medallion stamp is almost mythical, because so many people can't get it done. It's a prime example of how complicated the financial world has become. In the three decades that attorney Howard S. Krooks has been practicing elder law and estate planning in Florida, New York, and Pennsylvania, he has not found the process of estate administration any different or harder; it's more that financial rules have changed so much that it's a burden on people to get through basic tasks such as transferring accounts after a person has passed away. For him, the buck literally stopped with a medallion stamp. When his mother died, he had everything set up to pass seamlessly through a trust and beneficiary designations so the family would not need probate, but they nevertheless got jammed up trying to transfer IRA assets because one of the account custodians demanded a medallion stamp on the paperwork the beneficiaries needed to sign. He and his siblings searched far and wide to get it done and couldn't locate a bank willing to provide the medallion guarantee.

"I asked, 'Why are you requiring this? You're driving people crazy,'" Krooks said. He called repeatedly until he got an empathetic person who told him that the bank will sometimes look the other way if a notary stamp is provided in lieu of the medallion guarantee, and the family got the transaction done. "You may say that's not rocket science, but there are plenty of people who assume that what is required cannot be changed and don't have the wherewithal to keep calling and fighting," he said.

I got the same sort of runaround when I faced that challenge. At the same time as I was dealing with my mom's affairs, I had to get a medallion stamp to change my name on a 529 college savings plan account that I had neglected to do in the years after my divorce. College was closing in for my oldest, and I didn't want to have any problems withdrawing the money. I first went to the bank closest to my house and asked, but the people there said no.

I went into midtown Manhattan, the land of banks, to a big branch of a bank where I am a customer. The people there said it did not provide that service there but directed me to a different branch a few blocks away. When I got there, the customer service representative asked, incredulously, "Who sent you here?" And then laughed when I mentioned the branch. They sent me to a third branch one avenue over, and they flat out said no. I stopped on the way to my office at a branch of the brokerage firm I use for my retirement accounts to see if the people there could help. "We don't do that here," said the young man who handled the office.

I called the 529 plan's customer service and told them I gave up. They told me to mail in the form unstamped with a note to explain, and a few days later, my name was changed.

DO NOW

Download a power of attorney form from a legal website (or get one from a lawyer), and take it to the financial institutions to put it into force, even if you don't need it yet. See page 256 for more resources.

Government Agency
Power of Attorney Complications

When I was having so much trouble with my mother's power of attorney, I looked around for resources to help me through and found that my former colleague Michael Picón, an art director, had been going through the same thing while serving as a financial caregiver for a close friend. The friend was a gay man who was estranged from his family, and his husband had died. In the beginning of that financial caregiving journey, Picón encountered the same stalemate at the bank when he tried to use the power of attorney as I had. At that point, he was able to get his friend to go there in person to sort out the paperwork.

But that didn't help with other places where a durable power of attorney doesn't apply at all: the Internal Revenue Service, Medicare, Medicaid, Social Security, and the Department of Veterans Affairs (VA). The U.S. government doesn't recognize power of attorney documents, and it also doesn't have any centralized forms for its various agencies. To help somebody with any sort of government benefits, you have to approach each agency individually and jump through its particular hoops.

Picón managed his way through all of the roadblocks of dealing with banks like a champ—until he got to Social Security to deal with the benefits of his friend, who by then was too sick to go along with him. To be able to help, he needed a special form, the SSA 1696, to establish the relationship.[1]

"This was the case that broke me," said Picón, who later created workbooks to help caregivers keep track of all their documents called *The Power of Attorney's Notebook: Everything You Need for Managing Your Loved One's Estate*[2] and *The Caregiver's Notebook: Everything You Need for Managing Your Loved One's Long-Term Care*.[3] He added, "I was in the Social Security office, and these are not happy places. They are full of angry, tired, frustrated people. The people behind the desk are underpaid and overworked and out of patience. I had a briefcase full of papers and didn't have some things he needed. I cried. I just couldn't deal with it."

I had the most trouble with the IRS. To be authorized to find out information about my mother's taxes, I needed to mail the IRS a Form 56, the notice concerning fiduciary relationship.[4] I heard nothing back, so after a while, I called. Making my way through the phone tree took several tries because my choices kept dead-ending at recordings. I wrote down the next correct pathway and with help from an internet search, figured out a pattern—press one, then two, then one, three, two, two, three, and then wait for a real person.

How to Reach a Government Agency

- IRS: 1-800-829-1040
- Medicare: 1-800-MEDICARE (633-4227)
- Medicaid: 1-877-267-2323; but you may have to contact each state office individually
- Social Security: 1-800-772-1213
- Department of Veterans Affairs: 1-800-698-2411

The rep with whom I finally connected told me I had to fax the agency the form with a one-time-use number while they were on the phone with me, and it had to come over within two minutes or the call would time out. I wasn't ready with an online fax service, so I had to call back and do it again with a different agent. The fax went through, but then the new rep told me that the signature needed to be in pen and not photocopied, which is odd for a fax, but nevertheless, I had to do it again, explaining everything to another person. On the next round, the fax failed to go through in time. On my fourth attempt, it went through, and then all I was able to learn was that, yes, my mother's tax file was locked. To unlock it, I would have to file a Form 1310,[5] which would have to be mailed and could not be followed up by phone, so I set it aside to deal with when I did her final taxes (more on this in chapter 31).

The VA process for activating its version of power of attorney is perhaps the most maddening of all. It took Andre Morrow years to get the paperwork settled for his father, who had served in Vietnam. "I finally got a social worker to work with me. I had to pry, pry, pry," he said.

If your loved one can still speak for themselves, it's easier, and the key paperwork they need is their discharge. There's no reason to wait for a serious illness to register it in the system. "It's really crucial to get an initial application into the system as early as possible," said Dick Power, a retired army colonel who became a financial planner and practices in Massachusetts. If the veteran can't do this themselves, you will have to take extra steps to establish the relationship between them and the financial caregiver who will be helping them.[6] "You have to be on top of it, like when you do estate planning," Power said. "The reason it's so hard is that this is a federal organization following law. Banks can make up their own rules."

DO NOW

If you're caring for anyone who needs help with government agencies, start filing the appropriate paperwork now. See page 243 for more resources.

Going to Court When There's
No Power of Attorney

As much as the power of attorney is hard to use, it's even harder if you don't have it. If a financial matter comes up while a person is incapacitated, it can be a disaster for that person's family. The lawyer Eric Einhart, who is also a board member of the National Academy of Elder Law Attorneys, said he had seen foreclosure proceedings started on properties in situations where the owner got sick and did not have a durable power of attorney.

If somebody becomes incapacitated and doesn't have a legally designated power of attorney, it doesn't mean you will be frozen out of their accounts forever. But it is a big mess, to put it in technical terms. You need to go to court to be authorized to act on the person's behalf as either their guardian or their conservator, depending on how the state where the person lives defines things. Generally, the courts define a guardian as a person authorized to make decisions for the person, such as medical decisions, whereas a conservator handles their finances. Whatever the wording of the court, what that means for the people involved is legal fees and time, and the process could also cause conflicts between siblings or other relatives over who will have what powers.

Joy Loverde, the eldercare expert, had this happen in her own family. Her husband's aunt was living alone and thought her life was "hunky dory." Then they visited and discovered that she was giving money away to her cleaning lady at $10,000 a pop. "My husband asked his cousin, who is an attorney, to proceed with guardianship. It was horrific. His poor aunt, who I loved very much, didn't have a lawyer and was in court by herself. It was just the saddest thing," she said. "But it happens all day long."

It does, indeed, happen quite often, but there are no good aggregate statistics compiled in the United States as to exactly how much. A 2017 report by Justice in Aging estimated that 1.3 million adults in the United States were living under guardianship or conservatorship and their guardians controlled roughly $50 billion in assets.[1]

Many of the cases are solo agers or indigent adults who have nobody left to care for them. A court has to assign a legal guardian to manage such a person's affairs, and the state sometimes pays for their services. These are most of the cases that Shannon Butler sees as a certified master guardian in Minnesota, where she runs an agency called Ethical Solutions. She also has some private clients who are planning for a child with special needs, have no other family left, or have run into problems with a power of attorney being abused.

"It can be sad," she said. "When you have people fighting over money, it's complicated. The person isn't dead. It's their money."

Another big drawback of having to go to court for guardianship is that it's public, which was how the retired *Tonight Show* host Jay Leno made the news in 2024 when he needed to go through the process with his wife, Mavis, who suffered from dementia. Money, fame, and plenty of legal help are no fail-safe against the procrastination people exhibit when it comes to estate planning.[2]

Leno's situation was actually quite typical and was mirrored by the experience of the family that Annalee Kruger was trying to help, in which the children didn't listen and the mother predeceased the father with dementia. In Leno's case, he asked to be named conservator for his 77-year-old wife in order to establish a trust for her in case he, as her 74-year-old caregiver, should happen to die first, and he needed that because she had not designated a power of attorney agent. A doctor had to establish that Mavis was too incapacitated to sign papers on her own. Given the backlog of cases in California, the process played out over months and would continue to do so, because once a court-approved conservatorship goes into effect, there's usually yearly accounting involved until either it is dissolved or the involved party dies.

The case for Kruger's clients went further over the cliff to disaster. The mother who was the caregiver died first, and the parents had done no estate planning for their kids to access their bank accounts or deal with the bills and the house. So the siblings had to apply for emergency conservatorship over their father, which cost them $20,000. On top of that, they had to scramble and get the father into a stable living situation because he was undone by his wife's death. He was wandering off and needed full-time care, so the family thought a memory care facility would be best. But near the daughter who had the most availability to be his primary caregiver, there were only two secure memory units available. One was female only, and the other had a long waiting list. "They didn't understand that you can't get into just any facility. He has to financially qualify and behaviorally qualify. There might be a five-year waiting list," Kruger said. She helped them expand their search, and they found a place that was two hours away that had openings, but because of the state of the father, it would take him only if he had private full-time aides, which cost thousands of dollars on top of the facility fee.

"That's a very typical situation, when the caregiving spouse is the first one to die. Then what will be the arrangements for caring for the individual who is no longer able to do an estate plan?" said Sally Hurme, an elder law expert, who was formerly with AARP and authored a series of books and workbooks on this topic, including *Checklist for My Family: A Guide to My History, Financial Plans, and Final Wishes.*[3] Hurme also works on the National Guardianship Association's effort to gather data and participates in its annual review of guardianship and conservatorship appeals.

"Unfortunately, the guardianship court is not the best place to have to sort out personal issues and deal with family dynamics," she added. "But it's where you have to go as a last resort."

There's no true measure of how much worse things can get when there's no planning in place, but the basic financial equation is that you can download a power of attorney form from various internet sites for free or as little as $90, or you can pay for a conservatorship after the fact, which Kruger said averages the families she helps about $18,000 for legal fees and other costs.

The lawyer Jenny Rozelle explained it this way: "The work I have to put into cases like this is drafting papers, preparing for court hearings, showing up for hearing after hearing—you're not going to get probably anything below a couple of thousand."

Despite the cost difference, Rozelle typically has more than a hundred cases listed at once in Indiana's court database, and guardianship cases make up about a third of her practice. Her other work is split between preplanning and postdeath administration for people who have not planned. Typically, she'll be able to get a guardianship hearing within a few weeks of an emergency, then get temporary orders of administration within a few more weeks and then final papers in a few months. During Covid, everything took longer, and some states, such as California in particular, regularly have long backlogs.

If there's any fighting among family members, the process can take much longer, and the time involved and the price tag can grow exponentially.

Steps in Filing to Be the Guardian of an Incapacitated Parent or Relative

- File a petition in the right court (typically probate, surrogate, or family court).
- Notify all interested parties, such as other relatives.
- Provide proof of a medical reason why the person needs a guardian.
- Attend all hearings and provide testimony and further evidence.
- Return for all scheduled hearings and provide updates to the court.

The cases in the yearly appellate review of the National Guardianship Association read like a tale of family dysfunction.[4] "It's over issues from soup to nuts," said Virginia Tech's Pamela Teaster, who also helps review the cases. "'Mom liked me best,' or ancient wounds from when they were kids. It's over family members who took care of Mom and resent the others because they went off and did other things. Then there are the nefarious ones who want to take Mom's money. And the addicts, who are taking Mom's medicine and selling it, snorting it, or flipping it from the facility med cart. You name it, they'll do it," she said.

Naming a trustworthy person to administer a power of attorney could forestall almost all of this. "It's so much easier to preplan rather than being in a panic," added Butler. "You'll be overwhelmed and end up spending thousands on attorneys to get this figured out if you don't."

DO NOW

Send out a mass email to make sure all your loved ones over the age of 18 have a power of attorney in place. For anyone who says they don't, get them to fill out a form and have it notarized. See resources on page 256 for how to get started.

Part 2

• • • • • • •

The Costs of Care

11

The Costs of Staying at Home

The biggest financial concern of caregiving is, naturally, what the care costs. Planning is complicated because you never know what's going to happen next. If you don't have an infinite amount of money, you must figure out the best you can do with your available resources. A spectrum of care is available, and families generally flow from one type to the next as needed.

If an ill person wants to stay at home, the most economical scenario for couples is that one takes care of the other for as long as possible. That was what my grandmother did for my grandfather until she couldn't handle him anymore. He was a huge guy, weighing probably over three hundred pounds, and was ornery with dementia. It eventually got so bad that he needed to go into a nursing home. It was also what my mom did for my dad until he got too much for her to move by herself, as he was over a foot taller than she.

The medical-financial complex will pay for care only in certain approved circumstances. Since the 1950s, the eldercare system in the United States has defined six activities of daily living (ADLs), and if a person needs help with two out of the six, or sometimes three out of six, they can qualify for services of various types.[1] This is especially important for activating a long-term care insurance claim, qualifying for a rehab stay via Medicare after a hospitalization, qualifying for some home-based services such as physical therapy, and getting Medicaid approval for a nursing home.

The basic ADLs are: walking, feeding, dressing, washing, continence, and toileting. There's a lot of room for debate about the level of help needed for those tasks that will get someone certified for a claim by a medical professional. Some people hold off, thinking that they're getting by just fine, but there's a possibility that they could qualify for help at their level—and if they got that help, it could prevent a disaster such as a fall. By the time something bad happens, the care they need is much more complicated and expensive.

The National Institutes of Health identifies a secondary set of "instrumental" ADLs, which include transportation, help with finances, shopping and meal preparation, housecleaning and home maintenance, managing communication, and managing medication. Long before a loved one might need help going to the bathroom and getting dressed, they might need somebody to pick up groceries, mow the lawn, change lightbulbs, and so forth. These are often the tasks that family members handle, but if there's nobody offering free labor to do those things, you can pay for it.

The cost of hiring outside help for at-home care varies depending on where you live and what kind of care you need, and whether you hire privately or through an agency. The annual Genworth Financial cost of care survey is one of the most reliable estimates for how much people pay in various parts of the country for different levels of care, but there's no real way to know what the price will be until you start trying to hire people.[2] However, the survey is a good way of seeing the pricing hierarchy. Private pay is generally less than that of an agency, and assisted living generally costs less than private pay at a full-service nursing home.

My mom started with private, in-home aides, even though she hated everything about it: the expense, the lack of privacy, the loss of control, the endless logistics.[3] She came by her first caregiver through a friend in her building after his mother died, months before the surgeon agreed to operate on her back. Her friend made a simple, convincing argument: "If you don't sign her up now, she's going to get another job and then she won't be available if you do have surgery."

My mom thought that woman, whom I'll call Rose to protect her privacy, was sharp, which was about her highest form of praise. I fell for Rose well before I met her, because she got my mom cooking again. By that, I mean my mom directed and Rose was like a surrogate pair of hands. They had people over for dinner, and I heard joy in my mom's voice when I spoke to her on the phone as she told me about a new dessert she made that everyone loved.

Still, underlying it all, I had a lingering resistance to Rose because I felt guilty that she was doing my job. As the daughter, I was supposed to be the one sitting by my mother's bedside, taking her to doctor's appointments, keeping track of her medications, and cleaning up after her. The worst times Rose and I had together were when we were both in the confined space of a hospital room and there was an unspoken redundancy. Each of us raced to complete tasks before the other, such as filling my mom's water bottle. I think I made Rose nervous in the same way, because she could never sit still when I was in the room.

The reality of our situation was that we had to pay Rose and her coterie of helpers to care for my mom and I had to be okay with it. I couldn't be there full-time the way my mom needed me, and she didn't want me to take care of her more intimate needs such as bathing her and helping her in the bathroom. I would have, and I did it when it fell upon me, but it pained both of us. We could pay other people to do those things, but on the other hand, none of the aides could fulfill the financial caregiving role. My mom wouldn't hand over her ATM card to just anyone. It still usually comes down to a close family member or trusted friend to make important money decisions as the financial caregiver.

Before my mom's surgery, Rose regularly worked twelve hours a day, six days a week, and another woman took the overnight twelve. They alternated Sundays so they could go to church and sometimes had friends fill in. By the time the surgery happened, we had to bring on steady weekend help, because the hospital didn't like private aides to be there twenty-four hours straight. We tried out one lady, but Rose didn't like her, so she had to go. Then we settled on two others. My mom had to lay out all the care costs in cash before we could see about being reimbursed by her long-term care insurance. The total after the surgery for 24/7 coverage was $3,000 per week, or roughly $156,000 per year. After several rounds of raises, by the end it was more like $14,000 a month, or $172,000 a year.

What a Care Schedule Looks Like for 24/7 Coverage

Three Shifts

Day caregiver: Monday to Friday 8:00 A.M. to 8:00 P.M.

Night caregiver: Monday through Saturday morning, nightly, from 8:00 P.M. to 8:00 A.M.

Weekend: Saturday 8:00 A.M. to Monday 8:00 A.M.

Four Shifts

Day caregiver: Monday to Friday 8:00 A.M. to 8:00 P.M.

Night caregiver: Monday through Saturday morning, nightly, from 8:00 P.M. to 8:00 A.M.

Weekend day: Saturday to Sunday 8:00 A.M. to 8:00 P.M.

Weekend night: Saturday 8:00 P.M. to Sunday 8:00 A.M., Sunday 8:00 P.M. to Monday 8:00 A.M.

The other women were all loosely "friends of Rose." The night caregiver was actually her cousin or related in some manner. It was a pretty common scenario for the patchwork care market that is stitched all over the United States in various forms. Those particular women were all Caribbean and lived near one another. They had all worked for agencies at some point along their journeys and most of them at nursing facilities, too, but had left because the pay was bad and the flexibility was worse.

I was always on the verge of calling an agency to cover my mom's care, and the functional difference to my mom would probably have been minimal. It often comes down to personal choice and what options are available where you live, what the situation demands, and, as always, what the family can afford. It suited my mom better not to use an agency so she could consistently have people she trusted and keep control over the process. Because I was back and forth and had too much on my plate, I wanted to use an agency to handle all the staffing issues, especially the tax implications of getting everyone's documents and issuing them the proper wage statements.

We were in that predicament because my mom had outlived my father—not that he would have been much help in a care situation. Caregiving has always had a gender imbalance. Considering heterosexual couples, in which women statistically outlive men by 5.8 years, it's still usually the wife who takes care of the husband.[4] Then, in many cultures, it's expected that a daughter will step up for the mom. But it doesn't always happen that way.

Sometimes it takes a whole extended family to get into the act. Danielle Miura, a financial planner in California who specializes in caregiving issues, helped care for her grandmother as part of a four-person family team, because it took all of their efforts to do what was needed.

Warren Kozak, a husband caregiver, was the primary person there for his wife when she got cancer, and he took care of their daughter at the same time. When I spoke to him, he was 73 years old and still doing philanthropy consulting work, and his daughter was a young adult. Now that he's on his own, he's taking care of himself the best he can so his daughter will not be burdened. "When I was growing up, it was before Lipitor and stents and valve replacements, and all of the dads dropped dead in their forties and fifties," he said. "Now there are more widowers, because cancer is up. It's an equal-opportunity disease in terms of gender."

The stereotype also breaks down when divorce comes into play. That's how Elliott Appel ended up a caregiver at age 25 when his father was diagnosed with lung cancer, long after his parents had split. Somebody needed to step in. In the end, his mom helped, too, partly to relieve her son's burden, said Appel, who is now in his thirties, but also because she still considered her ex-husband a friend. Because of all he went through, Appel became a financial planner who specializes in helping widows and caregivers. "My dad and I had a complicated relationship, but you feel an obligation as family," he said. "If you're not there, who is going to be there to pick up the pieces? Nobody else is going to do it. You don't want to see somebody not eating."

Same-sex couples break all the actuarial norms, and that can necessitate special planning for longevity. Two men growing old together may need to account for more acute care expenses, while two women may need to plan for long lifespans and the extra costs they entail.

The care of a person living alone can be the most complex to plan for, and the burden often falls on family members, trusted neighbors and friends, or even a paid professional financial manager. "Solo agers should plan to surround themselves with professionals like trust officers and estate planning advisers. Buying long-term care insurance might also be a wise investment," said Joy Loverde. "Arm yourself with all the tools, including the legal documents. This is when planning is a must. It all has to be in writing, and you have to do it *now*. That's it. Get your ducks in a row."

It's always best in all situations to have conversations ahead of time about what's going to happen and who is going to do what. Big moves are hard. Transitioning a person with dementia into a nursing home can be heartbreaking. That's where a living will can come into play, more than a healthcare proxy to make acute care decisions, because it will lay out a person's wishes in more detail. Whatever you put onto paper, you still need to talk to your family, because what you want might not be feasible for them. If you put down that your wishes are to move in with your daughter when the time comes, you can't enforce it by having it in a living will. You have to come to an agreement. The same goes for saying that you never want to go into a nursing home. If you have dementia and your family needs to make decisions as to what to do to keep you safe, they will have to override you.

If you use an agency for home care, it will take care of vetting caregivers, staffing your needed hours, and dealing with recordkeeping for taxes. You'll likely pay a premium for that, of course, probably $5 to $10 more per hour. Your satisfaction level might also vary. After talking to dozens of caregivers who used agencies, I have yet to find one who was fully satisfied with the experience. Most of the people I talked to had been through several care agencies after having some sort of bad experience that made them abandon them.

Danielle Miura went through three caregiving agencies. The first changed shifts every ten hours, but the next worker would sometimes not show up on time and her grandmother would be left alone when the first worker had to leave. "It was a chaotic mess," she said.

The second agency was working fine until her grandmother got Covid. "They were like 'Sorry, nope, can't care for her anymore, not for a week,'" they told Miura's family at seven one night when there was no way to find another caregiver. The grandmother ended up spending most of the night alone, until Miura's uncle was able to get there and stay for the week. Then the family took up with a third agency that promised to stay if she developed Covid again. "We couldn't just have care workers leave," Miura said.

A caregiver from the first agency ended up working for the third agency by the time the family switched, so they had some continuity of care, but one thing Miura didn't like about any of the agencies was that she and her family didn't have much control over the caregivers assigned.

For Andre Morrow, the experience of dealing with an abusive caregiver made him see that he wanted to care for his dad himself and not take the luck of the draw. He worked out a way through the VA to get his daughter's hours covered, because she's studying to be a nurse.

DO NOW

Call a local care agency (or more than one) to find out its current pricing and availability and to get a sense of what it might cost to hire help. See page 242 for more resources.

12

Care Outside the Home

L iving at home is not everyone's best option, especially for older adults who are alone, or perhaps not for their whole care trajectory. At some point, many families consider a care center of some sort, whether they start out thinking that way or not. This goes beyond nursing homes for 24/7 care. There are many multitiered options that ratchet up care as a person needs it.

Assisted living, which can start with independent living, is an option where you can enter the facility living in your own apartment, have meals in a shared dining room, and participate in group activities. Some have shuttle buses to take residents to appointments. My grandmother's assisted living facility had a swimming pool. I visited many times, crashing on the couch, and it felt no different from when I visited my grandparents at their previous condo in a 55-plus community.

Facts About Assisted Living

- There are 30,600 assisted living communities in the United States.
- There are 1.2 million licensed beds.
- 56 percent are chain affiliated; 42 percent are independently owned.
- 18 percent of facilities have a designated dementia care unit, wing, or floor; 11 percent serve only adults with dementia.

Source: American Health Care Association and National Center for Assisted Living[1]

As my grandmother's spine deteriorated, she needed closer attention. She had run out of her own money, and my uncle and mom were footing her bills. My grandmother had all her faculties and was charming, so she negotiated one of the few Medicaid-designated beds in the facility's nursing section, and my mom helped get her approved. Her aide still visited her when she needed it, so she was not confined there. The last thing she did was travel from Florida to New Jersey for my wedding, just before her ninety-first birthday. She wore a sparkly long dress and was impeccably made up. She danced from her wheelchair and played with the great-grandchildren crawling around by her feet. Shortly after her return to the facility, she got an infection and passed away.

Assisted living facilities dot the nation, and fees vary by location. My grandmother's care cost $5,000 a month back in the early 2000s, before she was on Medicaid. At the end, my mom was still spending about $2,000 a month for my grandmother's out-of-pocket costs, which I could see as a line item in her budgets from that time period. Twenty years later, Genworth Financial reported that the median cost of nursing home care in the United States was $5,350 per month, but in many states you're more likely to come across fees ranging from $6,000 to $20,000 per month for private pay. When my mother was running out of Medicare-covered days at a rehab facility, we negotiated for her to stay on as a private-pay patient, and the cost was $12,000 a month.

A similar model is a continuing care retirement community, or CCRC. Think of it as the condo model of assisted living. Instead of paying rent, you typically buy a contract into the community with a down payment and then pay monthly fees for services. A typical buy-in will be along the lines of $300,000, with average ongoing monthly fees of $3,353,[2] according to the National Investment Center for Seniors Housing & Care, but the range goes from $100,000 to over $1 million, depending on the luxuries involved. Some CCRCs also have rental models, where you don't need to buy in, and the nursing facilities sometimes take in short-term Medicare patients needing rehab.

My mom was one of those Medicare interlopers, and the care she got at the CCRC rehab made me reconsider my parents' living situation in hindsight, because it would have been a relief to know that kind of facility was waiting for them when they needed it. But they would have had to make that decision together some twenty-five years earlier, and that wasn't what they wanted. My dad's dream retirement situation was at a condo by the water, with a pool an elevator ride away. My mom wanted privacy and the approximation of a home where her kids and grandkids could gather. There would have been no talking them out of that, even if I had been savvy enough back then to bring it up and had the options been as robust as they are now.

Kathleen Rehl, the author of *Moving Forward on Your Own: A Financial Guidebook for Widows*,[3] was 78 and at that phase of her life when I spoke to her about CCRCs. She and her husband were gung ho about their plan to move to a community in Florida. She had gotten the idea after her mother stayed at a facility similar to my mom's rehab; it was even run by the same company in a different part of Florida. Rehl liked the flexibility and the long-term planning aspect of the place she picked, which suited her after a career as a financial planner helping widows put their lives back together.

The decision for her was relatively easy, but she knew it wasn't for everyone. She told me about her friend Betty, who was in her late seventies and a widow. Betty wanted to join Rehl at the CCRC and was ready to make the down payment, but her family—particularly a son-in-law who was in the financial industry—was against it because it would constrain too much of her nest egg. "He said it wasn't appropriate for her," Rehl said, but she thought he sounded more concerned that he'd lose the management fee for a big chunk of her account. Betty kept talking about it, though, because she didn't want the trouble of her house anymore and was worried about hurricanes. The idea still fell on deaf ears with the family, and Betty eventually gave up because she didn't want to spend the legacy she intended to leave for her grandchildren. Betty's aging plan morphed into moving closer to her family when the time came but not moving in with them. It was not exactly what she had wanted, but she told Rehl, "I don't want to upset anyone."

Rehl tried to get Betty and her family to engage in long-term thinking. She was going strong and could live into her nineties. She didn't need to go into a nursing facility then, but Rehl noted that with a CCRC or an assisted living facility, she would get the greatest advantage if she moved in before she got sick. The unknowable cost of nursing care is what scares people the most and the one they try to avoid by making all those other choices first.

There's a good reason to fear the enormous cost of intensive nursing care and the type of facilities that provide it. For me, the eye opener was when my father first got sick. At first, we thought his stroke was a life-ending event, and we all rushed to his side to be there. Modern medicine saved him and then immediately wanted to spit him out. As soon as he turned the corner from imminent death, the social worker on his case at the hospital handed my mom a list of nursing facilities that would take him from there. My mom was exhausted and busy at the hospital, so driving around to each of them to pick one became my job.

The nursing facilities on the list the hospital gives you are mostly long-term skilled nursing care facilities, but many will take Medicare patients on a short-term basis—if they've had at least a three-day stay in a hospital to qualify them and a doctor orders it. Many families start their care journeys in this manner after a crisis hospital stay when the patient isn't quite ready to go home after a fall or a serious illness or they need some time to sort out the home care situation. So the patient goes to a facility of some sort, and then the family decides from there what to do. The patient can either stay longer and pay, find another facility, or go home.

I'd like to be reassuring and say that there are wonderful facilities on these lists and all you have to do to be a good caregiver is avoid the awful ones. I'd like to believe that there are flawless ones out there. But I didn't find any. I've talked to dozens of people who have been caregivers and too many experts to count, and none has found perfect places. I found facilities people could tolerate, and I heard stories that weren't that bad, but no ringing endorsements. The truth is that care facilities have a hard job. They generally suffer from staffing issues because there aren't enough caregivers available and they don't pay enough to keep staff on hand. That impacts response times, cleanliness, and food quality. Also, they are dealing with seriously ill patients, and it's not the facility's fault that their patients are sick. They can't always control the outcome of the illness. Public funding issues on the part of Medicaid, grants, and other local support aren't much under their control, either.

Nevertheless, people get mad at them. My mom blamed the first facility where my dad stayed for his getting an infection that led to further complications. She could just as easily have blamed all the root beer floats and cashews that my diabetic and heart-diseased father consumed over his lifetime, not to mention the pipe he smoked for most of his adult life.

Eventually, we got my dad to another rehab facility, where he was able to stay for a while and make progress. We had to go out of the way for that, about an hour from my parents' house, but it was worth the drive. The place—and the passage of a few months—got him back onto his feet and able to go back to Florida. That facility was not perfect, but we liked it. I think that's the best you can really hope for in any facility. As my mom would have said, it was sharp.

The difference between a private-pay multitier care center and a skilled nursing facility can be dramatic. For the most part, care in a skilled nursing facility is categorized as a mix of different payment plans, but many are Medicaid only. More than 50 percent of all people in any long-term nursing situation are paying via Medicaid, the government insurance plan for the indigent, according to the Commonwealth Fund.[4] That government insurance plan pays significantly less per patient than private pay does, around $3,500 per month per patient versus the $12,000 private-pay fee my mom was quoted. It takes only some simple math to see that a 100 percent Medicaid facility is going to have fewer bells and whistles than a private-pay one does.[5]

Given the state of retirement savings, most private-pay facilities reserve a few Medicaid beds for their ongoing residents who run out of funds, but it's hard to get one straight off the bat. Many facilities have a stated pay-in period of two to four years during which you must pay the full fee before switching over to Medicaid coverage. In some states, facilities get bad press for kicking out residents when they can no longer pay if they have no Medicaid spots available.[6] Some have also stopped offering Medicaid spots at all; the facility where my grandmother lived no longer even offers a nursing care option.[7]

Memory care is a subsection of nursing care, but it stands out because dementia presents its own complications. This illness is hard to care for at home, even with paid care, because patients often go through a wandering phase at some point and many have sleep issues that require multiple shifts of caregiving. Dementia also isn't always accompanied by other health problems, so a patient's life can stretch on for much longer than in other medical situations.

If your loved one has a cognitive issue, you need to plan ahead for the potential cost of care over a long period of time, maybe even more than a decade. On social media, I followed the saga of a former boss, Madeleine Smithberg, over her ten-year-plus critical care odyssey with her parents. She first moved them into an assisted living facility near her in California because they were both unraveling and could no longer live alone in their New York City apartment. Almost immediately after arriving, her dad got sicker and needed a different level of care, and then her mother's dementia worsened. Smithberg, a veteran comedy producer who worked for *Late Night with David Letterman* and was a co-creator of *The Daily Show*, approached it all with love and humor. When her parents had to go into different facilities because of their illness needs, she shuttled back and forth between them and wrote jokes about it. Her father passed away quickly, at 92, but her mother, who was younger, rallied. She made it through eleven more years to her ninety-third birthday, before passing away in 2024. Those were long years.

"I didn't know my mother would live that long and that it would be a marathon, not a sprint," said Smithberg, who was producing and starring in a cooking show called *Mad in the Kitchen* when we spoke and was starting to work on a memoir. "If I knew it then, I probably would have paced myself better. I sort of was living in every moment, and every moment felt like a crisis, especially with my dad. Every time my phone buzzed, I'd go into emergency triage mode," said Smithberg, who had to deal with her own breast cancer diagnosis and treatment in the midst of the chaos. "I really wish that I had adjusted my emotional timetable. It was very stressful. I think I could have made it a tiny bit easier had I practiced some breathwork as it was going on."

> **DO NOW**
>
> Get the nursing care list from a local hospital near your loved one and near you and any other potential caregivers to check out what facilities are available, and tour one or two to check them out. See page 243 for more resources.

Dive into Medicare

How will you pay for all of this? Between Medicare and long-term care insurance, I thought my mom was going to be all set. But of course, that was not the case. There was nothing much to do about it once I was in the thick of it, though, because the things I would have needed to do to help my mom had been set in stone years before, when I wasn't paying attention.

Many families run into the same situation, because decisions about these government benefits are made early on, usually before anyone gets sick.

When handling a loved one's finances, the most important thing to sort out is what costs are covered by insurance. For people under 65, that'll usually be their primary medical insurance, plus any short- and long-term disability policy offered by their workplace. You follow the rules and get what you can get. That's not to make it sound easy. It may be statistically less likely for somebody under 65 to need skilled nursing care, but it's monumentally harder when somebody young gets ill, especially if they're the family breadwinner. It's also difficult to plan for a child with special needs or somebody who is permanently disabled at a young age.

The strength of individual and workplace medical coverage is extremely variable, and the safety nets are weaker for those under 65. The gist is basically that you deal with the medical insurance available and move on to the step of how to make the money you have last. The ultimate safety net if you run out of money is Medicaid, so skip ahead to chapter 16 for that.

To help anyone over 65, you'll encounter Medicare, maybe for the first time. You don't have to know everything about the program as a financial caregiver, but you do need some functional knowledge. Most people have at least the understanding that Medicare is the medical insurance that covers Americans once they turn 65. Some people think it's free or that it covers nursing care or home health aides, but that's not the case. While politicians often promise reform—Kamala Harris proposed a Medicare long-term care benefit in the 2024 campaign but lost her bid for president—it would take legislative action that has not yet happened as of the publication of this book.

The basics are that Medicare is an amalgam of many different parts—an alphabet soup from Part A to Part N. Original Medicare consists of Parts A and B. Part D is for prescription drug plans.

Part A is generally free for most people, as long as they paid taxes while working. The Part B basic rate is set by the government each year, and there are surcharges above certain income thresholds, called an Income-Related Monthly Adjustment Amount, or IRMAA. The price of Part D plans is variable.

Medicare A to N Definitions

- Part A covers hospital expenses and short-term skilled nursing.
- Part B covers regular medical care such as doctor's visits.
- Part C involves Medicare Advantage plans, which incorporate Parts A, B, and D.
- Part D is the drug plan for traditional Medicare.
- Part E is the old Medigap plan, which went out of use in 2009.
- Parts F to N are various levels of supplement plans. Plans F and G are the most popular options, followed by N, according to the Congressional Research Service.

Source: Medicare[1]

Some people are automatically enrolled in original Medicare (Parts A and B) if they are already receiving Social Security when they turn 65. The rest have to actively sign up or face penalties if they are delayed for reasons other than that they are still working and covered by a qualifying employer plan. The monthly premiums generally come out of a person's Social Security check but are paid directly to the agency if the person isn't getting benefits yet.

If this was all there was to it, most people could probably handle it. But Medicare has a lot of coverage gaps. For starters, when my mom was enrolled, there wasn't coverage for vision, dental, or hearing. Medicare didn't cover long-term care beyond the stated limits. Most important, the program had a lot of co-pays and deductibles.

Basic Medicare Answers People Don't Like to Hear

- Is Medicare free? No.
- Does it cover a long-term stay in a nursing home? No.
- Does it cover home health aides? No.
- Will it pay for glasses or dental work? No.
- Do you get new coverage days every year? No.
- Are all my medical needs covered? No.

Because of this, many people sign up for one of two types of supplemental policies to cover the rest of the costs: a Medigap policy or a Medicare Advantage plan. The split these days is about 50/50 of people taking up one type or the other, tipping more toward Medicare Advantage plans over time.[2]

One of my own biggest misconceptions about Medicare was that one can easily change plans every year. Isn't that what all those ads are for every open enrollment period? And the big booklet that comes in the mail with thousands of plan choices? But no, Medicare is more complicated than that. Unlike the decision about when to claim Social Security, which is usually a onetime deal (although a lot of strategizing goes into it), with Medicare you have to make one big, important decision immediately and then make small adjustments every year.

The decision at enrollment about what path to pick—Medigap or Advantage—is monumental to the caregiver when the time comes. This is because it's pretty much functionally impossible to switch from a Medicare Advantage plan to a Medigap supplement, although you can more easily change from a Medigap supplement to a Medicare Advantage plan. Medicare Advantage plans can be cheaper initially, but if a person gets really sick, they can end up with limited options. Medigap is more expensive but has better coverage.

I'm not the only financial expert to feel confused. Andrew Crowell, the Los Angeles–based vice chairman of wealth management at D. A. Davidson, had the same feelings as I had when he was helping his mother after his father died. He was tripped up by the need to make any choices at all, not understanding what Medicare itself covered and didn't cover, what the famed "doughnut hole" was all about, and why there were two different routes to choose from and then many plans on either side.

His father had been covered under his workplace retirement benefits, and then after he died, his mother was on her own. Despite his expertise in money management, Crowell told me it was humbling to deal with Medicare and that he reached out to a lot of co-workers and even to clients when he found conflicting information. "Until you are actually living with these things, you don't know. I stumbled into it. When people are in their sixties and are healthy, they don't really talk to their children about this stuff. It's like renewing an auto policy to them," Crowell said.

If you end up being a caregiver, you might figure this out only when the Medicare recipient is failing and needs expensive care that the Medicare Advantage plan won't cover, and then it's not possible to switch to a Medigap plan.[3]

When my parents originally made their decisions, I wasn't a part of it. I was in my thirties, having babies and consumed with my own life. They didn't actually have much of a choice to make anyway. My father's teaching job at Franklin & Marshall College provided a Medigap plan for both my parents, and they happily took that. When my father died, the first communication my mom got from the college, where my dad had worked for almost forty years, was a letter with a perfunctory sentence of condolence and then the information that she'd be kicked off the plan at the end of the following month.

By that time, I was a personal finance columnist at Reuters and had passed my CFP® exam, so she consulted me. My advice was to call a Medicare counselor and work through the math, ask her friends about the plans offered in Florida, and weigh the costs. She did exactly that and picked a Medigap supplement plan because her healthcare costs were high and she wanted the most coverage.

Prescription drug coverage has been particularly tricky with Medicare, because there has always been a built-in coverage gap. If a person takes traditional Medicare with a Medigap supplement, they also need to elect a Part D prescription coverage plan. Part D is rolled into most Medicare Advantage plans. There's a penalty if you don't sign up for some kind of Part D plan as soon as you're eligible, either directly or through a Medicare Advantage plan.

Part D covers up to a certain amount each year, but then there's a wide so-called "doughnut hole" before it picks up again to cover catastrophic costs. The gap used to be much wider and harder to navigate. For my mom in 2023, Part D coverage tapped out at about $5,000 in drug costs, and she had to pay a 25 percent co-pay on drugs for the next $2,400. When she reached the "catastrophic" spending level of $7,400 per year, her drugs were covered 100 percent again; my mom always made it there. Legislative changes are constantly shrinking the doughnut hole, reducing the catastrophic coverage level to $3,300 in 2024 and $2,000 in 2025, but the future is uncertain.[4]

The key differences between Medigap and Medicare Advantage involve cost and availability. Medigap supplement plans have monthly premiums that go up as you age. There's also no hearing, vision, or dental coverage included. When I was handling the bills for my mother in 2023, the baseline Part B cost $164.90 per month, which came out of my mom's Social Security check, and is adjusted every year for inflation. She was paying $346 a month for her supplement, which also went up as she aged. The Part D average was $40 a month, but my mom's plan cost $72. On the plus side, everything she needed was completely covered and the insurance was widely accepted. If you're in poor health, that's usually the only plus that matters.

Medicare Advantage plans, on the other hand, function more like employer medical insurance plans from a health maintenance organization (HMO). All of your needs are bundled together for a zero or low premium: prescription drugs, vision, dental, and hearing, plus sometimes perks such as gym memberships. A private insurance company basically buys out your Medicare contract with the government and acts as a subcontractor. The downsides are that you owe co-pays just as you do with employer health insurance and your networks are limited.

If you're going through an expensive medical treatment, need frequent dialysis, or have other chronic health issues, the co-pays can add up with a Medicare Advantage plan. Your preferred provider might not be in network. You may face extra costs you don't anticipate and can't control, such as ambulance fees or lab costs. When I was doing a story on this for MarketWatch, Crystal Millican, a Medicare agent for the online insurance aggregator Boomer Benefits, told me that when she was helping her father go through his enrollment choices, she made sure that he signed up for a Medigap supplement plan because he was starting chemotherapy and she wanted to make sure it was covered in full.[5]

During my mom's illness, I kept expecting bills to come in the mail, but they never did because her supplement covered everything. I have a binder full of explanation of benefits forms, but for all the charges my mom racked up over 2022 and 2023, we never had to pay more than a few scattered bits.

Cameron Huddleston went through a similar caregiving experience with her mom, but with Medicare Advantage. Huddleston lives in Kentucky and is the author of the book *Mom and Dad, We Need to Talk: How to Have Essential Conversations with Your Parents About Their Finances,* the bible on having money conversations with your parents.[6] Ironically, the discussion about which Medicare plan to take was one she never had with her own mom. Her mom picked her plan when she was about to turn 65 and felt no need to consult with her daughter, who was in her midthirties then. But shortly thereafter, Huddleston's mom was diagnosed with Alzheimer's disease. It wasn't until years later, when Huddleston had to move her mom to a memory care facility in Tennessee, that she took an active hand in the matter to switch plans among the available choices each year, and then again when she moved her back to Kentucky, because Medicare Advantage plans are state specific.

At that point, Huddleston was stuck with the Medicare Advantage path for her mom, and she was generally satisfied with it. She shopped her plans yearly. "I reviewed all her options, and we picked the one where the premium was really low, like almost zero, with a low deductible, too," she said. The plan always covered a lot of the costs, but the ambulance trips were the biggest surprise. "Those were each a few thousand dollars," Huddleston said.

Others I talked to had less positive things to say. Michelle Petrowski did not have a good experience dealing with her mother's Medicare Advantage plan. "I'd tell anyone never to buy that," she said, endorsing Medicare supplements instead. The co-pays piled up after her mother was diagnosed with breast cancer. "She was denied care in many cases," Petrowski said. "So every time she got sick, we had to take her to the ER or else she had to wait weeks. It took forever to get her set up with chemo."

DO NOW

Find out what kind of Medicare plan your loved one has, and get a copy of the ID information. Log the information on your cheat sheet (page 234).

14

Fight for Your Benefits

The way many financial caregivers first interact with Medicare is at the hospital when their loved one has an emergency. The first thing you realize is that the clock is ticking. When I was there that first day for my mom's big surgery, I had no idea of the nuances involved, but by the next day, I understood that the goal of her care team from the moment she arrived was to get her out of there.

The feeling of patients about hospitals is generally mutual, especially since the advent of Covid. But when you are facing a medical crisis as a caregiver, the thought of the ill person going home is scary, especially if you don't already have caregivers and the setup you need. It feels safe in the hospital.

Medicare Part A governs hospital stays. This part of Medicare limits how many days are covered: ninety days per medical episode. It does not go by calendar year. That means if you're in the hospital in December for a heart attack and you stay there into January, you don't get a new set of days just because it's a new year.

Medicare Part A Coverage Summary, Before Coverage by Supplemental Insurance

- Days 1 to 60: $1,676 deductible (this amount and those that follow are 2025 numbers, which adjust each year for inflation)
- Days 61 to 90: $419 each day
- Days 91 and beyond: $838 each day while you are using your sixty lifetime reserve days
- Each day after you use all of your lifetime reserve days: All costs

Source: Medicare[1]

The only way the ninety-day clock will reset is if the person leaves the hospital setting and stays out for sixty days. If they go home for thirty days and come back for something completely different, it still counts as part of the same benefit period. The coverage limits were designed by actuaries to be enough for common situations, and mostly they are. The catch is that you actually get only the number of days the doctors approve for your medical situation, and that is almost always less than ninety days. That's why the people at the hospital start talking about discharge as soon as you set foot on a ward.

It can't be repeated enough that Medicare does not cover long-term care right now. Candidates for office often promise change, but as of this writing, no law has fixed it yet. The only safety net in the Medicare rulebook is that you get sixty extra lifetime days to add to your ninety days. These are not renewable, so you have to choose carefully when to spend them. When you go beyond the Medicare day limits, you will pay out of pocket, unless you have supplemental insurance that will pick up the cost.

After my mom's initial surgery in November 2022, these Medicare rules resulted in her doctors wanting to shift her very quickly to the hospital's in-house rehab floor for what they intended to be a two-week stay. By a quirk of Medicare administration, those days counted as hospital days, not rehab days. My mom had prenegotiated the move with the surgeon because the rehab facility had a good reputation for intensive physical therapy, it was ten minutes from her apartment, and her team of doctors could keep her on their hospital rounds. She clearly wasn't ready for rehab when they wanted to move her there, though, and then she clearly wasn't ready to go home.

We immediately started to renegotiate, and we were able to drag out her stay on the hospital floor by an extra week.

To lengthen her stay in rehab, the person we had to convince was the head of the physical therapy department, a humorless woman who scolded my mom for lollygagging and thought she was impeding her own progress. The stay-or-go determinant was a skills test. The PT head took my mom down the hall to the open space in front of the elevators and put her through her paces. My mom and I tag-teamed her as though we were first and second chairs on our mock trial team from high school. (Back in the day, my mom was the coach, of course.)

We tried small talk and jokes. We argued that she had been trying very hard, and we went through a list we kept of how many PT sessions she had and why she missed the ones she did. Many of the absences had a good medical reason: Her blood pressure was too low, or she was dizzy, nauseous, and generally too sick to do it. A few of the times, she was having tests done when the therapist came. More than once, the therapists mixed up her appointment with her roommate's. Mom was Ann and her roommate was Maryanne, so it was disconcerting but understandable. We always checked the meds.

We made little emotional impact on that woman. While my mom was excellent at using the grabber to pick up exercise bands from the floor, which was one of the tasks, she was not so great at walking the length of the area with her walker, then turning and going back.

My mom didn't pass the tests that showed she was making enough progress, which would have allowed her to stay at the hospital's rehab to continue to make more progress. She could do as well with therapy at home, the head of PT told us as she set my mom for discharge exactly a month after arriving. And, yes, she knew it sounded ridiculous that the more you need therapy, the less you qualify for it, but that's how the system works.

It was kind of half-time for us.

Once my mom was sent home, I hoped that she would stay out of the hospital for at least sixty days so that her Medicare hospital time would reset. My tally showed we had used up thirty hospital days, and if she went back in for an emergency, we'd have to be careful about using up more time.

She made it only forty days before she had another problem.

In round two, things were much more serious. She fell at home, which was why she had to go back to the hospital. Whose fault was it? Hard to say. Mine? I was the one who let her fall. Well, she didn't fall exactly. Her aide and I kind of lowered her to the floor gently when her legs gave out in the middle of transitioning her to a chair, but I was the one holding the bulk of her weight when she faltered, and I initially felt responsible.

I had just arrived with my kids. They had a week off at the end of January, and I grabbed the opportunity to go down there with them. We tumbled in at 5:00 P.M., and my mom and the daytime aide had dinner waiting for us. We ate together and laughed a lot as the kids caught my mom up on all their doings. I took a moment on her balcony to catch my breath and wrote in my journal, "Okay, phew, things seem manageable here somewhat." The kids and I then walked down to the strip of shops nearby for ice cream while my mom went to the bathroom, which always took forever.

When we got back, the night aide had taken over. She wheeled my mom to the living room, and we started to help transfer her to her recliner so we could watch a movie together. But as we were pivoting with her and I was holding on to the safety belt around her torso, my mom's legs gave way. They went right out from under her. The aide and I weren't strong enough to turn her around and hoist her onto the recliner at that angle, so down was the only choice. The kids grabbed some pillows, and we made a kind of nest for her to land on.

My mom was lucid and directed us the whole time, while I was trying hard not to panic in front of my kids. We clearly needed to call 911. When the EMTs arrived, my mom and I went off to the hospital in the ambulance, while the aide drove herself over and the teens stayed put in the apartment. I was having a true sandwich generation moment. They were old enough to understand that something very bad had happened but not adult enough to really be useful in a hospital setting overnight, so I chose to leave them behind on their own for the night.

It turned out that my mom had a hospital-grade, antibiotic-resistant infection in her spine that she likely acquired during surgery, and she needed more surgery to clean it out. This time around, I knew a lot more. I understood that the hospital's main goal was to get her out of there as fast as possible. And they weren't going to take her back again at the in-hospital rehab, either, because she was too seriously injured to participate. That was going to add a whole new dimension because she would need some kind of skilled nursing facility once she was released by the hospital.

We had sixty Medicare hospital days left. That countdown loomed large every day that passed, for both me and the staff.

What would happen if she used them up? She would owe co-pays through day ninety, which would be picked up by her Medicare supplement, and we could use up her lifetime reserve days; then we would have to start paying out of pocket. The potential price tag made me sweat, but we had to tough it out and see what happened.

My job was to keep all the balls in the air long enough to give my mom a chance to recover. Despite the infection and the two subsequent emergency surgeries she had the first week she was back in the hospital, she was not irreparably injured. The back surgeon, with his God complex and amazing ability to compartmentalize, said her mechanical spinal issues would heal. With time and physical therapy, she would be able to walk again and resume her normal life.

We all sincerely believed that. I still believe it now.

If not for everything else that went wrong systematically in my mom's body, she would likely have eventually bounced back from the initial surgery. The medical system, however, wrote her off and seemed annoyed at every turn when we tried to arrange "extraordinary" care for her. They saw a frail, bedridden lady who was out of it most of the time and beyond repair. So when her heart enzymes spiked after the emergency surgery, which indicated a cardiac event of some kind such as a heart attack, the cardiology department was slow to respond with any sort of treatment plan. After another emergency surgery a few days later to try to alleviate her pain, she was delirious, begging to die and trying to bite nurses. They wouldn't recognize that she was going through withdrawal from a pain med they had stopped giving her and wrote it off as dementia.

One day, Rose told me that my mom had been speaking Yiddish to her. I said, "We should tell the doctor; that's a bad sign." He didn't seem concerned when he was there next on rounds and said that patients often speak in different languages when they have cognitive decline.

"But she doesn't even really speak Yiddish," I said. "And she doesn't have cognitive decline."

My mom had taken high school German but knew only a bit of Yiddish; her parents spoke it around her when they didn't want her to understand what they were saying, and even they spoke it badly as they were both born in the United States and spoke primarily English. My father was the Yiddish scholar in the family; he mastered the language for his specialty in Jewish-American literature. There's no time for this sort of family history with doctors on rounds, though. The rush confounded me.

My mom's cognitive issue turned out to be a massive sodium imbalance—which was correctable with proper attention. She was mostly lucid afterward, but not totally. At one visit with the kids, within a few minutes, she told them she was seeing a naked man at the end of the bed and then whipped them at *Jeopardy!*.

She had a surgical wound from the top of her neck to the small of her back from two new surgeries that fused her vertebrae from T7 to S1. She had that kind-of heart attack in between the two surgeries. She was too nauseous to eat, and her arms were painfully swollen. Her current state could be blamed on an infection she'd gotten from the hospital itself, which required us to wear head-to-toe gowns and masks for a week when in her room and not to touch her skin with ungloved hands.

She clearly needed hospital-level care. There was reason to hope that if she could make it through her medical challenges, she could live another ten or maybe even twenty years. So why wouldn't that be enough to justify her staying put with doctors who knew her case, who could help her?

I told all that to the social worker who came with the list of nursing facilities as soon as my mom made it out of the ICU stage, after twelve days.

I said, "Look at her, she's in no position to go anywhere."

"We have to get the process started," the social worker replied, pushing the list toward me. She wanted us to go through the options and at least pick one or two for her to contact.

I knew we had to be strategic and play along while stealthily dragging our feet at the same time. There was no way the hospital could ship my mom off to another facility the way she was; it would be inhumane.

There are two key parts to stalling a hospital discharge: You have to be right, and you have to be nice. The goal is to keep the hospital from submitting the formal discharge order as long as possible for a Medicare patient, because once it does, it sets a process into motion. If you appeal the decision and lose, you're on the hook for the hospital charges until you decamp. If you appeal and win, it's not a permanent victory; you get to stay for the moment and then have to go through the cycle again.

Delay, delay, delay. My mom had taught me great debating skills. The first step is to keep control of your emotions and then make a logical, easy-to-follow argument.

"My mom is sick," I kept saying. "How could she possibly go anywhere?"

Then you have to have proof. In the hospital universe, this means having doctors on your side who will take the time to write formal notes in your chart. Our best advocate was the surgeon's assistant, the one who did rounds every day, while the surgeon himself came by only once a week or so. The assistant wrote out clear instructions in my mother's file that I was able to have the social worker read aloud to prove my case.

"Patient is recovering but needs to be monitored closely in the hospital setting," the social worker had to say to me. I nodded, pointed and said, "See?"

I got lost in that part of the journey as the mission overtook me. I did what caregivers tend to do and overwhelmed myself, only half finished tasks, and lost track of the days. I sent my kids back on a plane to New York as soon as I could—their first flight alone—and kept pushing back my own reservation. I tried to get to the hospital early every day to be there when the doctors did their rounds, but that was nearly impossible. I jumped at every beep from my phone with an update from the MyChart app, slept restlessly, and ate poorly. Why would anyone put Chipotle and Jersey Mike's as the main food places directly across the street from a hospital? I did endless billing paperwork for the long-term care insurance. I was constantly pulled in different directions, such as having to run around to all the local nursing facilities to pick one for my mom, because eventually, she would have to leave the hospital. Oh, and also, I worked full-time, remotely, filing columns from the cafeteria using the hospital Wi-Fi.[2]

Sometimes it felt uncomfortable to be so relentlessly tenacious with the hospital staff. Some people can go into situations like that and not give a second thought to doing whatever they have to do to get what they feel they are entitled to. They don't see themselves as pushy or rude. And way too many people go over the edge and yell, get exasperated, or berate people. I felt close to screaming or breaking down all the time, but I didn't. I would muster up the energy to ask calmly, one more time, for whatever it was that we needed at the moment.

We got through the entire month of February that way, because every time it seemed as though it was the day for my mom to be released, some part of her would tank. The ward doctor would come in the morning and say, "I hear everyone has signed off on you leaving today. Are you ready to go?" And then the specialists would come and tell us she wasn't going anywhere.

But then, suddenly, my mom seemed well enough to leave. Sort of. After five weeks, the surgeon started to change his mind that the hospital was the right setting for her, and I can't say he was wrong. She was depressed and losing her sense of reality. Hospital-induced delirium, it's called. So we had to make a choice about what to do next, none of which was a great option:

- She could go home and live with her full-time aides.
- She could go to a skilled nursing facility for rehab.
- She could go to a hospital-level nursing facility for an additional two weeks, then transfer to either a skilled nursing or her own home.
- She could move in with me or go to a facility in New York.

In terms of money, going home was cheapest. As it was, she was paying all the costs of her apartment and was out of pocket for the aides, because they were covered by the long-term care insurance only when the insured person was actually at home. But the logistics of it were mind boggling because she was bedbound and needed two aides and a contraption called a Hoyer lift to get her out of bed. She would need to call ambulance transport to seek follow-up care of any sort. Most of all, it didn't seem safe. So we ruled it out.

The stand-alone, hospital-level rehabs I visited were drab and depressing, and she could not see any of her same doctors, not even the back surgeon. She was at about seventy-five out of ninety hospital days at that point, so they would schedule her to stay at that level of care only for a short time. I got the feeling that most of the patients in those places usually died in that time frame and that they were simply places for them to go that weren't home. But that is just the kind of vibe those places give off.

So then it became a matter of choosing a nursing home for rehab. My mom wanted a private room and intensive physical therapy. There was one option. Most of the care centers in the United States are built around a roommate model, and it's very rare to find a long-term care facility that has single rooms. It's even rarer to find one that will cover a Medicare patient for one, as most charge extra for that luxury. There are experiments going on all over, though, and it's worth looking for a care model that suits the patient's personal needs if you can.

Keep in mind that picking a rehab is not all about personal choice. You have to be accepted to rehab. Given my mom's difficulties, the one we wanted rejected her.

I asked to appeal. Then I got impatient and called them directly. I'm a lifelong journalist, so cold-calling people on deadline is something I do. I stepped into the hall and I got the head of admissions on the phone, explained who

I was, and launched into my pitch: "My mom really wants to come to your facility. Her friend went there after her surgery and said it was really nice, and it's the only place she wants to go. I know her physical situation looks complicated based on her file, but she's a completely with-it lady, and she's going to be coming with full-time private aides. Maybe you should talk to her directly? Could I put her on the phone with you?"

I stepped back into the room, ready to gamble. My mom was not often with it. I turned on the speakerphone and said, "Mom, I have the director of admissions on the phone. Do you want to talk to her?"

My mom had the most charming conversation with the lady, telling her how much she wanted to go there, reiterating the story about her friend—which was true, by the way—and how she wanted to get better and needed time before she could go home. "I've had a hard time of it, but I know with physical therapy, I can get better," she said.

Who could say no to that? And off to rehab we went.

DO NOW

Ask a hospital social worker for a list of available rehab facilities proactively, and start asking around about them.

15

Appeal for More Coverage

Medicare covers one hundred days of skilled inpatient nursing care for rehabilitation, which are counted separately from hospital days. But as with hospital days, doctors have to approve them. At the start of a stay in a rehab, they'll assess the person and determine the likely length of care they'll need. They don't like to extend it. So if they say seven to ten days for a hip replacement or two weeks for major surgery, that's what they expect. There are ways to draw this out with a formal appeals process, but you need to follow the rules exactly.

I knew when my mom went into rehab that we could push to the outer limits of the hundred-day rule. I wanted to give her all the time possible to recover. We needed her well enough when she left to make it at least sixty days at home so her hospital days would reset. Then we'd go from there and make the next set of hard decisions. A long rehab stay is less rare than a long hospital stay. When my father went to rehab in New Jersey after his fall, he was there for nearly all of his hundred-day allotment.

My mom was going to be a challenge for the skilled nursing team, because the surgeon said there was nothing mechanical keeping her from walking, yet she couldn't move her legs. Her physical therapy sessions involved two people using the lift to get her out of bed and then placing her in a contraption that held her upright to get the blood flowing. The first time, she lasted seventeen seconds. Eventually she got up to fifteen minutes, but she still could not move around while upright.

I could tell the facility wanted her out of there immediately. I wanted a comfortable chair. I planted my feet and settled in. When the facility wouldn't let us put one of the facility's many recliners in the room for the overnight aide, we brought one from home.

One useful thing we did was keep track of my mom's physical therapy sessions, as we did at the hospital. Sometimes my mom wasn't up for therapy, and sometimes the therapist didn't show or have time for her session, because my mom was a complicated case. When the social worker first came to talk to us about discharge, we were able to argue that my mom hadn't been given her fair shot at therapy yet, and that delayed it a bit.

Next, the social worker tried to get me and my brother on a conference call, but we stalled them with an email that pointed to an upcoming appointment with the surgeon as a parameter. "We certainly don't want anything to change in her status before that point," we wrote.

The facility left things alone until that appointment. We asked the surgeon's office to write an after-visit summary letter and send it to the charge nurse. The key sentence: "I believe it is medically necessary for her to continue with the therapy she is getting, at least for another six weeks."

That didn't work the way we wanted it to. The head of my mom's care team put through a discharge order the following week at the staff's regular Wednesday status meeting where they decide such things. We got the official one-sheet notice called a "Notice of Medicare Non-coverage" that laid out the rules for appeal and the number to call that you get for any Medicare-related discharge.

The deadlines are strict, and that goes for both skilled nursing and hospital discharges. You have to call the Quality Improvement Organization (QIO) exactly as instructed with the case number within the time specified. The phone number will be different depending on the care facility. That call will trigger a review of the case file, which they get from the facility. That's why it's so important to have meticulous documentation. We tried to give a statement of support when we called in, but it did not seem as though the person answering the phone was even listening.

This is also where being right comes into play. There needs to be a legitimate reason for extending the Medicare coverage that the person reviewing the file can easily see. Not everyone can get doctors to cooperate with supportive notes.

If you lose, the stakes are that you will be responsible for the care costs past the date on the discharge notice. Medicare doesn't release statistics of appeal results, but for a MarketWatch story, Boomer Benefits told me that about only 20 percent of the appeal cases it helps with are successful—but it deals mostly with last-ditch efforts.[1]

For our family, not getting coverage was going to cost us about $400 a day, or about $12,000 a month, for my mom to stay at that facility. It was the beginning of May, and if she used all of her hundred days, that meant she would have until June 10. I marked it on my calendar. The financial goal was to get as many of the hundred days as we could and delay making any big decisions about what to do next. We were fighting for one day at a time.

The Medicare appeals QIO has roughly forty-eight hours to make a decision—by noon of the day before the discharge day of the notice.[2] We got our notice on a Wednesday, and the facility wanted her out two days later, on Friday. On Thursday, we heard that we'd won.

"Stuff it," I thought.

But then, the following Wednesday, the facility had its status meeting and set my mom for discharge again. "You've got to be kidding me," I said to the social worker when we spoke. "My mom's hundred days aren't up until June. Are you going to do this every week now?"

My biggest question to her was: Why did it matter to them? If they were going to replace my mom with another Medicare patient at the same rate, it shouldn't have made any difference to the facility as long as it was getting paid. And if it was concerned about turning her into a full-pay resident, we were ready to do that when the time came. But the difference for us was $20,000 or more at that point, and we were trying to make her money last.

There was no budging. So we went through the appeal again, with the letter from the surgeon that said she should have at least another six weeks still on file, and we won again.

My mom was hardly a unique case. The Kaiser Family Foundation reported on a situation the year before where a patient in a skilled nursing facility won ten successive appeals.[3]

I didn't want to go through that. And I was mad. My mom taught me that when you get mad like that, you write a letter. When I was eight years old, she had me write a letter to PBS because I was upset that it canceled the series *The Paper Chase* in 1979. I don't know why I liked a show about Harvard Law School students at that age or why my parents let me watch it, but I did. I got a letter back on a note card decorated with Big Bird thanking me for my feedback.

In the ensuing years, I had learned to be a little more effective. I also learned some research skills as a journalist. I called the office of the chief executive of the retirement community where the rehab was located and spoke to the assistant, who asked me to email them, so I did.

I don't know what happened on their end, but the discharge orders stopped.

My Letter to the Rehab Facility CEO

Dear Sir,

My mother is a patient at your facility and has been there since March 3, after being discharged from the hospital. She has received very good care at your facility.

I'm writing to you today because your staff keeps putting in discharge orders for her even though her surgeon and Medicare agree that she needs continued care. We have now won two appeals.

Your staff meets every Wednesday, and they intend to put a discharge order in for her every week, even after we keep winning the appeals. My mother has 30+ days left of skilled nursing coverage under Medicare Part A, and she needs all of it.

My mom had an infection in her spinal cord and had several surgeries since Jan 24. She was walking prior to that and has no dementia or other cognitive issues. She arrived at your facility weak and unable to walk. After six weeks, she can roll herself in bed, hold herself in a sitting position and tolerate sitting in an upright position in a wheelchair. These are all huge victories. We are trying to get her to a point where she can go home with a 24/7 caregiver, but right now, it takes more than one person to get her out of bed with a lift. With another month and proper pain management, she could make a significant amount of progress toward that. Your staff says that she is not making "functional gains" and should just go home as-is.

I'd like to ask if you could address this situation and have them measure her progress more realistically—it's about inches, not miles—and let her have the time that Medicare says she is allowed. We have tried to talk to the team, but that has not been effective and they suggested we needed to escalate this higher. It would be helpful if we didn't have to constantly deal with appeals and could just focus on my mom's recovery.

Please see attached documentation from her surgeon.

Thank you for your time and consideration.

Sincerely,

Beth Pinsker

In talking to experts about the appeals process, I discovered that it's hard to assign blame for why this happens. It's the system. That goes for hospital and nursing home discharges, medication denials, treatment delays, and any other occasions when you have to tangle with approvals from government or private insurance companies. They go by manuals that have coverage guidelines and don't look at the human side of things. There are places where patients and caregivers can get help, such as the Medicare Rights Center, the National Council on Aging, AARP, and Boomer Benefits. For private insurance issues, there are public and private patient advocates, and many workplace HR departments have help available. You can also go to state medical insurance assistance agencies. Most of all, you have to use your common sense and dig in your heels.

DO NOW

If you have a loved one in the midst of care, make sure you can put your hands on the statement of rights from Medicare that the facility should have handed out when you arrived with your loved one. It should be available in your medical file and have the date of arrival and contact information for questions. See page 244 for more resources.

16

Get Medicaid Relief

Medicare does not cover long-term care, but if your pockets are truly empty, there's Medicaid.

About 90 million Americans are on Medicaid, roughly 60 million of them over age 65.[1] It's the payment provider of last resort for about half of all patients in full-time nursing care facilities, according to the Commonwealth Fund.[2] Medicaid also can cover at-home care by professional caregivers or family members who are certified, day programs, and other healthcare needs.

For a financial caregiver, dealing with Medicaid can be merely tedious or can be a nightmare. It all depends on how and when you come to it. There are typically two pain points: getting enrolled and getting care once you're approved.

When Michelle Petrowski was taking care of her father, she had an easy time with the enrollment part of Medicaid. Her father had been diagnosed with multiple sclerosis before he was thirty, but he was forty when it got bad. Her parents were still married at the time, and they went through the process with a lawyer to get her dad on Social Security Disability Insurance (SSDI). That can lead automatically to Medicaid if you are below the income threshold, which they were. When her parents divorced a short time later, her dad went on Medicaid, while her mother's circumstances improved for a while and she got private insurance. "With Medicaid, the only snafu you can have is that the person can't have assets. He didn't have anything, so that part wasn't too hard," Petrowski said.

This process will be much harder if the person applying for Medicaid is too ill to deal with enrollment themselves or even sign the papers. Then you'll have to go through the steps to be named their representative because of the quirk that the government won't recognize even a legal power of attorney.

One good aspect of Medicaid enrollment is that there's no restricted calendar period to sign up, so you can embark on the process at any time. It's not an impossible task, or else millions of people would not already be enrolled. Getting approval is a matter of presenting the needed medical proof and wading through the financial red tape that for most people looks back at five years of financial records, such as tax returns and bank account statements.

This five-year look-back period is a big hurdle for some families, because they don't realize that the rule exists until they are in an emergency situation where the ill person needs care and the family can't afford it. You have to start planning very far in advance if the person has assets. Then you hurry up and wait. The time before an eligibility decision is made can vary by state. New York, for example, says four to six weeks, New Jersey more like ninety days.

Generally, the maximum income level is set at 133 percent of the federal poverty level, but state rules differ for seniors and the disabled, and those income limits are sometimes more generous. Legislative reform could change the numbers in the future, but when I was dealing with my mother's affairs, an applicant's assets were capped at around $2,000 in Florida, and that had held steady for many years.

Medicaid's Five-Year Look-Back

What Counts

- All financial transfers by the applicant and spouse
- Gifts to family members (even below the annual federal gift tax exclusion)
- Gifts from family members (including payment for healthcare services)
- Donations to charity
- Retitling of houses
- Sale of household items, such as jewelry or other items

What Doesn't Count

- A primary residence
- One car

- Household belongings
- Assets of the "well spouse" up to a state's limit
- Life insurance below a certain face value
- Burial plots and prepaid funeral costs

Source: Medicaid[3]

The income requirements depend on what kind of care you are seeking, whether it's general assistance, home-based care, or inpatient nursing. When I was running the numbers for my mother in Florida in 2023, she would have needed to have income below $2,829 a month and assets below $2,000 for inpatient care. Medicaid would have counted her Social Security and pension, plus any IRA distributions she took per year, but not the IRA itself. She would have had to spend down a considerable amount first and then restructure her assets by giving away gifts and setting up trusts (more on that in chapter 24).

You might want to seek help to figure out the paperwork for all of this, even if you have to pay for it. You'll save time and headaches that way and might make back the outlay by getting benefits sooner. It can cost $3,000 or so to go through the paperwork with a lawyer—one who specializes in eldercare law would be best. If you think about the math, that's a fraction of the monthly fee at a private-pay facility. Some nursing facilities will help you with the process if you have been paying them privately but have run out of assets.

One aspect of Medicaid that is constantly changing is the ability for family members to be paid as at-home caregivers for loved ones. Each state Medicaid program has some version of a Consumer-Directed Personal Assistance Program, which provides for family caregivers, but approval criteria and payments vary. There are also efforts in the private sector to help family caregivers, and various advocacy groups, like AARP and the National Caregivers Alliance, are always pushing for change. It became a national initiative in 2023 when Joe Biden issued an executive order[4] to increase compensation and improve job quality for family caregivers, along with long-term caregivers and early educators. But progress is slow and administrations change.

If you're getting a loved one on Medicaid for long-term nursing care, the lawyer fees can go up to $10,000 or more if you add in the work of structuring assets so the person can qualify and also assistance in finding placements and getting through wait lists. "The benefit of working with an elder law attorney is that we are constantly talking to facilities, asking 'How many beds do you have, and when will there be an opening?'" said Jenny Rozelle. "I have somebody right now I need to get in somewhere. We're filing for Medicaid, but it doesn't happen overnight and you don't want the facility to get nervous that they won't get paid, so you have to keep talking to the business managers."

Medicaid has a third qualification beyond income and assets for getting care: You have to qualify medically. Just because a person is diagnosed with dementia or another serious illness does not mean they automatically get approved to go to a nursing home. Medicaid has several service tiers, each with its own enrollment criteria. Generally, Medicaid doesn't pay for independent or assisted living, unless the particular state allows some cost sharing.

Another hurdle is that you have to get your loved one into a facility you like. The competition for placements can be so intense that some families send their loved ones out of state, which requires filing again because Medicaid enrollment is not national and each state has its own rules and application procedures. Pam Krueger, an investor advocate, helped her family with that situation when her brother-in-law was ill. "We had to go in search of a facility that had a Medicaid bed, because he ran through savings and lived beyond it. We wanted to find facilities that had the care that was needed and the quality," said Krueger, whose firm, Wealthramp, helps connect people with fiduciary financial planners. She started to make calls and sent her niece out to scout facilities, but it was like finding a needle in a haystack. They had no luck with any place near Boca Raton, Florida, where she and most of her family lived. "We finally found what he needed in St. Louis," she said. "He didn't want to move there, but that was the best possible care. Now he's super happy there."

This is when advanced strategizing really pays off. If you get a placement at a multicare-level assisted living facility or continuing care community and pay for as long as you can, you may have better luck getting one of its Medicaid slots. That worked for my grandmother. But you have to watch closely and communicate with the administration often, because their situation can change and new management might not honor verbal agreements made with old staff. My grandmother's facility, for instance, no longer offers nursing care and therefore doesn't take Medicaid at all. In some states, this sort of situation has led to residents' essentially getting kicked out when they can no longer pay, which is, surprisingly, not against the law if it's done within the state's parameters, which may require proper notice and an avenue for appeal.

It's hard to think of everything at once, though, and family situations change. My college classmate Maggie had been very happy with her mother's memory care at an assisted living facility. When her mother's money ran out, Maggie and her husband picked up the cost, which started at $9,000 a month and grew to $12,000. But then Maggie split from her husband, and the payment was suddenly a stretch. She started to look into getting her mom onto Medicaid, but the facility didn't accept it, so she also had to look for a new one. Maggie reached out to A Place for Mom, a for-profit referral service, and a consultant directed her to a number of places in her area that would take Medicaid after the patient was full pay for two years. That didn't necessarily mean her mom could qualify for Medicaid in that time, however, because of the five-year Medicaid look-back period. It would depend on when she spent down her assets and if the payments to the assisted living facility were categorized as gifts from the family. My friend could have still been on the hook for the full cost for five years, or a portion of it, until her mom was properly signed up.

Also, she soon found out that the list from the agency she contacted wasn't necessarily comprehensive but rather was the facilities it contracted with for referrals. She was able to find an even better recommendation from a stranger in a bagel shop who happened to overhear her talking to a friend about her situation, and that was where her mom ended up going. "I wish I had known all this earlier," Maggie said wearily.

Still another way you have to plan ahead is to keep the patient's income and assets under the limits the whole time they are enrolled in the program. Once on Medicaid, a person's Social Security payments typically go directly to the facility and the patient is allowed only what is known as the "Personal Needs Allowance," which varies by state but is set federally as low as $30 a month. If a person gets a large gift or windfall of some sort, they have to report it to Medicaid, and that could jeopardize their benefits or temporarily suspend them.

Alex Murguia talked about how he had to pay constant attention as he managed his parents' finances through this process on the podcast *Retire with Style,* which he co-hosts with the retirement expert Wade Pfau. At the time, Murguia's father was 95 and had dementia, and he was in a nursing home on Medicaid. Murguia's mother was in an assisted living facility, spending down her assets with Murguia and his siblings covering some of the costs. When his dad's balance from his personal allowance started to go over the limit, Murguia had to use it to buy things such as shampoo and body lotion. As his mother reached the point of needing nursing care, her facility actually nudged Murguia to finish the paperwork to put her on Medicaid, and he was grateful for that and its assistance with it. "If you're helping your parents out of pocket because they have no money, this is where Medicaid can actually help them out in a great way. There's no stigma to it, it just is what it is," he said.

> ### DO NOW
>
> Look at your state's rules for Medicaid assets, and use the worksheet on page 249 to calculate your loved one's assets to figure out if you need to start planning for an application.

Deal with the Department
of Veterans Affairs

I f your loved one is a veteran, there are many additional services and benefits available, especially if the person served during wartime. Dick Power, who has helped many vets steer through the system as a financial planner, told me that the quality of healthcare, home care, and nursing care may be better than what's available through Medicaid and Medicare. At the same time, the Department of Veterans Affairs (VA) can be even more frustrating in terms of paperwork, red tape, and access.

The most important step is to register the vet in the system. The key paperwork needed is the Certificate of Release or Discharge from Active Duty, also known as the DD214.[1] This is a record of the service member's time in service. You can file online, by mail, or in person at a veterans affairs office. "Massachusetts has an office in every town hall. They know how to process these forms. It's daunting if you aren't familiar with the military, but for a vet it's the normal stuff you're used to filling: name, rank, and serial number," said Power.

If you have to file for somebody else, you'll need to work with the local veterans affairs office to prove your relationship and get authorization. "They have their own thing, and nobody can really explain it," said Shannon Butler, who often has to deal with the VA for her guardianship clients in Minnesota.

"One thing that's useful to do is to get in touch with veterans services officers to help you do this, like the American Legion, state departments of veterans affairs, or veterans services officers [VSOs]," noted Power, who added that some people like him act as pro bono financial advisers for veterans. Andre Morrow, the caregiver from San Jose, said he had to show his Social Security card and birth certificate as part of the process to be authorized to handle his father's affairs.

The VA can provide both basic and more advanced medical care, akin to what a senior would get on Medicare or Medicaid but through VA clinics. In a highly populated area, there will be more options, but there may also be more vets competing for resources. In rural areas, you may run into long commute times.

Once Morrow got through all the paperwork to get VA benefits for his father, his family was able to get a variety of benefits. "We were able to put in a stair lift, modify grab bars, get a medical bed and a scooter. I never knew they did that," he said.

The family was also able to access some funds for caregivers, including a stipend for one of his daughters, who is a certified nursing assistant (CNA). It wasn't easy. "I've gone through three appeals. When I was finding out what you can do, I heard horror stories, like eight years into it, the person passes, and you're still not getting back pay," he said.

Who Can Qualify as a Paid Caregiver Through the VA

- Must be at least 18 years of age
- Must be a spouse, child, parent, stepfamily member, or extended family member of the veteran
- Or must live full-time with the veteran or be willing to live full-time with the veteran if approved
- The veteran must be rated 70 percent or more disabled, be enrolled in VA healthcare, and need more than six months of continuous care

Source: U.S. Department of Veterans Affairs[2]

That said, Morrow made more use of the VA benefits than of Medicare. His dad is 100 percent disabled and served during a war. Getting the designation for full benefits took years of work, starting with his mom sending letters to their senator. "He went from being forty percent to sixty percent, and now he's one hundred percent disabled; then you're taken care of," Morrow said. "The care system has gotten better. They just built a center one mile from our house."

If it ever comes time for Morrow's father to need inpatient nursing care, the VA would be on tap to provide that as well, and the facilities would likely be VA run and serviced only for vets, not in conjunction with Medicaid or private facilities, depending on future legislative changes.

VA benefits vary based on the person's service history and the kind of disability they have. For those who were severely injured during service, there may be additional benefits as well. One of Power's pro bono clients, for instance, is 100 percent disabled, as he lost one leg below the knee and has PTSD and some ADHD because of his service. He gets a $60,000-per-year stipend, plus his healthcare is covered.

On the contrary, another friend of Power's served before the start of the Vietnam War, and he would qualify for benefits only if he had injured himself during service and was disabled. There are also income considerations. Power himself wouldn't qualify for any additional stipends because he has assets, but his healthcare would be covered if he developed something serious because he served during wartime. It all comes back to the DD214 and what category a person falls into.

There are other VA financial benefits as well, including education stipends and a mortgage program that allows you to buy a house with no down payment. There are also death benefits, which can be monetary for some, such as spouses and minor children, or ceremonial. "Every veteran gets a free headstone if you apply for it," Power said, and also spouses and dependent children in some circumstances. You can even order one for a vet who has been deceased for some time. Power's father never used his own benefits from being a veteran of World War II, but Power is considering applying for one for him. "He's in a local church cemetery, and I never thought of it until now," he said.

DO NOW

Find out if your loved one has their service records available and has filed with the VA. If not, get the process started and find out what services they may be eligible for.

18

Wade Through Long-Term
Care Insurance

M y mom had an old-fashioned long-term care policy that I was grateful for, even if using it almost drove me off the deep end. Besides
Medicare covering the hospital costs, it was the only money we had coming
in from outside sources to help with her care.

Most people have three major complaints about long-term care insurance: You pay endlessly escalating high premiums for decades; it's extremely
difficult to qualify a claim; and it never provides enough money to cover all
expenses. All are good points. The flip side, however, is that the costs of
long-term care can be so catastrophic that you need any help you can get to
pay for it. In talking to people about long-term care policies over the years,
I've never heard anyone complain that the payouts were a problem. Most
called their policy a lifesaver. It certainly was for my family. Beyond the cash
infusions, my mom felt comfortable hiring help in the beginning only because she knew it wouldn't bankrupt her. In turn, having aides on hand
meant I didn't have to be there every second, which saved me.

The way I first encountered the long-term care policy was sorting out my
mom's overdue premium payments and handling the ongoing claims, which
was a mind-boggling amount of nitpicky paperwork—and I'm a person
who's pretty good at that sort of thing.

It was really my mom who did the hard parts, which were to buy a policy
in the first place, manage the payments for years, and start her claim. She
was relatively unusual, because only about 3 percent of Americans over age
50 have a long-term care policy, according to the Life Insurance Marketing
and Research Association (LIMRA).[1] Another research group, the Commonwealth Fund, found that only 9 percent of those currently in nursing
homes are using any sort of private insurance to pay the costs.[2]

My mom got her long-term care policy in 1998, right after her fifty-second birthday—the age I was when she had her surgery and got so ill. What made my mom so forward thinking, since so many people don't think about this until they are in their sixties or later? Much of it was about trying to avoid the fate of her parents, who ran out of money when they needed care.

My grandfather had early-onset dementia, and that can be hereditary—unless his dementia was from something more like chronic traumatic encephalopathy (CTE) resulting from blows to the head. Beanpop, as I called him, was a college football player in the days before modern helmets and then for years was a bad guy professional wrestler under the name the Green Hornet. Most of his stories about those days ended with his getting hit over the head with chairs by angry fans. This matters to me for my own planning, because you have to cull through family history to know your own risk factors.

My grandmother was in assisted living when my mom took out her policy; my mom and uncle were paying for it, but the only thing really wrong with her was her spinal condition. A more important thing that happened that particular year was that my uncle—her brother—got cancer, and I know that scared the hell out of her. It scared all of us. I was a young adult then, as were my cousins, and none of us was shielded from the details as if we had been kids.

Another force that collided back then was that my brother and I were out of college and my parents finally had a little extra money on hand. My mom made the leap. My dad already was diagnosed with type 2 diabetes, so he couldn't get the same kind of coverage. The best they could do for him was a nursing home–only policy, which he didn't end up using. When he needed help, they had to pay a care agency directly at $18 an hour.

Will I Get the Disease My Parents Had?

Not every condition that leads to long-term care is hereditary, but many are linked. During your application process, your potential insurer will ask you many health questions, including about your family medical history. About 20 percent of applications are declined, according to the American Association for Long-Term Care Insurance. Your current health conditions will be considered much more than your family history, but it will be considered. Insurers have a list of immediately unacceptable conditions if you currently have them, including:

AIDS or HIV infection

Alzheimer's disease

Amyotrophic lateral sclerosis (ALS)

Cirrhosis of the liver

Cystic fibrosis

Dementia

Hemophilia (other than von Willebrand disease)

Active hepatitis C, non-A, non-B, or autoimmune

Kidney failure

Memory loss

Mid to advanced multiple sclerosis

Muscular dystrophy

Paralysis

Parkinson's disease

Post-polio syndrome

Schizophrenia

Sickle-cell anemia

Systemic lupus erythematosus

Sources: American Association for Long-Term Care Insurance,[3] Genworth Financial[4]

Over the years, my mom used her long-term care policy three times: in 2001 and 2005 for short periods after back surgeries and then full-time starting in 2021. Her policy had no 90- or 180-day waiting period as many newer ones do; she could start using benefits as soon as a doctor certified that she needed them. She was allowed up to a cumulative 1,460 care days, or about four years, with a daily reimbursement rate that started at $120 in the original contract and ended at $387, thanks to inflation increases. Over time, she paid in about $67,000 in premiums, and by the end, she received back more than $100,000 in claims.

The premiums my mom paid were reasonable, compared to what people pay when they buy policies later. She started out paying $1,436 per year. Ten years in, she was paying $2,666 after yearly increases. The biggest jump happened in 2021, right before she went on claim, to $6,285. Wait another ten years and buy in your sixties, and these amounts could double. By the time a person hits 70, the numbers start to make no sense.

The best time to buy is actually earlier than my mom did it, especially if you can get a group policy through your workplace—as long as it's what's considered "portable," meaning you can take it with you if you change jobs. I got access to one of those in 2004 when the company where I was working was acquired by another company, whose parent company also owned a long-term care insurer. My mom's decision to get a long-term care insurance policy greatly affected me, because I saw how it worked for her when she used her policy for those early surgeries, so I jumped at the chance. My payments started at $14 a month because I was in my early thirties and were up to only $54 by the time I got to my fifties. Of course, by then the insurance company was teetering on the edge of solvency, so who knows what will happen in the future if I ever need to go on claim. The company that owned my mom's policy went bankrupt in 2017 and went into receivership.

Thus is the state of the long-term care industry. Most of the companies that issued policies like my mom's priced them in a way that wasn't sustainable. The house is always supposed to win, and it can't maintain a deal where people get out more than they put in. For the customers, however, the math of the return on investment isn't as linear as that. My mom's long-term care insurance paid her about $33,000 more for claims than she paid in premiums, but she also paid out of pocket at least $75,000 for the full-time aides during her illness that the insurance didn't cover. If she had invested that $67,000 in premium costs over time instead of paying it to the insurance company, she might have grown it to roughly the same $100,000 and been at exactly the same place. It still wouldn't have been enough to cover all of her expenses, and it would have fallen very short had her illness lasted longer. If she had needed care for several more years, it would have been a catastrophic cost and depleted all her savings. Protecting against that kind of thing is the exact purpose of insurance. You have to balance covering for the unknown against the cost to the person's monthly budget, but peace of mind is hard to put into dollar terms. You never really think about that when it comes to insuring your house against fire or your car against wrecks. You find a monthly premium you can afford and pray that nothing bad happens, but you can sleep at night knowing that if it does, you won't be destroyed financially.

If you discover that your ill loved one is paying an exorbitant amount for long-term care insurance, you might question whether continuing the payments is worth it. I spoke to accountant Larry Pon about one family that faced such a decision for a story I did for MarketWatch about how to have family money discussions.[5] The family elders had to go to their kids and tell them that they either needed help now to keep paying the premiums or help later on to pay for care. Pon tagged along for that conversation to explain the math: that splitting a couple thousand per year now to keep the policies going would likely work out to be less than paying $12,000 a month down the road. The kids decided to chip in.

> ### Three Ways to Lower Long-Term Care Insurance Premiums
>
> 1. Freeze the policy as "paid up."
> 2. Downgrade the policy.
> 3. Go on claim.
>
> Source: MarketWatch[6]

There are actually more options than paying 30 percent or more increases every year. Most involve downgrading a policy in exchange for lower premiums, the way you would work with your car insurance carrier to raise your deductible in order to lower your monthly bill.

One option lets you designate the policy as "paid up." This means you don't need to pay any more premiums but your benefits are frozen in time; if the policy promises to pay out $300 a day today, it will pay out $300 in the future, even though inflation runs at an average of 2 percent per year and much more some years. The cumulative rate of inflation from when my mom bought her policy to 2023 was nearly 90 percent.

Another option is to change the parameters of the policy to lower the monthly premium, such as reducing the inflation adjustment, lessening the number of days covered, or lengthening the amount of time you have to wait before you can use the benefits. If your loved one has a policy that has an unlimited number of covered days and no maximum coverage amount, insurance companies are especially eager to convert those.

One last-ditch strategy is to go on claim. If you qualify for care by not being able to do at least two of the six standard activities of daily living, you can get some help at home and knock out that premium. The risk, of course, is that you might outlive your benefit days. But if the policyholder is 85 years old or so and the policy provides something like five or six years of benefits, it might be worth it. You have to weigh saving that $6,000 or $7,000 in yearly premiums versus the possibility of having to pay for years of nursing care that might cost that amount or more per month once you run out of benefits.

In my mom's case, once she was on claim for ninety days, she stopped having to pay premiums. The reason we got angry past-due notices was that she kept regularly missing paperwork, so they'd pause her claim and send a bill for the premium again. My mom's files showed several instances of the premium amount going out and then reimbursement checks coming back when she got caught up and the claim was reinstated. When it was my turn to write her checks, I thought the process was absurd, because I had to overnight mail payment to the company, and then when they sorted the problem out, they sent back a check (by regular mail, of course). That is the kind of red tape that leads to the second most common complaint by long-term care users: that it's really cumbersome to use.

The paperwork nearly toppled me. Before I could submit time sheets for the caregiver hours, I had to submit documents to recertify the caregivers for the claim and get a doctor's note to justify that my mom continued to need care. That meant collecting driver's licenses and fresh W-9 tax forms from the caregivers. Then I had to beg my mom's primary care doctor to return the form that said she was sick enough to need care. Since she was in the hospital and couldn't walk, I thought that could have been simpler.

I had to catalog each caregiver's hours on a form each week, signed and properly dated. Rose kept track of everyone's hours on scraps of paper, which she handed over to me on the weeks I visited. I had to include a copy of the processed check from my mom's bank account, arranged by caregiver. My mom did this by copying her bank statements, cutting and pasting the check images onto a new sheet of paper, and then scanning them.

My digital-everything brain cringed at the disorder. Wasn't there an app? Couldn't we track this electronically? Why was I trying to write dates and times in tiny squares? And how the heck was I doing it wrong every time? I cried more than once. I called the help line many, many times.

The process was arcane mostly because the insurance company receivership had no interest in investing in technology to make the process easier. The company did have a website, but it wasn't of much help for the claim-filing process. The customer service reps, however, were lovely and patient with me.

The worst news in all of this is that if your loved one doesn't already have a policy, what's available now won't compare even to this kind of subpar, onerous experience. After witnessing a care situation up close, you might also be inclined to check out policies for yourself, especially if you are in your fifties or sixties. Being a caregiver can be a huge wake-up call that you need to consider a policy, and sooner rather than later. You won't find too much for yourself, either.

This is the situation Victor Ricciardi was in when he went looking for a policy at age 55 and in good health, after dealing with caring for his parents. They had purchased prime long-term care policies through work thirty years prior, when they were in their sixties, and he wanted what they had, which he found very useful in covering the majority of care they needed. He said they probably used about $200,000 in benefits between them before his father died in 2024 at the age of 91.

Ricciardi is a behavioral finance professor and the coordinator of behavioral and experimental research at the Social Science Research Network (SSRN), so his day job is trying to understand why people make financial decisions. When he thought about his own procrastination on many estate-planning tasks, it came down to setting priorities, which turns out to be easier to talk about in theory than in practice. Long-term care insurance shot to the top of the to-do list after his parents got sick. "I'm not married and have no kids. I don't have a will. I don't have a power of attorney named. I have it all on my to-do list," he said.

The policy he chose was a hybrid life insurance and long-term care policy, which is the main option available today that is affordable and at the same time provides enough benefits to justify the cost.[7] Most major life insurance companies now offer some type of hybrid, so it's possible to shop around. These policies attempt to address one of the major concerns people have with traditional long-term care insurance, which is that there's no re-turn on investment if you never use the policy. With hybrid policies, even if you never engage the long-term care feature, your heirs will at least receive a death benefit.

Since hybrid policies are relatively new, the jury is still out on whether they are easier to use on claim, but it's already clear that they are not less complicated or confusing. Ricciardi tried to explain his policy to his stu-dents, and they got confused as soon as he started talking about how the policy's cash value was based on the underlying investments that the life insurance company uses to gauge growth.

It's also hard to figure out how much coverage you need in a hybrid sce-nario. Chris Chen, a financial planner based in Boston, tries to run all sorts of projections for clients but is stymied by the lack of available data. Some digital data-mining solutions are on the horizon, but for the most part, all Chen can do now is go by national averages. "We take a guesstimate," he said. That guesstimate may turn out to be too low down the road, if the per-son gets sick earlier than expected and needs more care than they budgeted for. You can also buy too much because you expect a worse outcome than actually comes about. That was what happened to Chen's father, who bud-geted for long-term care based on California prices and ended up aging in Nevada, where it was significantly cheaper. "He bought way more than he needed," said Chen. "He was covered for ten years, but when he went in for dementia, he stayed five years."

From a financial standpoint, you want to get as close to the mark as you can. The best way is to be as honest about your health conditions as you can and then add a little cushion above and below your estimate. Then you need to figure out how much you need to save today to fund the amount you might need in the future. You need to either invest that "today" amount right away or buy the equivalent coverage. "It gives you a good benchmark. Then you can decide when you're looking at a policy if it's more or less ex-pensive than what you can do on your own," Chen said.

But hybrid coverage as a combination of long-term care insurance with what? If people understand life insurance at all, they usually know about term life insurance, which they often get automatically through work. This kind of insurance is meant to provide income replacement for the benefi-ciaries should a principal wage earner die. Of the 52 percent of Americans who buy any sort of life insurance, according to LIMRA, most of them have term coverage up until the age when they intend to stop working, around 65 or 70.[8]

Hybrid policies, however, most often use whole life insurance as the base. This is a type of permanent insurance where you pay yearly premiums in exchange for a death benefit. Some have level pricing so the cost doesn't change over time, and some charge a lump sum to start. Either way, you build up cash value that you can borrow against. With long-term care added onto a policy, you can access the built-up funds to pay for care. Medical underwriting is usually required to qualify for the policy and to use the benefits. If you do tap into it, your heirs may get less when you die, depending on the terms, but they will still get something. A typical policy might call for a lump-sum payment of $100,000 with a death benefit of $140,000, and there would potentially be $450,000 available as long-term care funds.

Other hybrid policies have variable life insurance as the base, the difference being the kinds of investments that the insurance companies use to measure the growth of the cash balance; instead of a fixed rate, it might be determined by a variable rate or a specified market index. Some companies also attach long-term care insurance to annuities, mostly single-premium immediate annuities.

It's also possible to exchange a current whole or variable life insurance policy with one that has a long-term care add-on, called a rider, under what's known in the industry as a 1035 exchange. This allows you to enjoy certain tax advantages in switching, rather than cashing out and repurchasing, akin to rolling a 401(k) retirement plan over to an IRA.

Some workplaces still offer group rates for traditional long-term care policies, but more are now offering hybrid policies. These plans typically work a little differently from the individual plans on the market, because instead of pegging the benefit to the amount of cash value or premium value built up, they accelerate the death benefit to cover long-term care costs. If you end up needing the care, you're basically taking that money out of the pool that would be left for your heirs. A typical policy of this type might cost $3,500 per year and provide $400,000 in long-term care benefits, paid at $8,000 a month for fifty months, and a $200,000 death benefit, which would be lower if the long-term care is used. The big caveat with these policies is that they aren't usually offered with inflation adjustment, so if you buy in young, the monthly amount will not go nearly as far down the road.

When I wrote a story about this for MarketWatch, Jesse Slome, the director of the American Association for Long-Term Care Insurance, told me, "For some people, it's going to be outstanding, because they'll put in money and never need the benefit and their heirs will get a death benefit. For a more significant number of people who buy it and need long-term care, the benefit will be sufficient. They'll make do and manage with that."[9]

DO NOW

Check on the status of your loved one's access to long-term care insurance, and figure out if they need to negotiate pricing or consider taking out a new policy. A list of resources is on page 242.

19

Hospice

Medicare comes back into play at the end of life to cover hospice care, but what that means might be different from what most people think. I was totally confused about hospice. I thought it was a place. My romanticized vision of it was a peaceful facility, most likely by the seaside, where my mom would have a quiet room all to herself. I imagined our spending her last days telling family stories and letting her know we loved her while nurses dealt with all the bodily details to make sure she was comfortable.

Hospice is actually more of an idea than a place, at least as far as Medicare is concerned. The goal is to provide a dignified death without invasive medical intervention, but that is not an immediate or easily quantifiable experience. It could mean days, or it could mean years. It's covered for as long as a doctor says that the person's condition is terminal and the person wants no further treatments.[1] Medicare allows six months before requiring recertification, although only about 12 to 15 percent of people make it that long.[2] You never know, though. Former president Jimmy Carter officially went into hospice at his home in February 2023 and celebrated his hundredth birthday while in care more than a year later.

Medicare covers the medical care involved, such as the prescribing of pain and anxiety medication, but not room or board. At home, the nursing care provided is sporadic and can be, as it was in our case, cursory, at least until death is imminent. Family, volunteers, and paid help do everything else. Depending on the person's medical condition at the start, it may seem no different at all from their life before they elected to go on hospice. It's also not all or nothing, as we found out. You can sign into and out of hospice if you decide you want to go see a doctor. It's really only a state of mind on any particular day.

What Is Hospice?

According to the Hospice Foundation of America:

- Medical care for people with an anticipated life expectancy of six months or less, when cure isn't an option and the focus shifts to symptom management and quality of life
- An interdisciplinary team of professionals trained to address the person's physical, psychosocial, and spiritual needs; the team also supports family members and other intimate unpaid caregivers
- Specialty care that is person centered, stressing coordination of care, clarification of goals of care, and communication
- Care that is provided primarily where a person lives, whether that is a private residence, nursing home, or community living arrangement, allowing the patient to be with important objects, memories, and family
- Care that includes periodic visits to the patient and family caregivers by hospice team members. Hospice providers are available twenty-four hours a day, seven days a week to respond if patient or caregiver concerns arise
- The only medical care that includes bereavement care, which is available during the illness and for more than a year after the death for the family/intimate network
- A Medicare benefit to which all Medicare enrollees have a right; hospice care is also covered by most private medical insurance at varying levels and in almost every state by Medicaid

Source: Hospice Foundation of America[3]

Nothing much changes until the sick person gets very close to the end. Then the family enters the "crisis period," which is when your loved one could be placed in a facility; some of them actually are by the sea, depending on where you live. But we're talking about no more than ten or so days or for brief respites or emergencies.

Choosing hospice involved a family and medical discussion for us, and we were not all on the same page at first. My mom had to convince a lot of people that it was really what she wanted to do. There was a lot of talking involved, not only about our values and beliefs about the end of life but also about practical considerations, such as interviewing various hospice providers to see which one we liked best. My mom stuck to her guns the whole time.

"Don't you think I've had enough?" she asked one doctor who came to check on her when she ended up back in the hospital from rehab because of another minor infection.

"Can you make me better?" she pointedly asked another. When he said no, unfortunately, he couldn't, she replied, "See? That's why I just want to go home."

That was where my mom's living will came into play the most. It was a document she created when she had no expectation of being ill, so her thoughts about it were not influenced by panic or pain. It was basically a reiteration of everything she had always told us verbally: She didn't want to be kept alive by machines, she didn't want to live in a vegetative state, and she didn't want to be kept alive, specifically, on a breathing tube. Our family had to face all of those decisions throughout her illness, and it helped tremendously to have that clear statement of her wishes to fall back on rather than have to sort through our feelings each time.

We flubbed it a few times. During surgery, my mom had to have a breathing tube. One time when she was coming out of anesthesia and realized that the tube was still in, she got really mad. It was only temporary and they took it out quickly. She gave all of us the "what for" immediately, and the doctor had to explain to her that it was medically necessary for an operation, and it was never intended to be permanent. Nobody was trying to slip one by her.

When the hospice people came around to evaluate her at the hospital, they took the living will into account with her current opinions of what she wanted, and it helped ease the process that she had been consistent about expressing her wishes. But they didn't rely on it solely, because my mom was not incoherent. The living will is mainly for your loved ones so they know what you want if you can't speak for yourself. My mom was able to say for herself what she wanted all the way to the end, but we had the kind of relationship in our family where she wanted us to be part of the decision and on board before she did anything. It took a while.

My mom and I used to watch soap operas together every day after school when I was in elementary school and junior high, and I knew she loved stories. I asked her, "Don't you want to see how everyone turns out? Where the grandkids go to college? Who wins the next presidential election?" She said she did want to know all of that, but she knew the kids well enough to know that they were doing great and would be happy in their lives.

I told her that I needed her and loved her and wanted her to stick around, no matter in what shape. She told me she loved me and was proud of me and said, "You got this. You're doing great. You can handle this."

I said the same thing back to her, that she could handle what was in front of her, too. But she said no, she couldn't, and I could tell by the way she looked directly at me and did not waver that she meant it. I realized that it was actually on me to accept that it was her life, her choice. She seemed at peace, and her calmness helped me. She set the tone.

Not every family will get that. People tend to desperately want to do something, anything, to fix a bad medical situation, and everyone, both the sick person and the caregivers, has their own beliefs about how much intervention is worth trying. It's hard to let go and accept death, and when family members are not on the same wavelength or are at different stages of grief, it can be a big swirling pot of emotions. One thing you can count on, though, is that the situation is always going to dictate the timeline, despite your protestations.

One thing that made it hard for me to accept that my mom wanted to stop treatment was that we never really understood what was making her so sick. Before we agreed that it was time, I marshaled all the doctor forces I could to run tests to see if there was something that medicine could fix. None of them could come up with a plan. I was eventually able to see that if the doctors couldn't fix my mom, I couldn't keep her alive by sheer force of will. It was what was happening. It was devastating, but it had to proceed on its own course.

So we asked for hospice. The hospital sent in a general doctor—they called him the "hospitalist"—for his first evaluation, and he merely came into the room, checked her charts, and left without speaking to anyone. He came back a while later, didn't remember anything about my mom, and cut me off when I started to ask him questions.

I finally had my *Terms of Endearment* moment, except unlike Shirley MacLaine screaming for her daughter to get her pain medicine, I went to the desk and demanded another doctor for my mom's case. That wasn't so easy. The hospital administration told me I couldn't switch doctors unless I found another one with privileges who would take over her care. I asked for a list of available doctors, and they didn't have one.

I stormed off down the hall, thinking, but not saying, "You don't know who you're dealing with here! I'll be damned if we're going to go through this experience with that awful doctor."

Sitting on a hard chair by the elevator, I blitzed phone calls to every doctor my mom had in her phone contacts, the way I track down a lead on deadline. I kept calling until I got a live person in each office, then told our sad tale. Every time I hung up, I bawled for a few seconds, then collected myself and tried again.

As we entered that last, hardest part of my mom's illness, what got me through moments like that was a framework I had built up over a long time that included therapy, anti-anxiety medication, and self-care in the form of junk food. I was able to keep a lot of balls in the air that way, at least temporarily. What I liked least about it all was the responsibility, and a lot of that stemmed from the fact that it was my mother I was caring for and we had a turnabout of traditional roles. When one of my kids is sick, no matter if it's minor or major, I don't have any doubt in myself. Around my mom, I wanted her to be the one in control and making all the decisions. Even though I was past 50 at the time, I didn't feel capable of being the adult. I faced times like those with the doctor by thinking about how mad my mom would have been if she had the energy to understand the situation, and that powered me through as her proxy.

It took me a few hours, but I found a doctor who would take her case, and a little while later, it was as though Marcus Welby himself walked into my mother's room. He was charming and talked directly to her on the side of the bed where she could hear him. He understood her desire for hospice and said he'd sign off on it. For a few minutes, I felt strangely happy.

We set the plan into motion with the hospice operator we liked best from the interviews. But another thing I didn't understand about hospice going into the process was that you can choose the hospice, but the hospice also has to choose you. My mom was rejected.

Then I had more doubts about whether we were doing the right thing. If hospice didn't want her, had we made a mistake by asking for it? And if she didn't go that route, what else could we do? We would have to figure out if we could care for her at home and where she could go otherwise. Dr. Welby stepped in and got a second hospice to accept her, and we set about getting the equipment we needed at home: a hospital bed, reclining wheelchair, oxygen machine, mechanical bed lift, and other supplies. All of it was covered under Medicare's hospice benefit, which takes over all the practical medical aspects of care management.

If my mom had gone back to the rehab where she had been staying—if it would have taken her—all of the equipment would also have been covered there, but the daily cost of her staying there would have been $400 a day out of pocket (partially reimbursable by the long-term care policy), and on top of that, there would have been the cost for the private aides. Her going home meant that the aides were covered by the insurance and the housing fee was her regular mortgage payment.

Because of the lack of a true terminal diagnosis for my mom, we had no idea what we were dealing with in terms of a time frame. The surgeon kept telling us that all she needed was time to recover. We took her home thinking that we could be hunkering down for a long time.

DO NOW

Have that hard talk about what your loved one wants for their end-of-life wishes following the prompts on page 257. Allow for the possibility that these conversations may evolve over time and change of circumstances.

Part 3

. . . .

How to Make the
Money Last

20

Calculate Your Burn Rate

We had big plans for hospice. Rose and I talked about putting my mom into the fancy reclining wheelchair and taking her to a friend's apartment for dinner. It had been about six months since my mom had seen anyone who lived in the building. The only person she let visit her while she was in the hospital and rehab was her first cousin Bunny, who lived nearby.

She was going to enjoy quiet during the day, catch up on her board paperwork, watch movies in the living room, and get a little sunlight on her balcony. We started out great. We got right down to watching a movie when she arrived, my mom in the wheelchair and me next to her in the recliner, holding hands. The trip in the ambulance and up the elevator in a stretcher had been hard, but she looked relaxed. The hospice team kept a steady stream of deliveries coming, including wipes, bed pads, and a ton of bandages and other first aid supplies.

That evening after we used the lift to put her into bed, I made us cheese omelets for dinner; then we had ice cream sundaes and watched CNN. Before bed, my mom and I talked about her plans. It might sound like exactly the wrong time for long-term thinking, but everything had gone so fast for us that that was when we got down to figuring out what she could afford based on how long her money would last.[1]

Up until then, we had been in emergency mode and most of her care was covered by Medicare. Hospice functioned the same as if she were home living her regular life, but with a toll-free number to call if we needed something. I'm not trying to minimize that logistical support, because it was crucial, but it didn't help us much with the all-important basic "activities of daily living" or the instrumental ones, either. My mom needed a functioning household, and I couldn't be there every minute of what we expected to be a long haul. That meant, most of all, food shopping, cleaning, doing laundry, and all the other necessary tasks, which would not be easy for the caregivers to do if my mom needed 24/7 attention and couldn't be left alone. So that, in turn, meant increasing the caregivers' hours and making their pay enticing enough to keep them on board.

Back-of-the-envelope calculations aren't really good enough for this sort of financial planning. You need to run several changing scenarios at the same time and figure out a range of options. Professional financial advisers use software that runs what are called Monte Carlo simulations—yes, like the casino town in Monaco—that assess the probability of various outcomes given a bunch of variables. My mom's situation mirrored the scenario we most often hear from readers at MarketWatch and what friends and other family members ask me about. It always goes something like this: Mom is 80 and has $500,000 but was recently diagnosed with dementia. How do we make the money last, and what happens if the money runs out?[2]

That $500,000 is a sort of arbitrary demarcation. If you have more than that at the start of a serious illness, you probably have enough if you spend wisely, or at least you'd have quite a while before you'd need to make big decisions. Your financial planning will revolve mostly around maximizing the growth of the money as long as possible by investing wisely, spending carefully, and minimizing taxes.

"The money will last as long as you don't spend it" is the simple answer, said Susan Hirshman, the director of wealth management for Schwab Wealth Advisory and Schwab Center for Financial Research.[3]

To set up a plan in a case like this, Hirshman does an analysis of the current costs and what the expected time frame is. Whereas retirement planning often stretches thirty-plus years and accounts for ages up to 100, an illness scenario might be ten or twelve years or, realistically, much less. "Planning is about making the best decisions with the information you know today," Hirshman said. "Plans are living and breathing. We adjust over time. Like if we assume we have to sell the house in ten years, we might have to change that to eight years depending on what happens."

With liquid assets such as stocks, bonds, CDs, and money market accounts, Hirshman looks for how much cash the ill person needs over, say, the next six months to three years and then assesses their risk capacity for keeping the rest of their savings invested in stocks or other long-term fixed income instruments such as bonds. "I don't want to have to sell when the market is in an inopportune place. But if the market goes down today, you have to ask if you have time for it to recover before you intend to use it. Thinking ahead is one of the most important things," she said.

Tax Implications of Withdrawals

- IRAs and 401(k)s: After age 59½, withdrawals count as ordinary income and are taxable.
- Roth accounts: After age 59½ and the account being open five years, there are no tax implications.
- Brokerage accounts: Selling investments might cause taxable capital gains.
- CDs: Early withdrawal penalties may apply.
- Checking and savings accounts: There are no penalties, but accounts may have minimums required or fees, and interest is taxable as income.
- Real estate, hedge funds, and other illiquid investments: Consult a professional to assess the terms of the contract.

To that end, Hirshman will then look at the accounts in which the money is held. In tax-deferred accounts such as IRAs, selling investments doesn't cause any taxable gain, but withdrawing the money from them adds to taxable income. Following a five-year holding period, money in a Roth IRA, for those over 59½, can be drawn out at any time with no tax repercussions. For assets in a taxable brokerage account, you'd have to worry about taxable gain on anything you sell. She weighs the pros and cons of where the money is and figures out if it makes sense to change the investment situation.

The financial planner Chad Holmes, who specializes in multigenerational inheritance planning and wrote the book *The Inheritance Playbook: Helping Your Parents Pass the Torch, Not the Tax* about his strategies, said that professional software isn't good enough for the types of scenarios he maps out over long spans of time from grandparents to great-great-grandchildren who haven't been born yet. "The software is trying to solve for the growth, spending, and inflation of one couple, but what if we try to add in another generation and maximize?" he asked. Even for one couple, he finds the answers that the software spits out are lacking, because there are too many unknowable assumptions. "We have to average and be conservative, but really, planning is everything, and you have to reevaluate all the time," he said.[4]

One thing about planning after illness strikes is that you can narrow down the time frame somewhat, even if you still have no idea what will happen. And if you look objectively at the situation, you can see that if you're dealing with less than $500,000 net worth at the start of a serious illness, you might have to make some hard choices. That means putting Medicaid planning and possibly selling a house on the table, especially if dementia or another slow-going diagnosis is involved that could cost $200,000 or more per year for care.

Of course, most people in the United States have far less than $500,000 saved for retirement, so this is what they will face. The median net worth, including property, of those 75 and older is around $250,000, according to the Federal Reserve Board's Survey of Consumer Finances. Half of Americans rely only on Social Security for income in their later years, which is why the decision about when to claim to maximize your benefit matters so much.[5] When you have little saved, you can get by on a regular basis with only a monthly benefit check, but it's hard to cope with the cost of a major illness. That's why so many people talk about there being a retirement crisis in America.

The picture at the family level is much more nuanced, though. Just because a person has little or no retirement savings doesn't automatically mean that they are struggling. Quality of life depends greatly upon whether a person lives with family members or on their own and whether anyone is helping them with cash infusions of any sort. It also depends on whether they own the house in which they live and can tap into it for emergency funds.

When a financial caregiver comes into the picture in any of these circumstances, you have to first assess what the person needs now and then think about what they might need in the future. You need to talk openly about the decisions you might need to make, such as: Are you going to sell the house where the person is living and move them elsewhere? Will they live with you or go to a facility? Do they still need a car? When should you liquidate investments? If you take large chunks out of savings, what will you pay in income taxes, and will that increase their Medicare premiums with income-related surcharges?

It's best to think about these things earlier than we did. It's ideal to have family members or trusted friends involved all along. There's no reason for this to be a big secret, even though we are all conditioned to treat information about our money as private. My whole life, I never knew how much my parents made until I went through the box with their tax returns after they had both died.

Many people I've talked to over the years know that they need to do something to plan for what's going to come, but they don't know what to do or how to start the conversation. "I have really been stuck on how to get my mom and my sister to focus on planning for the future," my friend John Sparks said to me. "I don't know if it's fear or complacency or something else, but they don't seem to want to talk about these things. My mom has made some significant financial mistakes, and I seem to be the only person who is trying to prevent worse things happening in the future."

John's mom was 83 and living alone when we had that conversation. She had been widowed for twenty-five years and was living off resources that her husband left. My friend was an expert in the bond market and had long tried to offer his mom advice on investing and the importance of budgeting and estate planning, but she met most of his efforts with mistrust. John felt a sense of impending doom because his mother was starting to experience hearing and memory loss and he expected that she would become yet more difficult to help, even as her need for help increased. "I've tried to figure out in an amateurish way what the assets are and what the spending is, but I can't figure out where the money is going. I've made a simple spreadsheet for tracking things like utilities, property taxes, and insurance for her to fill out, but she hasn't done it. That makes it hard to see what the present looks like, let alone the future," he said.

One of the keys to having a successful financial discussion with a loved one is not to tackle it all at once; it's not one conversation and done. That's the big lesson Cameron Huddleston emphasized in *Mom and Dad, We Need to Talk: How to Have Essential Conversations with Your Parents About Their Finances.*[6] Huddleston herself took about two years to get through the process with her mother. The big impetus for her to get started was her mother's Alzheimer's diagnosis. That set a countdown into motion to get things done, such as meeting with an attorney about estate planning and talking about end-of-life planning before her mom declined too much.

"She never specifically asked me for help, but because I knew she needed it, I stepped in," Huddleston said. She started out helping with paying bills and getting her organized, then had her mail transferred and got access to all her accounts. By the time her mom moved in with her two years later, Huddleston had a plan going and was fully in charge of the money. "If your parents need caregiving help, get as much information as you can as soon as possible," she implored. "And get help—from family and friends and anyone else you can. My husband helped a lot. And find people you can talk to for your own support."

My friend John still had time, which was a good thing, and he made use of it after we talked. He could have helped his mom little by little as best he could until there was an emergency. In that way, he'd at least have been more prepared to take over when the time came. But instead, he and his mom started to move toward each other. He let her know that he was there to help, without threatening that he was going to take over completely before she was ready, and she let him know that she was ready for a little help. "Recently, there have been some steps forward," he said in a follow-up with me. "After she missed the deadline for the required minimum distribution from her IRA, she agreed to automate her distribution going forward. She also says she now agrees with reallocating her IRA to reliably fund those distributions while also preserving the principal."

Another thing that helps is if you can get the ill person to see what it's like to be in the shoes of the financial caregiver. If stubborn parents understood the repercussions of their procrastination on their children, maybe they'd have a little less resistance to change, for instance. They might feel bad about the possibility of leaving a mess to clean up, where somebody is always scrambling to make stopgap decisions rather than thoughtful ones. If you're the one who is the parent, think about how you want to leave things for your kids and if they could handle it.

My mom and I didn't make much progress along that path until the start of my dad's illness, and she started then only because she needed somebody to talk to about her worries. When they had to pay for caregivers for my dad, it blew up their budget and she was terrified. There was significantly less money then, too, because most of my mom's available funds came from death benefits after my father died.

The big decision my mom made then was to sell their house in New Jersey and live full-time in Florida instead of being snowbirds. It was a sad decision for her, but the stairs in the New Jersey house were too much for both of them and there was too much upkeep needed. I offered to help clear it out for staging because my mom was busy caregiving, and I dived into the local real estate market to figure out what we could get for the house. I asked questions about her mortgage and what she'd do with the proceeds. That led to discussions about what she owed on the condo in Florida and if she should pay some of that off first or if there was other short-term debt.

Another option to consider when you need to raise cash and the main asset is a house is to do a reverse mortgage. These have gotten a bad rap over the years because of shady sales tactics, but federal reforms have turned them into a good option in some circumstances, particularly when a home-owner over 62 has a lot of equity built up but little cash on hand. The biggest hurdle is getting over the myths about how a reverse mortgage works: You don't lose the title to your house, you can't end up owing money after the term is done, and your heirs can still inherit the property if they pay off the lien.

You can usually borrow up to 80 percent of the equity in a property as a reverse mortgage. That means if you have a house worth $430,000 and a remaining mortgage balance of $100,000—which is the average, according to the National Reverse Mortgage Lenders Association—you could borrow around $264,000. You would no longer have to make mortgage payments, and you don't have to pay back the loan as you go.[7] The payoff amount will be settled after you die or sell the property. There are protections, too, such as that if the sale price ends up being less than the amount due, you won't owe more. If there's an excess, that's profit for you. As an example, if you take out a reverse mortgage for $150,000 on the $430,000 home and then sell it for $600,000, you'll walk away with cash. If you sell it for $125,000, you'll just walk away. If your heirs want to keep the house instead of selling it, they will need to come up with the money to clear the reverse mortgage payoff.[8]

By the time my mom was in hospice, we were down to the nitty-gritty, and what she had was her condo and her retirement nest egg. She wasn't at the point to consider a reverse mortgage. So what I did next was some basic financial planning, which you can do at any point along the way and should do at regular intervals as circumstances change.

The first step was to calculate the burn rate then and for the immediate future; that is, how much the person is spending per month. I did that in a simple way when my mom first got sick in order to pay her bills. That was only six months prior, but the situation was different now. This is how fast things can change, and you can't really get around it. You have to make adjustments and hope the plan you originally set into place will be flexible enough to handle shocks.

What Kind of Financial Professional to Hire

"Financial adviser" is a generic term, and anyone can claim to be one. You want to choose one who is a fiduciary, which means they are bound to give advice in your best interest and not because of commissions or any other reasons. This does not pertain to how they are paid; some are paid by hourly fee, some by flat fee, some by a percentage of assets under management.

Who Is a Fiduciary?
CERTIFIED FINANCIAL PLANNER® (also known as a CFP®)
Chartered financial analyst (CFA)
Registered investment adviser (RIA)

Who Is Not a Fiduciary?
Call center employee at a brokerage
Broker-dealer at a firm who does not have any fiduciary designations
Representative at a bank who does not have any fiduciary designations
Insurance salesperson

I didn't consult a professional, because I ostensibly was one and I had access to a lot of experts to ask questions. One of them was Wealthramp's Pam Krueger, who had worked through her own parents' finances as they aged and helped many clients.[9] "The back of the napkin is useful to calm you down, but you're missing a ton of variables. This is all about stress-testing assumptions," she told me. The basic calculator on your phone won't cut it, either, because you need to calculate growth at the same time as spending. For instance, if an aging parent has $500,000 and spends $15,000 a month, you need more than simple subtraction because the $500,000 is growing (or should be), at the same time as you're taking money out. It's crucial to have access to financial tools that can handle more complicated equations, which is easiest through either a professional adviser or a financial services company. There are some free calculators online that can help you if you're willing to dive into the math. I keep a basic savings distribution calculator open in a tab on my phone and run numbers all the time, not only for my mom's situation but for college savings, for my own retirement projections, and for articles I'm writing.[10] (For more calculator resources, see page 250.)

When you contemplate the basic "Will Mom run out of money?" scenario above, the mom with $500,000 would get to zero in three years and one month if no other income was involved, assuming a 7 percent growth rate. You have to change the calculations and use more powerful software to add what comes in from any other sources. If you catch the situation before the person makes a choice about when to claim Social Security in the first place, there are tools available to help maximize the amount they can get (see page 244 for resources). The good news is that numbers perk up when you start to add income. With $2,000 a month in Social Security income, the nest egg would last an extra six months. That might not sound like a lot, but it could make a difference when you're measuring a health situation by days and weeks and you'd much rather deal with that than stress over money. Depending on how the person's money is invested, they could also make more or less than a 7 percent return.

How Long Will $500,000 Last When Spending $15,000 a Month?			
Year	Withdrawals	Interest	Balance
0			$500,000.00
1	$180,000.00	$29,171.91	$349,171.91
2	$180,000.00	$18,268.53	$187,440.44
3	$180,000.00	$6,576.93	$14,017.37
4	$14,017.37	$0.00	$0.00

"It's all about identifying the variables of the health condition and the likelihood of going from level one care to level two to level three," said Krueger. "And it's all about cash flow. It has nothing to do with the money that's left over for heirs. It's about what will keep the person in good care."

With my mom, I counted up her expenses and then looked at her savings on hand. It was late June, and we had enough cash to get her through July and August at the current rate. That meant we had some hard decisions to make about spending more and where we'd get more cash to pay for extras and anything past August. She was now going to need overlapping caregivers, not one at a time, or else they wouldn't have time to run to the store or even go get the mail. I also wanted to talk about moving my mom to New York, and that would cost $20,000 (or more) for a medical flight on a private plane with emergency equipment and special staff, which I priced after searching online for providers and looking at their reviews. Then we'd need to pay the facility I had picked out in New York and new aides as we barreled forward in our new normal. Or if she stayed in Florida, we'd have to consider if she needed to go to a facility there at $12,000 a month.

When trying to figure out how long the money will last, it matters when you spend big sums. It's called sequence of returns risks. If you spend a lot early or there's a dip in the market that reduces your investment returns, your plan will be permanently dented. This is why financial advisers sometimes worry about new retirees splurging on a lot of travel first thing, because they spend down their resources and then have a smaller pile compounding interest. It's not always your own fault. People who retired in 2007 or 2020 were hit with major downturns in the global economy that were beyond their control.

The best way I can illustrate this is with a smaller time span of what happened to the college savings for my two kids. My older child was born in 2006 and my younger in 2008, and I started saving in a 529 account for each at birth, at the same rate, in age-based portfolios that adjusted over time. When we were getting ready to use the money for the first one's college tuition, he had less than his younger sibling, despite having two extra years of savings. What happened? The recession in 2008 knocked down everything we had saved up to that point, while the younger child saw only the upswing. Then the older one got hit with a double-whammy of another downturn before his account slid into safer investments because he was close to using the money. He had no time to stay invested and recover, while the younger child hung on.

When my mom started spending more money, she wasn't going to have time to rebound in the market. With her, we were only talking about right now. She had her savings, which were being depleted. So we were staring at the idea of spending her principal, and we'd keep going until it was all gone.

DO NOW

Look at the sample financial equation on page 121, and substitute your own numbers. Calculate the burn rate of your loved one's monthly expenses, then how long their money will last at that rate. Bonus: Calculate how long the money would last at higher burn rates if more care is needed.

21

Make Peace with Spending Money

It's scary to have a finite pool of money to work with and not know what's coming next. I made my peace with it quickly because I could run the numbers and see that my mother's money would last long enough for us to get through at least six months of hospice, and then we could see what happened from there. She probably realistically had enough for a few years at home, considering what was left on her long-term care policy and in her savings. It was harder for everyone else involved—including my mom—to contemplate because they had a vague sense of panic that we were spending money with no tomorrow.

This worry plagues most people when it comes to retirement planning, so much so that it sometimes paralyzes them. It makes others scrimp and deny themselves things, even if they can afford them.

When it's not your money you're spending, the psychology gets weirder, especially because if you don't spend the funds, it could be your money at some point.

"In theory, people should be more rational when making decisions for other people," said Andy Reed, the head of investor behavior research at Vanguard, somebody I call often to ask why people make the money decisions they do. He added that when you're making money decisions for other people, "emotions don't play as big a role, so you can focus on numbers and be more patient doing the math, which should lead to better outcomes."

But as a student of human nature, Reed knows that this is difficult when you're talking about family money. "Emotions might be revved up even more, and the stress is ramped up," he said. "This is a special wrinkle, and it might show that advisers would make better decisions than the people involved."

The trouble with having an adviser make rational money decisions in an end-of-life situation is that sometimes the best decision isn't what's cheapest or most economical. "The rational choice is obvious only in hindsight," Reed added. "What makes sense in dollars is not what makes sense on the human level. You throw the math out and do what feels right."

When my mom was in hospice and we were talking about the future, we had only bad options, some of which involved spending vast sums of money that were hard to fathom for us because we had all lived pretty restrained financial lives up to that point.

Even the smaller sums worried me. At one point, I had to make a choice about paying $700 extra for an air mattress for the medical bed in my mom's room at home or take whatever standard one came with the package paid for by Medicare. I thought about it for a minute, years of frugality tugging at my brain, and then plunked down my mom's credit card. This is what money is for. Would I regret in a year or two that we had spent that money? No, but I would regret it if my mom had any sort of preventable discomfort in her dying days.

The biggest cost I had to manage all along was the aides. They were dangerously burnt out. They needed vacations. To provide that meant paying double—for their vacation time and for somebody to cover for them while they were gone. It also meant risking that they'd leave and not come back, which meant making their return enticing with raises. I felt as though I was in the middle of a human resources maelstrom, which I had long tried to avoid in my career. I hated being a manager.

I told myself repeatedly that it was my mother's money and we should spend it whatever way was best for her needs. I would be careful with it out of respect for how she handled her life, but I would not hold back on getting her what I thought she needed, even if it meant spending her savings all the way to zero. That was the way Madeleine Smithberg looked at it, too, until it actually came to spending it all as her mother's dementia illness progressed. Smithberg's father had been a good planner and had left his mother in good stead, but there are very few fortunes that are enough to cover $15,000 a month indefinitely. "It's a very loud ticking time bomb," Smithberg said. "My brother started worrying about two years before the money was going to run out. He said, 'This is going in one direction, and we have to figure out what to do.'"

Her mother exhausted the long-term care insurance. She "graduated" from hospice. "She ran out of money one month and one day before she died," Smithberg said. At that point, Smithberg and her brother decided to pay out of pocket for what she needed, instead of trying to put her on Medicaid and move her to a facility that would accept it. She still had Social Security to contribute, but nothing else. "My brother said, 'Things will have to change, we'll have to tighten up this ship, Maddie,'" Smithberg said. "And I said, 'What do you think I've been doing, getting the most expensive adult diapers?' I had been taking care of all the logistics up to that point. The facility charged thirty dollars a day for what are called hygiene products, that's nine hundred dollars a month, so I'd buy them myself and take them to her. It was already a pretty tight ship."

For Tanya Edwards, a freelance writer, it was easy to spend her mother's money on her care but not on herself. When her mom got sick with Lewy body dementia, a disease that causes hallucinations and cognitive decline, she was an only child in New York trying to care for her divorced mom in Michigan. After a few years and a few turns for the worse, she and her now husband decided to move near her mom until the end, since Edwards had a flexible job and her partner was between gigs. They got an apartment but needed a car to be able to get to the nursing home to visit daily. "Could I spend my mom's money on that? I didn't have anyone to ask for permission," she said. In the end, her mom died with $4,000 left, and the car Edwards bought is in her driveway where she now lives in Connecticut.

I thought my family was heading the way of Edwards's and Smithberg's and we'd have to spend what we had until it was gone, after which my brother and I would pick up the slack until my mom could go on Medicaid. The start of that was breaking into the principal of her retirement savings, and fast. We had to put our hands on more cash since we had enough on hand for only two months.

Up to that point, my mom had not been spending much from her nest egg and had been taking out only the minimum amount the government required her to, known as her required minimum distribution, or RMD.[1] She was basically skimming interest off the top, and the account kept growing. Going forward, she was going to run into the same problem as early retirees who get hit with a market downturn: The more we spent now, the faster the nest egg was going to dwindle.

What Is a Required Minimum Distribution (RMD)?

The IRS requires people who have tax-deferred retirement savings, which includes IRA, 401(k), 403(b), and 457 plans, to begin taking money out of those accounts starting at a designated age and according to a formula that the government supplies. Before 2023, that age was 70½; then Congress changed it to 73. It is scheduled to go to 75 in 2033 if no other action occurs.

The required minimum distribution (RMD) formula is based on the account value as of December 31 of the previous year. To get the RMD amount, divide this amount by a "life expectancy factor" based on the age of the person.

Example: An RMD for an 80-year-old person with a $500,000 IRA balance would be around $24,752 according to AARP's calculator.[2]

Our complication was that we couldn't take the money out ourselves. Other people may have more liquid savings than my mother, such as money in a brokerage account, savings account, traditional IRA, or Roth IRA. My parents were teachers, and as is common for this profession as well as for civil servants, all of my mom's money was locked up in annuity contracts with an insurance company. We had to call the financial guy who managed her account and talk about getting an early and enlarged distribution for the year. I had not executed the power of attorney with him, but since my mom was able to be on speakerphone with him, she could grant me permission. He encouraged us to wait as long as we could to withdraw money because my mom had to meet certain contract milestones in order to avoid fees and surcharges. The most consequential deadline was five years since she inherited my dad's account, which meant waiting until October, when it was then the end of June.

The other thing we had to consider was that if my mom took her annual required distribution—or really any amount—while she was still alive, it would hit her tax bill as income for the year. However, if she died before the end of the year and had not taken at least the RMD, my brother and I would have to take out that money and it would hit our tax bills, split between the two of us. I wrote about what happened to families who forgot about that, and there were stiff penalties involved—at the time it would have been 50 percent, but it dropped the next year to 25 percent, or 10 percent if caught quickly.[3]

I had to stop and think about all that for a while and ask more questions, because I didn't understand why my mom's annuity contracts were set up that way. The word *annuity* in that situation was confusing on its own. My mom had three tax-deferred contracts with an insurance company that were referred to as annuities, but the money was not annuitized. That meant that it actually functioned more like a retirement IRA account than the type of annuity most people know about, where you put in a lump sum and you get a monthly payment for the rest of your life. My mom's money would run out eventually if we kept spending it, while an annuitized monthly payment would have paid out a steady amount for her lifetime.

The advantage of her contracts were that they had built-in risk management, which meant she couldn't lose more than a certain percentage a year, even if the stock market tanked. On the other hand, she also couldn't gain more than a certain amount, even if the market soared, and she had little flexibility of access.

Annuitized payments are tricky, too. Years ago, I interviewed a retired teacher named Shirley Wolf from Kentucky for a Reuters story.[4] She had a pension that folded in her Social Security payments, and the rest of her savings was annuitized in her tax-deferred retirement plan, which is called a 403(b) plan for teachers, rather than the 401(k) you'd get from a private-sector employer. She was 67 at the time and was having a hard time paying out of pocket for her Medicare premiums and other healthcare costs. She wanted to buy a new car but couldn't put together the money because she couldn't access her pool of savings for lump-sum withdrawals. It was all set up as annuitized monthly income, and she had to save what she could from it each month.

Financial experts tout annuitized payments as being important for replacing a paycheck in later life, but they're not usually an all-in strategy. Most advisers actually advocate for more of a diversified approach. Some call it a bucket approach and show drawings with literal buckets that have different types of savings in them to illustrate the point. You want one bucket of tax-deferred savings, as in an IRA, 401(k), or 403(b). You want another with some taxable money that is easily liquid, such as cash, fixed income, and stocks. You also want some tax-free growth accounts, such as a Roth

IRA or Health Savings Account (HSA). That way, you can manage your tax burden as you go through retirement, pulling from different accounts as needed.

In the same vein, you want some monthly income, such as Social Security, a pension, or an annuity, and you also want some liquid savings you can access if you need them for emergencies or even travel. You can look at these as buckets, too.

The Bucket Approach to Investing

 Bucket 1: Tax deferred: You put in pretax money, get tax-free growth, and pay income tax on the withdrawals. Examples: traditional IRA, 401(k), 403(b), 457, SIMPLE, SEP.

 Bucket 2: Taxable: Subject to capital gains tax on transactions, dividends, and interest. Examples: brokerage account, money market account, savings account.

 Bucket 3: Tax-exempt growth: Taxed going into the account but not taxed coming out if rules are followed. Examples: Roth IRA, Roth 401(k). Funds deposited into Health Savings Accounts are also tax exempt.

My parents didn't do this, and they never had any other savings outside of what was in their annuities. They also both claimed Social Security earlier than they probably should have, by not waiting for their maximum benefit at age 70 or even their full retirement ages. My mom had already been on Social Security Disability Insurance because of her back problems in her fifties, which automatically turned into claiming Social Security at the first possible age of 62, permanently reducing her possible retirement benefit by 25 percent. My dad claimed at 62 when he transitioned to retirement, rather than his full retirement age, which was 65 and 8 months. The longer you wait, up until the maximum of age 70, the more you get per month from Social Security.

But there's also nothing inherently bad about the way my parents handled their affairs. Their financial situation worked for them while they were well, but I'm not sure they understood all the implications of this approach once they got sick. Had they both lived longer, it could have been a stretch to afford what they needed. As somebody who deals in financial education for a living, I find that troubling. People should understand what they are doing with their money, and if that means keeping it simple, that's what they should do.

I could have intervened earlier to get them to invest differently, but it's very hard to see what's ahead and people don't like to give up control. Until my father got sick, I had no idea at all what kind of money my parents had or how it was invested, just as I didn't know how much they made in salary. I'm not sure my mom would have been forthcoming if I had initiated such a discussion. She might have said, "We have enough, don't worry."

Thankfully, she did have enough because she got sick so young, but that didn't make my job as a financial caregiver any easier. The annuity guy was trying to do the rational thing and maximize my mom's savings by not breaking into her contracts before the deadline, but I needed to consider the quality of the rest of her life over everything else.

Procrastination ended up winning over all my plans. The money manager stalled the distributions. My mom stalled on making a decision about moving to New York. We basically stuck with the hand we were dealt and made the next play.

DO NOW

Go over the assets of your loved one using the guide on page 254 to figure out where you could get emergency cash if you need it. Think about what road markers there might be that would make you need to change a living situation or hire more care.

When to Stop Trying to Juggle

Before I flew home after settling my mom into hospice, I set up a video feed in her bedroom through an Amazon device that connected to my phone. That way I could look in on her anytime I wanted, without relying on the aides or my mom to pick up the phone. They all thought it was an invasion of privacy. My mom was particularly concerned that the camera was unflattering with her in bed—what if she was "indisposed," as she put it? But I insisted because I didn't want to have a minute of stress caused by not being able to reach them by phone.

Then on a Monday morning in early June, I took off on a plane for New York. My daughter was nervous about a big test on Tuesday morning, so I promised to drive her. I had to give a work presentation at noon at my midtown office and then had other in-person meetings. I planned to go back to Florida soon, tag-teaming with my brother for the rest of the summer.

I got through much of my Tuesday, but as soon as I turned my phone back on after my presentation, I had six messages from Florida. I called immediately from a corner of our busy office.

"Something's wrong," Rose said.

"What do you mean?" I asked.

"It's like a light went out, I don't know how to describe it," she said.

"Like a stroke? Or a heart attack or something?"

"Maybe, I don't know," she said. "She just isn't right."

"Do I need to come back?" I asked, already running through logistics in my head.

"I think you do," she said.

I froze for a minute, not sure what to do. Go straight to the airport from the office without going home first and gathering clothes and take the next flight out? Go home first and try to fly out that evening? Calling 911 didn't register in my brain. She was home because she wanted to be home. I opted to go to my next meeting.

I sat down across from the managing editor to talk about an upcoming special project, and I said, "So after this, I have to go back to Florida because there's another emergency and I think this is it, but I don't know at this point. I might have to be off for a while."

You never know what you're going to get at a workplace when you say something like this. "I'm leaving now, and I don't know when I'm coming back" is risky, and not everyone gets a good response. I was met with compassion and wisdom. The editor had just been through the experience with a parent, and he not only understood but said all the right things about knowing when it was time to shift focus to the emergency at hand.

I had tried so hard all that time to keep everything going that it was really hard to stop. The first thing I did was curse the hospice that turned my mom down because she wasn't terminal. How did anyone decide that she wasn't sick enough? But then I packed up and flew out the next morning, while my brother made his emergency trip plans. The situation I walked into back at my mom's in Florida was a complete reversal from what I had left forty-eight hours before. I think we were dealing with one of those situations where the sick person hangs on while their loved ones are in the room and then slips away as soon as they leave for a minute. I had gone back to New York thinking we were in for a long haul, but my mom was waiting to be left alone so she could let go.

What the Family and Medical Leave Act (FMLA) Covers

Workers are allowed up to twelve weeks of unpaid, job-protected leave per year for the following reasons:

- The birth and care of the child of an employee
- Placement with the employee of a child for adoption or foster care
- To care for an immediate family member (i.e., spouse, child, or parent) with a serious health condition
- To take medical leave when the employee is unable to work because of a serious health condition

Source: U.S. Department of Labor[1]

At the end of life in hospice, you get assigned what is called a crisis team—nurses, social workers, supervisors, and others—to assess what's needed. So in place of one nurse who was set to stop by on Tuesdays and Thursdays, a succession of people started to come into my mom's condo. They set up a schedule to provide constant care to monitor and dispense medicines, most of which were narcotics for pain relief. I didn't know if my mom had hours or days or weeks left, and they couldn't tell us much, either, except that she had reached the end stage and it would take the time it would take.

That was when Medicare's hospice coverage would have kicked in for that idyllic refuge by the sea for my mom's last days, or at least some kind of suite in a facility where we could hunker down. But my mom shook her head when we asked her about it, and it seemed logistically hard to move her at that point. So instead, the hospice team set up 24/7 coverage in her room, turning a card table into a makeshift medicine staging area and ordering supplies on an expedited basis. Everything would now be hand delivered as soon as we needed it, any time of day or night. Throughout that stage, the hospice nurses mostly sat in a chair near my mom's bed and recorded her symptoms and dosages on their forms, while our private aides managed her personal care. There wasn't much to do because my mom was not eating or drinking. My brother and I sat by and held her hand, talked to her, and were together.

Many kinds of help are available at this stage. Hospice provided all sorts of counseling as part of the service: somebody for my mom to talk to, somebody for the family, a religious counselor, and even music therapy. We could also have found our own help if we wanted. There are eldercare services such as end-of-life doulas, also called death doulas, who can help you through the last days, which are not easy for anyone.

Nicole Daigle, the doula from Chicago, said that a typical engagement for her starts when a person comes home for hospice—although she wishes families would contact her much sooner. She can help with equipment logistics, care coordination, education, and family dynamics, or she can sit by the bed and hold the dying person's hand if the family needs a break. "Death is still such a taboo topic in our country that people find themselves in this situation where you don't realize what you don't know until you're trying to navigate it, and at that point, you're overwhelmed," she said. Doulas vary in pricing and can charge either by the hour or a flat fee. Daigle used a sliding scale but ballparked $50 an hour as a typical charge.

If the dying person is conscious, she will direct her efforts to them, but most of the time, when she gets there, she's interacting mostly with the family. She can also be a support for people who don't have close family members to be there. In the case Daigle described earlier, where the woman hired her to help her with her wife's death, she stayed on for about six months. First she helped the client get organized. "We made sure the paperwork was all laid out, which I especially emphasized with any LGBTQ+ clients, because even when the law is the law, you want to make sure that whoever should be in the room should be allowed there—and the person making decisions should be the person you want," Daigle said. She was there through the death and funeral; then she helped the woman close out credit cards and take care of other financial tasks; and finally, she directed her to resources to help with grief.

There's no such thing as an "easy" death. No matter how well you think you will handle it, it's harder than that, and you're going to need support. I found myself on the internet a lot, searching for what my mom was going through at that particular moment and trying to figure out a timeline of what would happen next. I scoured message boards where people poured out their anxiety as they waited for their loved ones to pass. It was my own version of group grief therapy. The post that spoke to me the most was by a young man who was at his grandmother's bedside and in agony as the days went by. "How long can this go on for?" he wailed. He posted many times over the course of eleven days before she finally died.

I had the hardest time just sitting still in the cold, dim room with my mom. I was never alone with her, because one of our aides and a hospice worker were always there. I couldn't get comfortable. We flipped between CNN and repeats of *Everybody Loves Raymond* all day and night. We made small talk. We held up the phone for my mom to talk to family members and friends so she could have some last, mostly one-way conversations with people. During one call, we talked to a cousin who told us the good news that he and his wife were expecting a baby. My mom loved babies more than anything. A few hours later, when I was going through a closet in the guest room, I found two perfect baby sweaters my mom had knit at some point, one in yellow and one in a neutral pastel. My mom had knit something for all the babies in the family up to that point. I'm not one to believe in signs, but that was one. My cousin's baby would eventually wear one of those sweaters for her baby naming, celebrating being partially named in honor of my mother. The other sweater is waiting for its recipient.

On one of the early days of crisis care, my mom said she saw her brother, who had died more than twenty years before. She started narrating the scene as she was experiencing it, and we all stood on edge, telling her it was okay to go to him, that he would protect her. We tried to ask her: Do you see anyone else? Is there light? But she didn't have words for it. I had so many questions for her: Why didn't she see my father? If she could tell us about my uncle, could she tell us anything else about how she was feeling? How much did she understand about what was going on? Was she still okay with all of this?

We were in suspended animation, and I could barely keep track of the days. They stretched on and on. I had to start doing things, so I took a shift in the room for a while, then tried to organize. I went to the bank and emptied the safe deposit box. I sat at my mom's computer and used her phone for two-factor identification as I culled through her credit card bills to cancel any services she had that we would no longer need, such as her newspaper delivery, identity theft protection, and Netflix. I then changed the email address on all accounts that we had to keep open: electric, cable, home warranty service, and her cell phone. I paid particular attention to her Ancestry account, because she had spent a lot of time researching our family history back to the 1800s, and I wanted to preserve that.

I sorted through the drawers to find what I would need next: her life insurance policy contract, her birth certificate, her retirement account information, and whatever else was there that I didn't know about, such as cash hidden in little envelopes. I found a giant ring of keys and realized I needed to check her condo storage lockers.

I had Rose show me where there was one that she knew of on the lobby level, near my mom's parking space, and we sorted through it. It didn't contain much except extra kitchen tile, wheelchair spare parts, and an old walker. I knew that there was another storage locker that held my grandmother's paintings and maybe some other treasures.

I asked the office for information, but the building had recently changed management, and they didn't know all the nooks and crannies. I texted the old manager, who was a friend of my mom, and he had some vague memory of my mom renting a storage locker from another tenant, off the books, and thought that they might have passed away by now. My last chance was to go back to my mom and ask her. At that point, she could squeeze once for yes and do nothing for no. I asked if there was another storage locker. She squeezed once. I asked if it was on the lobby level. Nothing. I asked if it was on the basement level. Nothing. I asked if it was on the subbasement level, and she squeezed.

Weeks later, we did eventually find another storage locker, on the lobby level, but it contained only beach items. If there is another on the subbasement level, it remains a mystery. Maybe she threw out all my grandmother's paintings. I'll probably never know.[2]

My brother and I also talked—quietly, in the other room—about funeral arrangements and how they would go. We made hotel reservations in Philadelphia near our family cemetery and kept pushing them back as the days stretched on. We lined up a rabbi and talked to family friends who lived nearby about hosting a lunch after the service, knowing it was coming but not exactly when, to put everyone on standby. We worked on an obituary. I sorted through my mom's recipes, because I thought it would be nice to give out some handwritten ones after the funeral and have people write memories on index cards in return, kind of a take-one-leave-one situation. We also had to figure out how we were going to pay for everything.

My mom had one of those life insurance policies designed to be just enough to cover her funeral and last expenses, but it would not pay out until we had the death certificate, which could take weeks. We had to pay the caregivers their last checks, and we wanted to give them some severance pay, because, like me, they had not been planning on my mom dying so soon. We had to cover the cost of the apartment until we decided what to do with it. There was the funeral itself, plus flights, hotels, and all sorts of incidentals. It all added up to more than $20,000.

This is where the power of attorney and joint bank account debate comes back around. If you haven't thought it through, you will get stuck at a time like this, when your brain is on overdrive and you aren't making good decisions. Once the person dies, their power of attorney designation is no good. You can't use their credit card to pay for a casket, for instance. You can no longer legally access the bank account on which you held power of attorney. In some cases, a bank will close access to even a joint bank account temporarily, until it receives a death certificate and you transfer the funds to the living joint signer in a new account.

We had one reader at MarketWatch who wrote in saying that her father's plan for this was to leave $20,000 checks for her and her brother hidden in the house and they could cash them after he died.[3] But checks aren't good for very long and banks move fast to close accounts, so you can't guarantee access to the funds. I advised her to get her father to go another route, adding a joint signer or giving the money to them in advance.

It may seem ghoulish to start moving funds around as somebody lies dying, but if you need access to cash immediately, you have to do what you must. It's better morally and legally, assuming that you have proper power of attorney or joint holdings, to do it before rather than after. The caveat here is that there's little oversight, and this can cause problems between siblings or other interested parties. The last thing you need is a big family fight over who touched Mom's money in the middle of everything going south.

Take what Michelle Petrowski had to go through when her mother was in a coma and dying in Florida, while the rest of the family was in Arizona. Petrowski said her mother had specifically asked her, in front of her mother's husband, to use whatever funds she had left to pay for a funeral and give the remainder to her husband. But when her mother was very sick, Petrowski found that the stepfather had used her mother's credit card, even though he was not an authorized user.

"At the time, I was so pissed, I was going to call the police and have him arrested," Petrowski said. "I asked the credit card company to file fraud charges, and they said it was up to us. As her executor, I could have done it, but by then my mother died, so I let it go."

One person I interviewed about estate planning told me that they had a plan with a neighbor to secure the house as soon as her mother died, because she lived in a different state and it might take her a few hours to get there. "I sent her drawings of the house and where everything valuable is. I've had it all appraised. When my mom dies, I'm having her get a locksmith out there to change all the locks. I don't trust my sister's family at all," she said.

I knew my brother and I weren't going to fight like that. I offered to put the funeral costs on my credit card and then pay myself back out of the life insurance funds when the bill came due. The rest of it we'd front, and it would come out of whatever was left from my mom's savings. It was all going to come around eventually, when my mom's money became our money.

But we kept pushing everything back, day after day, because my mom wasn't ready to go yet and we had to wait.

DO NOW

Think about a plan for your life if you had to stop everything and help in an emergency for an extended period of time. Use the conversation prompts on page 242 if you need to.

Stop Procrastinating on Basic Estate Planning

M y mom died on a Saturday morning, and to keep it simple, I'll say she went peacefully in her sleep. It wasn't like that at all, of course, but at the very least, she was out of pain. There was relief in that. She had been home for exactly two weeks and one day, and she had lingered in crisis care for twelve of those days.

When it happened, I thought of the first lines of Joan Didion's *The Year of Magical Thinking*, the best book on grief I've encountered.[1] "Life changes fast. Life changes in the instant. You sit down to dinner and life as you know it ends," were the first words she wrote after the death of her husband, John Gregory Dunne.

You sit down to dinner and life as you know it ends.

We were waiting and waiting for it to happen, agonizing over the days, wailing like the young man on the message boards. And then it was done in an instant, just like that. It shouldn't have been surprising, but it was, and it hurt even though we were expecting it and had been preparing for it.

Anyone who thinks there will always be time and that important things can be left to do another day is either delusional or has never faced an untimely death. My mom was only 76 and should have had many more years with us, a decade even. If she had waited to put her affairs in order, we would have had a much harder time after she died, and I don't know how I would have handled that in the state I was in.

My mom's estate plan is one thing I'm proud to say came about because of my financial planning knowledge. In 2014, I wrote a column for Reuters headlined "What Should Be in Your 'Death' File" that went through all the paperwork you should leave in an easy place for your heirs to find so they don't have a big mess to deal with.[2] I told the story of a man who went to find what he could after his father died. On the desktop of his dad's home computer, he found a folder marked DEATH, and in it was everything he needed to proceed settling his dad's affairs. The folder had a copy of his dad's will, a list of financial accounts and insurance policies, copies of his various identification papers, and directions for where to find everything else. It was a huge relief to the family. And so then the man turned to his mother and asked her to do the same thing, which was even more important, because the surviving spouse is the one who really needs to take care of estate planning.

Planning Needed by Life Stage

- When turning 18: Once you become an adult, you need to execute at least a power of attorney, healthcare proxy, and HIPAA authorization, or even your parents or other family members may not be able to help you in an emergency.
- As a working adult, particularly if you are part of a couple: You need to make a will and take out life insurance and make sure you name beneficiaries to all financial accounts, plus you should consider your long-term care insurance options no later than age 50.
- When buying a house: You need to add a plan for the house by designating it in a will, setting up a trust, or adding a beneficiary to a transfer-on-death deed.
- When having a child: You should name a guardian for any child born.
- At retirement: Consider setting up a legacy plan for your assets, decide how you will pay for long-term care, and figure out if you may need Medicaid in the future.
- At an advanced age: Start giving away assets if you can while you are living, update beneficiaries and trustees, and make sure your power of attorney agent knows everything about your finances.
- When one spouse dies: The surviving spouse needs to revisit their will, trusts, and all beneficiary designations and assign a power of attorney and healthcare proxy.

When the first spouse goes, everything is a little easier. Assets are easily transferred to the other when one dies if instructions have been drawn up. Such a will is called a "sweetheart will" because if one member of the couple dies, they leave everything to the other spouse and vice versa. When people have mostly joint accounts and name the other spouse as a beneficiary on life insurance or retirement accounts that are not jointly owned, the process usually goes pretty smoothly—but not always. Many spouses do not have joint accounts or may have one or two accounts each of their own.

It helps to build contingencies into a sweetheart will for what will happen if, for instance, one spouse dies and the other is too incapacitated to serve as executor. The worst scenario is if two married people die together in an accident, or within a very close time frame. If the will doesn't specify what happens if both die simultaneously, it will be too much for their heirs to deal with estate complications and their grief at the same time.

The circumstances don't even have to be unusually rare or even unexpected. I have a friend who ran into this when his parents were both sick and declining for years and then passed within six months of each other. His mother passed first, and the process of transferring her assets to his father was still going on when his father died. So then their estates were stuck in limbo, and it took more than a year for him to settle first one estate and then the other, and meanwhile, his inheritance was tied up.

My mother and father had sweetheart wills for many years prior to my dad's death, but my mom updated her own plan very quickly after he died in 2018. What clinched it for her was that she read a great story in her local newspaper a few years before about the estate planning a surviving spouse needs to do. She liked to clip out articles like that for me and give them to me when I visited. She got out her scissors, started to cut out the article, and then realized that I was the one who wrote it; her newspaper syndicated my death file story.

Estate planning is not on every grieving spouse's list of things to take care of urgently, but it should be. Every adult needs to have some kind of documentation in place that says, at the very least, who should handle their affairs for them after they die, just as they need to name a person who can do that if they get sick, who has a power of attorney and healthcare proxy.

At some point, many people do come to the realization that they need to get their affairs in order, and that goes even if you have a negative net worth when you die. Typically, this realization hits at retirement age and beyond, and it starts with a basic will. While less than 50 percent of Americans have some type of will overall, that number does go up as high as 79 percent in the 65-plus age group, according to Gallup in one of the more optimistic surveys of will completion.[3]

This explains at least somewhat why more people make a plan for the care of a pet than name a guardian for their minor children: People who are older than 65 are much more likely to have a pet at home than a minor child.

In fact, at any age, people are more likely to have pets at home than children, as there are about 87 million households with pets in the United States[4] in contrast to about 60 million households with children.[5] Trust & Will, an online service to create estate documents and handle estate administration, told me that 94 percent of its users make provision for a pet in case of their death, but only 40 percent name guardians for their children. In an ideal world, all parents should name a guardian for their kids. The consequence if you don't is that if the parents die, the courts have to get involved. But most parents nevertheless fail to do so.

Writing a will is not one of those tasks that you can do for somebody else. A person has to be of sound mind and a willing participant in the process or it isn't legal. I have seen it happen in plenty of families that a solo adult died without a will. In one family, the widowed matriarch simply refused to decide how to split up her assets among her children and told them they were "vultures" anytime they tried to talk to her about it. A colleague whose divorced father died in his early sixties had "writing a will" on his to-do list but didn't get to it before he died of a heart attack out of the blue. She was a CFP® professional, too, but she couldn't close that particular deal. If you can't convince the people in your life to take care of their advance planning and you're the one on the hook to close things out, it's not impossible to do, just more difficult.

One attorney told me that they simply gave up trying to convince people to write wills and do other advanced estate planning. Instead, they focused on estate administration on the other end for people who had not planned. "Most regular folks just drop over dead with no plan at all," they told me. "My practice picked up when I stopped trying to concentrate on planning."

I asked estate attorney Adam Schneider how he splits up his time at his practice in San Diego, and he told me he spends only about 30 percent of his time on advanced estate planning. The rest of his efforts go to probate cases and estate administration, most of which could have been eliminated if the deceased had done planning. "I'd say probably less than five percent would end up with any court action needed," he said.

All this avoidance for what? Estate planning sounds like a complicated procedure intended for rich people, but it's not really. "The word *estate* conjures up a Newport mansion, but the reality is that everyone needs an estate plan," said David Peterson, the head of advanced wealth solutions at Fidelity Investments. "You need to ask, 'What happens to my stuff?' It all needs to go somewhere. You might want certain things to go to certain people and some protections, especially for minor children. Even kids right out of college have something, like the beginnings of 401(k) plans or digital assets. Do you want one of your parents looking at your dating apps? You might want to put somebody you trust in charge of shutting that down."

In terms of complexity, there's actually very little that goes into writing a will or any of the other estate-planning documents when you're the client and not the one drawing up the papers. It's not any more difficult than going to see a financial planner, for instance, or even filling out basic medical forms. Most of the language is standard, and the lawyer completes it after asking you a series of questions or giving you a packet to fill out.

The hardest part may be finding an attorney, but even that is not too hard. Some workplaces provide legal services as a human resources benefit. I found my estate attorney by networking through my daughter's elementary school parent community for a free one-hour consultation with an estate attorney that led to a full engagement. My mom asked her friends for recommendations, and I directed her to the National Academy of Elder Law Attorneys to find a reputable estate attorney who specialized in dealing with seniors. Sometimes estate attorneys will do lectures at local senior centers or other community events.

My experience as a financial caregiver was so much easier because my mom followed through on taking care of this to-do list item many years before we needed it. What did it cost her? A few hours of time and $4,700. This was what she got:

- Durable power of attorney
- Designation of healthcare surrogate, otherwise known as a healthcare proxy
- Declaration of anatomical gift
- HIPAA authorization
- Living will
- Living trust
- Assignment of digital assets
- Last will and testament

That may still sound like a lot of hassle and cost, but I would later find out that we would have ended up paying as much or more on the other side if she had not invested that money in the beginning. And the hassle to me would have been gargantuan. Dying in the United States is expensive. Transferring assets costs money and often requires professional help. People who are inheriting often have to weigh whether the cost to get the money that's left to them is worth it. Somebody has to pay on either the front end or the back end.

The biggest decision my mom had to make was how to split the responsibilities and the assets, and it wasn't much of a struggle for her. She named my brother and me as co-trustees for everything and split it all 50/50, which is the default most states take if you don't specify anything. It may not have been ideal—most lawyers advise against designating joint decision makers to avoid fights—but it worked out fine for us.

I had a much more complicated decision to make when I did my first planning years ago because I'm divorced and my children were very young then. I named my mom as trustee on all the financial paperwork but picked a family friend to be guardian for my children should something happen to both me and my ex-husband. I had to update those plans after my oldest turned 18, to put him in charge until the younger child is also of age. I might change things again down the road, depending on what life throws at us.

If you die without a will, the default the state takes is generally split decision making and an even division of your assets among your heirs. Some people get stuck and decide to punt and let the state figure it out. "They'll say, 'I just want it to go equally, and I don't care to pay for a plan,'" said Howard Krooks, the elder law attorney, who is also a past president of the National Academy of Elder Law Attorneys. The results of letting it go are rarely good. For one thing, families change, and there could be new relatives, divorces, and blended families, or some family members could run into mental health issues, disabilities, addictions, or other problems.

When you're intentional about the split, there are plenty of choices besides an even share for all heirs, even when there are two children and especially if there are more than two or several generations. There's what people consider "fair," which is splitting things into equal parts. And then there's what's "equitable," which attempts to take other factors into consideration.

The most common way this happens in families with two kids is when one sibling makes considerably more than the other, so their parents leave a greater share of their estate to the one with less. Or perhaps a surviving parent leaves more to the one who took care of them, to compensate for their time and effort.

Bruce Steiner, an attorney in New York, told me about two families he had seen deal with an equitable split. In one, the sibling who got less contested the will. "He said, 'If my mother had said she was going to do it, I'd be okay with it, because I don't need the money, but she never said anything about that, so I wonder whether that is what she wanted or did my sister convince her to do it,'" Steiner recounted. In the other family, the parent had laid out their plan ahead of time, and the sibling with the smaller share was fine with it.

People making estate plans can get creative with equitable splits, depending on their assets. Steiner had another case where the parents had put one child through medical school, so they left their business to the other child. Some give money to one child and property to others. Some leave the family farm to the child who stayed home to work the land and cash to their other descendants who moved away.

In over thirty years of practice, Krooks said he had seen families split things up every which way, yet the only factor he could see that mattered in terms of saving the heirs from fighting was whether the family elder discussed what they were doing with the heirs first.

"Whatever you decide to do is okay," said Krooks. "But I'm a big proponent of talking to family while they are still here. I know what I advise about talking it out is not easy to carry out. In some families, talking hasn't happened for years. However, it establishes a firm communication to everyone involved, so later on if anyone wishes to change what Mom or Dad would have wanted, it will not be so easy."

Estate lawyers can help tremendously with the communication part of the process by making sure everyone is in the loop. But if money and time are tight, self-serve estate-planning documents can work fine for some straightforward circumstances. Interfaces change over time, but when my mom was planning, Trust & Will, the online estate-planning service, said its users averaged thirty-three minutes to make their plan, which included those who stopped and started. If you complete the process straight through, it said, it would take ten to fifteen minutes. With most services like this that offer estate-planning documents, you can connect with a lawyer to review the documents before you sign or to get further help if you run into problems you can't solve on your own.

Generally speaking, it's better if you get legal documents personalized by somebody who knows the rules in your local area. Something is better than nothing, though, so if getting started online is what gets you there, that may be the best option for you right now. The music legend Aretha Franklin's will was handwritten and found stuffed between cushions in her couch, and a judge still found it valid.[6] So you never know.

Getting started is the important part. Usually, behavioral finance science has some sort of explanation and possible solutions for procrastination problems like this, but there haven't been many studies on why people won't engage in this kind of estate planning. "Trying to find the best messaging to get people to do estate planning is a dog's dinner kind of thing to think about," said Pamela Teaster, the Virginia Tech professor. "Rather than scaring them or guilting them, I think you treat it as another thing you do for your children because you want to be a good aunt, mother, dad, or whatever and spare them all the things that might happen if you don't do it."

In 2024, researchers at the Center for Retirement Research at Boston University did a study on why people don't write wills.[7] They found that the most commonsense answer—that they don't want to think about death—didn't rate highly, and only 5 percent chose it as their primary reason. The number one reason given by nearly half of the respondents was that they hadn't gotten around to it yet. Pure procrastination.

"When there aren't deadlines and when things are confusing, people stall," Harvard economics professor David Laibson explained to me. Behavioral finance experts like him look for ways around people's mental blocks about money, testing nudges, self-imposed deadlines, and other solutions that will get them over the hump. It might be easier to get estate planning done, for instance, if everyone were guided to have all their needed documents in place by the time they were 50, the way the medical establishment sets guidelines for getting colonoscopies or the shingles vaccine. But what if you're 40 and you don't know that six months from now you're going to have a stroke or get into a car accident? What if your life changes significantly at different milestones, for example, you get married at 60?

People who procrastinate on estate planning suffer from all sorts of what are called biases, the most pertinent one being overconfidence. This is when people think that they've got everything handled. You feel almost invincible just being alive, so why should you worry about what will happen to your affairs after you die? That's for another day.

"You could call it passive overconfidence bias," said Thomas Gilovich, a psychologist who teaches at Cornell University. As the co-author with Gary Belsky of *Why Smart People Make Big Money Mistakes and How to Correct Them: Lessons from the New Science of Behavioral Economics*, Gilovich has not delved as much into end-of-life planning issues as he has everyday money issues.[8] But when we were talking, he did find ties between the money mistakes that have an immediate impact and ones that linger. "I think people are aware in some abstract sense that this is all looming, but it's something for later. For some people, the issue is that later comes sooner than they expect," he said.

One nudge in the estate-planning world that has had success in recent years is that hospitals now regularly encourage incoming patients to fill out a healthcare proxy form when registering for surgery. In that vein, the Center for Retirement Research asked its survey respondents if they would complete a will at the same time as they initiated a mortgage so they could set up an inheritance plan for the property. The answer was a resounding no. People didn't like the idea. They felt overwhelmed and preferred not to make those decisions together.

Instead, what prompted people most—relatively speaking because the percentage who had a will was low—was having a child, which created a feeling of responsibility and the need to name a legal guardian in the event of disaster where both parents die.

One thing that Vanguard's Andy Reed sees as a motivating factor for doing estate planning is watching others go through a hard time. For him, the impetus to write a will came from watching his father struggle with handling his grandfather's financial affairs as he declined with dementia. Reed and his wife had set up a simple estate plan after their first child but had not updated it for their second child. "Watching what was happening with my grandfather really pushed us over the edge to get our estate plan done," he said. "But it didn't push me to deal with my parents. Baby steps, I guess."

That was echoed by David Peterson, who has had plenty of clients go

through this. He sees people in preretirement age as the biggest procrastina-
tors. "They either have no estate plan or only have a basic estate plan from
when their kids were born. But they are generally not taking action unless
they had some executor or trustee experience that drove them crazy. If you
have that experience, then you get proactive about it," he said.

People in early retirement are also often not good at getting estate planning done, he added. "Their primary task is to figure out the retirement
thing, so they are naturally putting off estate planning," he said. "Once they
get older, they see the death of peers, maybe other family members, and
they get concerned about taxes and gifting. If anyone has lived through the
burden of administering an estate, they want to do all they can to get organized to help their own families after they pass. And if grandchildren are
born, that's a motivating factor to create or refresh a plan."

In a couple of decades of writing about estate planning and personal finance, the only thing I've seen actually move the needle was the rock star
Prince dying without a will and the endless headlines that ensued about the
fight over his estate. He seemed to serve as a cautionary tale for many, as if
he were a distant family member. Within a month of his passing in April
2016, I wrote a story for Reuters about the significant uptick in will writing
that services such as Nolo, Rocket Lawyer, and LegalZoom were seeing.[9]
Similar jumps in interest have happened with other major celebrity estate
fights, but none so big as that. Unfortunately, the interest eventually waned
and the aggregate national stats never shifted. Even as Prince's estate fight
has stayed in the news over the years, it hasn't changed that everlasting ratio
in the United States, that about 30 to 40 percent of people take care of estate
planning and a vast 60 to 70 percent do not.

DO NOW

Make an appointment with a local estate attorney, and find out what it would cost
to get your own documents in order and those of your loved ones. Put it onto your
calendar, and make it happen. See page 254 for more resources on finding an
estate lawyer.

Decide What Planning
You Need to Do

My mom kept things simple with her estate plan, creating a will and the most common type of trust, a revocable trust, also known as a living trust. A trust is a legal arrangement that is set up to hold property and assets. A will, on the other hand, is a set of instructions for actions to be carried out after your death. The difference between the two might seem like semantics to most people, but when you're the financial caregiver, it becomes clear that the two are distinct. Not everyone needs a trust, but if a person did need one and didn't create one, their administrator has to do extra work.

It's hard to convince people to think beyond a will as the only document you need before they die because it's how we collectively refer to leaving our last instructions, almost a brand-name like Xerox or Kleenex. Sometimes people figure that they don't even need a will because they don't have enough assets to bother. In today's complicated and regimented financial world, though, a simple will is often not enough to handle your affairs effectively because it is not good at dealing with complications such as blended families, conditional inheritances, and jointly owned property.

As a legal instrument, the most important step in writing a will is to name an administrator who will be recognized by the court to handle your estate. A will is also the most effective way to name a guardian for a minor child. In order to be valid, a will has to be administered by a court after death in a process known as *probate,* and that takes time and resources to carry out. Once you file a will with your county court and the administrator is officially recognized, that person will have the power to close a bank account, empty a safe deposit box, and carry out other financial transactions. They basically hold the power of attorney in the postdeath period.

A will provides control over who gets what, but not usually what they do with their inheritance. Distributions are usually whole and immediate by the end of the probate period. If Grandma leaves you $50,000 and says she wants you to spend it on your education, you can honor her wishes or not, but you will get the $50,000 into your hands regardless.

There's only wiggle room for her to say something in the will such as that you will get the money only *after* you go to college if the will contains a provision to turn it into a trust after death, which is called a testamentary trust. Similarly, there's little room for what-ifs that might change the inheritance dynamic, such as divorces, the birth of children, or changes in fortune. If Grandma leaves you $50,000 by name instead of saying "$50,000 to each grandchild," she might unintentionally disinherit any of your siblings born after she last updated her will. Whatever is signed as the official last will is what the court goes by. There can be surprises, much as in the movies, when what's in the will doesn't match up with what the heirs expect. Lots of ex-spouses, rather than current spouses, inherit property and other assets because the deceased forgot to update their will. Children can be disinherited, either intentionally or unintentionally.

It's also important to know that anytime you go through probate it's a public process. Because anyone can see the records, it opens up the possibility of disputes about who should be named administrator and how the estate should be distributed, and it also alerts creditors. That's why we know so much about celebrities whose estates go through probate but not about those who planned with a trust.

It gets even trickier when you want to put a time-delay element into an inheritance, such as a provision for a minor to receive some inheritance money at age 21, more at 25, and the rest at 30. If you do that in a will, you need a testamentary trust, said David Handler, an estate attorney based in Chicago, who specializes in trusts and estates. Lawyers use much the same language for a testamentary trust or a separate trust, so you're not really saving much time or money by including the language in the will. The big catch is that if you add the provisions as a testamentary trust in a will, your heirs will have to go through probate to get the process started, and that costs money.

On the other hand, a trust is a recognized legal instrument and can take effect without court approval. That's why most estate attorneys today prefer to put any complicated conditions into a stand-alone trust in order to avoid probate and then they use a will as a "pour-over" document, meaning any odds and ends that are left over and not accounted for in the trust "pour over" to the trust after the principal's death. That way their clients need only a little bit of probate or possibly none at all. One common exception is a couple with young children making a will primarily to name a guardian in case they should die—which can't be done in a trust. Some lawyers, such as Jenny Rozelle, find it fine to insert a simple testamentary trust in that case, just to name a financial trustee until the inheritors come of age.

A trust creates much more flexibility and control than does a will. Pick any sticky family situation, and you can probably take care of it by creating a trust. I learned an alphabet soup of trusts during my CFP® certification training, and still get some of them confused, such as GRATs and GRUTs (grantor retained annuity trusts and grantor retained unitrusts, trusts that differ based on how payouts occur).[1]

That's all for professionals, though. You typically can't form a trust and administer it without a lawyer, so you don't have the burden of having to understand the underlying legal structures of all the different types of trusts. For practical purposes, all you have to do is share your situation and what you hope to accomplish, and the lawyer will guide you to the right kind of trust and, hopefully, explain to you how it works at the level you wish to understand.

First on the list of priorities is telling the lawyer everything—really every-thing. "People have assets all over the place, and they kind of forget about them," said Fidelity's David Peterson. "When I first started, we were doing a plan for a client based in New York. And we start doing the planning, and they hand over their compilation of their assets, and then later on, we find out he forgot to tell us he owned a big rental property."

Justin Miller, the national director of wealth planning at Evercore Wealth Management in California, spends a great deal of time explaining trusts to clients and uses flow charts to illustrate what's going on.[2] "The simpler you can make it, the better. A picture is worth a hundred thousand words. And tell stories when you can," he said. "I can talk about IDGTs [intentionally defective grantor trusts] for ten weeks, but they won't get it until you tell them a story of how they prevent a surviving spouse in a second marriage from fighting with the deceased's children from his first marriage. People connect on a biological level with stories."

Miller told me about one wealthy couple that had come into his office to go over a complicated estate plan and there were stacks of documents on the table. The husband was ready to sign, but the wife wasn't comfortable. "She was afraid there wouldn't be enough money for her," Miller said. "There was all this documentation, but it was still a matter of explaining how it works."

So he got out his color-coded flow chart to map out what would go from the husband to the wife, the children, the grandchildren, and charity. The husband had made some previous gifts and still had about $20 million left. When he died, he wanted his heirs to owe no estate tax to the IRS. The wife, who was younger, but in her late eighties, had her own separate property worth about $7.5 million. She was worried that it wouldn't be enough to sustain her lifestyle. Miller colored all the trusts that the wife could draw upon in green and showed how whatever was left in them at her death would go to the husband's children. There were also direct gifts to charity and to the children and grandchildren, shown in different colors. "If the wife ever needed money, those trusts would be there, and because she got to see those three green boxes, she was comfortable doing the private foundation that was irrevocable," he said.

Those numbers are a little steep for most people, but the process is still the same: Map out your assets and where you want them to go, putting in conditions as necessary. Here are some of the most common kinds of trusts and how to choose among them.

Revocable Living Trust and Joint Trust

The most common situation is the one my mother had—and I have with my own property—which is a revocable living trust set up to seamlessly pass on a house. A trust of this sort is a simple legal document that establishes it as an entity—capable of having its own tax ID number after death—that can hold ownership of assets. You name a trustee and set the parameters of who can make decisions about the contents of the trust and how the assets can be handled.

My mother's trust, for instance, named my brother and me as co-trustees and allowed for us to inherit her property in a 50/50 split and do with it as we pleased. We could sell her condo or keep it. We could divide her jewelry or give it away. It was simple and easy—as long as we both agreed on what to do.

A joint trust is a revocable living trust for a married couple and can be particularly useful for those in a community property state such as California, where all property of a married couple is considered joint, because it delineates the ownership ratio of shared property. It functions similarly to a sweetheart will in that if one spouse dies, the other inherits. But many estate attorneys prefer to create separate trusts for married people, especially in states that keep marital assets separate. "I did a joint trust once in a separate-property state, only at the insistence of the client, and I regretted it," said David Handler. "It was horrendous to administer, and it created a lot more issues than I foresaw."

A revocable trust is especially important for property a person holds out of state or jointly with anyone but a spouse, which would lead to a second probate if it were passed in a will and even more headaches.

The biggest problem most people have with revocable trusts is that they don't understand that they are a two-step process: You create the trust, and then you put assets into it. It's like filling a bucket: The trust itself will do nothing if you don't put assets in. Most lawyers will take care of retitling a house as part of the process, because in many places you can't do that on your own. "No layperson can prepare and file a New York deed," said Michael Ettinger, an estate attorney in New York, so he'd blame the lawyer involved if a house didn't end up in a trust. That said, things happen. Houses are sold, new houses are bought, and along the way, the assets somehow don't end up in the trust.

Another mistake that Justin Miller said he sometimes sees is that people go to the trouble of creating a trust and intend it to cover retirement accounts but then neglect to change the beneficiaries of their retirement and investment accounts accordingly. The beneficiary designation then wins out. "They might draft the trust to split the account equally among three kids, but in the investment account, it's pay on death to one kid," he said of mistakes he's seen. "Then you have to completely ignore all those expensive documents they've paid for."

Marital Trust

The evil stepparent trope could disappear in one fell swoop if all blended families set up some kind of marital trust. Throughout my years writing about personal finance, I have heard every version of this story: Dad died without an estate plan and all his assets went to his new wife, who then cut off the children from his first marriage. Sometimes it's a stepfather who is demonized; sometimes it's the kids from the first marriage who are called out for inheriting a house and then unceremoniously kicking out the surviving stepparent who had been living there.

All of these fates can be avoided. For wealthy families, a marital trust also serves a tax purpose: moving money out of a large estate and making use of the unlimited spousal exemption to avoid the estate tax threshold.

But there are other flavors of marital trusts that help regular families. For blended families of any means, a qualified terminable interest property (QTIP) trust can serve to clearly delineate the path of the person's assets. One common usage is that a QTIP trust sets up a plan for a spouse from a second marriage to live in a house after the other spouse has died or to have access to a certain amount of funds for the rest of their lives. Then when the second spouse dies, the remainder of the estate goes to whoever is designated, like children from a first marriage.

Fidelity's David Peterson described how that worked in his own blended family after his mother died and his father remarried and had two more children. "My father's IRA was going to pass to his new wife, and the big question was 'What if she remarries and then dies? Then the money goes to her new spouse.' For my dad, once I opened up his eyes to that, he said, 'I want all five kids to inherit,' so he created a trust," he said.

If you choose to set up a marital trust, you might also want to consider having a third party as a trustee to avoid conflict, David Handler said. This can help address the problem of the spouse's children from a first marriage looking over their shoulders constantly, waiting for the stepparent to die. In some cases, he said, the children are roughly the same age as the stepparent or younger, and depending on how long everyone lives, they might end up never inheriting anything. Or, the stepparent could use up all the funds and there will be nothing left by the time they die, and there's constant conflict over this.

For this reason, some people choose to leave separate inheritances to the children from a first marriage and to their current spouse. "Leave one pile of assets to the kids, or maybe some life insurance, and leave another pile to the second spouse. Then if anything's left, it's a bonus for the kids," said Handler.

Qualified Personal Residence Trust

A wealthy person who thinks their estate will owe federal or state estate taxes could benefit from a trust—still unlikely, given the high federal exemption limit, unless it changes, but more likely in certain states such as New York and Washington. A multimillionaire family may want to put their house into an irrevocable trust called a qualified personal residence trust (QPRT). These were much more popular prior to 1996, when the federal estate tax threshold was much lower, and they may come back into fashion again if that amount is lowered in the future. This kind of trust removes the value of the house from the person's estate but allows the principal inheritor to live in the house for the remainder of their lifetime. The conditions for setting one up properly are complicated, and you have to abide by the rules or you could risk nullifying the trust.

Jeanne Wiener, the CPA from California, had this type of setup for her mother's house in Washington, because that state has a $2 million estate tax exemption and Wiener tried to keep lowering the value of the total estate over the years to below that level. "I'm always chipping away at it," said Wiener, practicing what she preaches to clients about tax-efficiency. Her only problem with the plan is that the house continues to appreciate as her mother ages. In order to assure a fair division of assets later, Wiener took the unusual step of executing a nonjudicial agreement with her mother and her sister that the home would be valued at date of death for determining the division of the estate. She said that if she knew in the beginning that her mother's need for care would cross the ten-year mark and keep going, she would have left more liquid assets in her accounts and made fewer irrevocable choices.

Medicaid Asset Protection Trust

If you don't go the living trust route, you're most likely to go the way of the Medicaid Asset Protection Trust, to prevent a person's assets from being "spent down" to the last penny for care. If you want to get an individual onto Medicaid and that person has assets, you need to shield them in some way—and you need to do it a good five years before the person can qualify for benefits because of Medicaid's look-back period. "Even middle-class people can be severely financially compromised by a long-term care stay," said attorney Michael Ettinger, so planning ahead is worthwhile.

The sweet spot is between ages 65 and 75, unless there was a diagnosis prior to that, Ettinger told me. Age matters more than the person's current health condition because that can change at any time and the person needs always to be five years ahead of needing Medicaid. The reason a person might want to wait until about age 65 is that this particular kind of trust requires the trustees or managers, who are often relatives, to take control of the trust immediately. After the death of the person, what's left is distributed to the designated heirs.[3]

Say, for instance, that a Medicaid trust contains a house and an investment account and is being managed by the child of the ill person. The trust would need its own tax identification number and would file its own tax return (via the trustee) to handle any capital gains or income taxes due on the investments and the sale of the house, should that occur. The ill person could continue to live in the house and use the assets of the trust for their care, to prepay for a funeral, or to modify an existing house, or they could go into a facility and pay for a couple of years until they qualified for Medicaid, all managed by the trustee.

"It's a big shift, and you have to be ready to do it," Ettinger said. He added that the primary person will still retain control, because the trustee can be changed.

The whole point of this kind of legal structure is that it preserves the home and other assets so that the person or their spouse can continue to live there without having to sell it to pay for long-term care or for the heirs to pay it back to Medicaid after the person dies.

Special Needs Trust

Much the same as with Medicaid trusts, families often turn to special needs trusts for loved ones who are disabled and receive government benefits. In many cases, parents will set one up to provide for a child who will still need care after they're gone. In this circumstance, it might be best to have a professional trustee who is not a family member but is paid by the trust, such as a bank or trust company, or at least have some kind of institutional representative as a co-trustee, because you might not know who will be available to administer the trust after you're gone. At least with a business entity, you'd have some sort of succession in place, Justin Miller suggested.

There are two main kinds of these trusts: first-party special needs trusts and third-party special needs trusts. In a first-party trust, the assets are owned directly by the person the trust benefits. Over time, the trustee uses the funds for that person's benefit, and then when the person dies, if there are funds left over, Medicaid may claim back its cost of care before any heirs would inherit. In a third-party trust, the funds come from others—such as parents or grandparents either while they are living or after their death—for the benefit of the person, and Medicaid can't claw back funds after they die.

What this means is that families have to be very deliberate about how they give money to those with special needs. If a well-meaning grandparent leaves money directly to a grandchild with a disability, for instance, it's not as efficient as placing it in a first-party trust, and perhaps it would be even better to give that money to the child's parents so they could put it into a third-party trust.

Families can also make use of an Achieving a Better Life Experience (ABLE) account, which function like a 529 college savings account in that the growth in the account is tax free and the funds can be used for the benefit of the person who has special needs.

Jenny Rozelle, the estate attorney in Indiana, told me that many of her clients think that you can't leave anything to a person who has special needs because you will jeopardize their benefits, but that's not true. "It makes my heart sad when people say, 'I can't leave them anything.' You can," she said. "You have to tread with caution, but there are ways to leave assets to somebody on government assistance or gift them assets; it just has to be appropriate."

Charitable Trust

There are many ways to leave a legacy to charity, and most of them do not involve setting up a trust or doing anything other than writing a check, but the key similarity among all the methods is that nothing happens by default.

Charitable giving has to be intentional, so if you mean to leave money to a nonprofit or any other kind of group outside your blood family relations, you have to do something about it before you die.

Those with a higher net worth employ a variety of trust structures in which either the money is left to the charity directly or it's set aside for another person while they are living, such as a spouse, and the remainder goes to charity. The goal is to support a favored charity in the most tax-efficient way, which is why it pertains primarily to those who would hit some sort of estate tax threshold. That level has been high for many years—it was $12,920,000 for a single individual (double for married couples) in 2023 when my mom died, and we were nowhere close to that and didn't have to worry about it. But estate tax laws change over time and sometimes drastically, and there's no crystal ball that can tell you when or how that might happen. You can always check the IRS website for the latest amounts. "We can only advise you on what we know today," Fidelity's David Peterson said. "You build in as much flexibility as you can into your plan and revisit it every three to five years because family situations change, people are born and die, and tax laws change all the time."

If you have a net worth somewhere in the neighborhood of what you think the next estate tax exemption amount will be, you might want to consider some of the more complex strategies that estate planners have in their toolboxes. Or you can choose to go a simpler route, because estate tax changes probably won't affect most people anyway. "The number of people who pay estate tax at seven million dollars is still going to be some small fraction of one percent," said the estate attorney Bruce Steiner.

Peterson said that many of his clients skip setting up complicated trusts and instead reduce their estate by using annual gifting to move large sums of money out of the estate. The IRS allows each person to give up to a certain amount each year without needing to file paperwork or touch their lifetime exclusion amount. For my mom in 2023, that was $17,000, but it changes nearly every year due to inflation adjustment; in 2025, it was $19,000 per recipient. For those with a lot of resources, it can add up. Peterson gave me an example that he sees often, of a senior couple who gave the maximum yearly to each of their two children, their children's spouses, and four grandkids. Two people giving eight gifts apiece is almost $300,000 at the 2025 amount. "If they do that after age sixty-five for the remainder of their lives, maybe fifteen years, that's around four million dollars that they could move out of the estate, without considering the growth on that money had they kept the funds."

Another option for families is donor-advised funds, which allow you to open a charitable giving account into which you deposit money for charity and take the tax deduction in the year you give. You don't have to distribute the funds right away, but the gift is permanent immediately. The account can grow over time, tax free, and you can make the grants as you wish. These accounts have built-in legacy options to carry out your wishes. An account can also be named as the beneficiary of an IRA to spare heirs the tax burden of paying income tax over ten years on inherited accounts.

Spendthrift and Discretionary Trusts

For the ultimate control beyond the grave, spendthrift and discretionary trusts are for when you want to put conditions on the assets you are leaving. Popular culture is full of examples of eccentric spendthrift trust clauses. Take the 1999 film *The Bachelor,* in which the main character has to be married by his thirtieth birthday in order to inherit his grandmother's fortune. Or the various versions of *Brewster's Millions,* such as the 1985 film with Richard Pryor, in which the main character had to spend $30 million in thirty days in order to inherit $300 million. "These kinds of crazy conditions are in the movies a thousand times more than in real documents," said Handler.

Not all conditions are equal. For instance, a clause in a will about the heir needing to be married could be thrown out if the recipient challenged it— and it has been in some test cases.[4] Handler said he has had clients who want to put a clause into the trust that the inheritor will inherit only if they marry somebody of the same religion, and others who wanted to restrict an inheritance if the heir doesn't have a prenuptial agreement with their intended spouse. He has also had clients request him to limit the money going to troubled heirs by requiring drug testing or a stay in rehab prior to distributions being made. "You have to be careful of the consequences. You could end up cutting off your heirs, and is that what you want?" asked Handler. All of these conditions are hard to define and police, and some trustees balk at having to enforce them. For that reason, Handler usually talks his clients out of being too specific.

Most of the time, spendthrift clauses are about encouragement rather than punishment, and that makes them easier for the trustee to oversee. The conditions can be as simple as putting in age limitations so that the recipient will receive a certain amount at, say, age 25, then more at 30, and the remainder at 35. Or Grandma specifies that her grandchild will receive $50,000 once they have completed college.

The most creative provision Jenny Rozelle has seen, which was suggested by a client and now copied by others, was for the trust to match the beneficiaries' W-2 wage statements each year, so the more successful they were, the faster they were given access to the money. "The client's goal was to make sure that none of the beneficiaries would become suddenly unmotivated to work," she said. But not everyone agrees with that approach, since it's easy to argue that it favors richer children over poorer ones, doctors over teachers.

There's a good side to discretionary trusts in that they offer protections for the recipients from creditors and in the case of divorce, because the beneficiary is not considered to be the owner, so others cannot make a claim on the trust. So if you have an heir who has $100,000 in debt, you can leave them $100,000 in a trust and the creditor can't come after them for the money owed. Some have stretched this to use it as a tax avoidance strategy, but the IRS might strike down such a use.

DO NOW

Think about your family circumstances, whether you need a trust, and what kind of trust it should be. See pages 257–58 for more resources.

Part 4

· · · · · · ·

Settling the Estate

Starting Estate Administration

One of the most important things I did before we left Florida for my mother's funeral was to go online and set up forwarding for my mother's postal mail, paying for the longest period of time available. I remembered to do that because of a conversation with a financial planner who regularly helps people deal with the loss of a loved one; when her father died, that was the only task she could manage. "My brain turned off," she told me, "but that was one thing I could do."

When you look at checklists of things you need to do after somebody dies, they are full of tasks like this that you need to complete if you are the responsible party. You can find many such lists put out by your financial institution, AARP, most personal finance websites, and caregiver organizations.[1] I did not find that any one was better than another after I cross-referenced a dozen of them. There's no mystery as to the steps involved. The devil is in the details.

Assuming you secure the person's phone and have access to it and their email, forwarding the mail is always the other main thing at the top. Sounds fairly straightforward.[2] But what if you don't get to this step right away and mail collects at the deceased's residence with nobody to collect it? That's a detail you need to handle by making a call to a friendly neighbor, among the hundred other calls you need to make all at the same time. What if you don't choose the option to extend the forwarding and mail starts to be delivered to the old address again? You'd face something like I did when, not thinking, I forwarded my mom's mail and didn't include my father's name because I figured he was no longer getting mail after being dead for five years. It turned out that he was still getting a few letters that I needed to follow up on. I learned that in order to forward the mail of a deceased person, you need to show proof of death and also estate administration papers. Since my mom never had to do probate to settle my father's affairs, I'd have had to start from scratch, and that was simply too overwhelming to contemplate, so I let it go. If you've been trying to get in touch with my father and wondering why he never gets back to you, this is the reason.

The other beginning steps of estate administration can feel too over-whelming to contemplate in the first few days. But you don't have to do the whole list all at once. Just doing that one thing with my mom's mail was enough for right then. It meant I was free to go home to Brooklyn and deal with the funeral and all the other things that needed to happen immediately. The paperwork could be left for another day, because at least everything would come to my house. I could get back to the vexing question of how much food to order for the lunch after the funeral, which I had no idea how to plan.

A funeral, like a wedding or any other rite-of-passage celebration, can be as frugal or as expensive as you want. The average cost is $8,300 for a funeral with a coffin and burial, according to the National Funeral Directors Asso-ciation, and $6,280 for a ceremony with cremation.[3] We had extra costs be-cause we had to transport my mom's body from Florida to Pennsylvania, plus we added on various other incidentals because we had to stay in hotels and feed everyone for a few days, since nobody in the family lived nearby anymore. We already had a funeral plot for my mom, but this can be a big expense if you have to pay for a plot as part of the funeral package. If we'd had to buy my mother a plot to be with her family, it would have cost us nearly $9,000, well above the national average of $3,000.

It's easy to get decision-making fatigue. You have to think about not only where to hold the funeral but also all the other little details, such as picking out a casket or urn, ordering flowers and programs, and a hundred other things. No amount of preparation is too much when it comes to saving your family on the other end, if you can do any of this in advance. When Stepha-nie Kerch, a semiretired editor from Chicago, was dealing with her mother's funeral in 2001, she thought her mother had worked it all out because she was a meticulous planner and had set up the cremation and everything else she wanted ahead of time. Then the funeral director asked Kerch to provide clothing for her mother, because it was required at the time. "I said, 'Are you freaking kidding me?' My mother had identified a linen shroud in her wishes. I didn't want to have to go through her clothes. And I hated the idea of something melting on her," she said. She ended up picking a suit her mom had made for herself that she had never had the chance to wear. "It was beautiful and brand new, and it finally got its wearing."

I found it especially helpful that my family developed a long relationship with a funeral parlor and cemetery and all my brother and I had to do was call them and say we wanted whatever my mom had done for my father's funeral. Nevertheless, I still felt overloaded. Beyond going with the same choices, we had to think about whether we wanted web streaming of the ceremony, which wasn't a thing when my father died. For the lunch afterward, we had to get a rough head count and work through the menu with the caterer a friend suggested, but I had no idea who would come or how much to order, because that was my mother's specialty from working so many years on her own catering jobs and having grown up working in my grandparents' catering business. I longed to ask my mom how much lox we would need.

Some families prefer to gather at somebody's home after a funeral and have a potluck, some go to restaurants, while still others wait to have a memorial service at a later time. All religions and cultures have their own death rituals to follow, and some people prefer to create their own. There's no right way to do it. Regardless, it costs some kind of money to get it all done. Even transporting the body from the place of death to a funeral parlor for cremation has a price, and somebody ends up responsible for that bill in the short term, even if it can be reimbursed later from the funds of the estate. If there is no money for this and nobody steps forward to pay, the state will usually cover the costs of a simple burial or cremation. You can find out what's available in your area from the coroner who certifies the death.

We managed a sweet ceremony for my mom and a lovely lunch afterward at a friend's house. I spoke about the ways she impacted her loved ones and the world during her many eras—a Taylor Swift shout-out to please my daughter. It was all a blur.

Funeral Costs to Consider

Transport to the funeral home

Lodging and transport for immediate family if needed

Embalming

Casket or urn

Burial plot if not prepaid

Musician

Flowers

Programs and other items, such as a display portrait and guest book

Funeral home charges

Officiant fees

Cemetery or cremation fees

Meal afterward (or any associated costs for other cultural practices)

Thank-you cards

Headstone or monument

Perpetual care of grave site

After the funeral, I wanted to get started right away on that long list of things that needed to be done, but Covid had other plans for me. After the first night of mourning at my brother's, I started to feel as though I had a sinus infection coming on—not an unusual thing for me in farm country in the middle of summer—and I packed up my crew early to get back to Brooklyn before I felt worse, since I was the only driver. I got us home, took a test to be sure, and the second blue line sent me into quarantine. I couldn't do anything, so I didn't. It was painful and horrible but also probably the best thing that could have happened. I needed time, and I wouldn't have listened to centuries of religious wisdom to pause after a loss and take a minute to reflect. I listened to my body, though, because I had no choice. I could barely sit up, and I couldn't talk.

When I regained my voice, my first call was to my mother's estate attorney, thinking that she would be one-stop shopping to handle all of our needs. She was not available. She was traveling out of the country and, as a solo practitioner, did not have anyone covering her clients while she was gone. Her answering service was curt and said I could make an appointment in about a month. The attorney seemed annoyed when I followed up with an email to her directly to ask some questions. As with the last doctor in the hospital, I needed a different vibe in order to go through that difficult experience, but I didn't know if I could switch lawyers midstream or if that would jam up the process in some other way.

As it turned out, it was pretty easy. I got a referral from somebody I knew, and we got started. We still, of course, had to wait for the death certificates to arrive. The funeral and Covid had eaten up a good ten days. The copies— all fifteen of them that the funeral home had encouraged me to order—came pretty quickly after that.

The dynamic with the new lawyer was right for me. I realized at some point along the way that I was surrounding myself with mother surrogates with all of the professionals I engaged, including the estate attorney, my tax accountant, and my therapist. I would have called my mom to ask what to do at every turn, but I had a group of women I hired instead. It wasn't the same, obviously, but it got me through.

The estate attorney, Gayle Owens, based in Orlando, said that the trust was straightforward. The ownership of the condo and all my mother's possessions passed to me and my brother immediately upon her death, and we could do with them as we wished. Score one for estate planning.

There were a few complications, though.

The first was that my mom's bank figured out immediately that she had died and shut off access to her account within days of her death. I wasn't expecting it to happen that fast and had left money to cover automatic payments and the last checks to the caregivers, about $12,000 worth of expenses. I also expected her last pension and Social Security payments to be deposited to help cover all of that. None of that happened, and because the cash was left in the account that had no joint signer and no beneficiaries named, it was locked in there until we filed probate paperwork with the court.

I don't tally that as a mistake so much as a miscalculation. It could have easily gone the other way and the account would have been overdrafted if the payments came out of the account, because the pension and Social Security payments never landed.

To start fixing things, I had to go back through my mom's paper statements and see what bills had to be paid manually, such as her credit card and electric bills, because I no longer even had digital access to her account with all the recordkeeping. I had to send off one of my own checks to a caregiver who hadn't been able to cash her last payment in time.

The credit card company was happy to accept a final payment from me, but that's not always the case. When Bruce Helford called to pay his mother's credit card debt after she died, which had soared to $70,000 while she fought terminal cancer, they told him, "Oh, no, we write that off. You don't need to worry about that at all. The company is fine with that," Helford told me in an interview for MarketWatch.[4] Helford, a producer of the ABC show *The Conners,* was so mystified by that response that he wrote the scenario into an episode of the show. In his re-creation, the character of Beverly, who has dementia, starts charging up her credit card and her family gets worried because she has no way to pay the bill. Then they learn that credit card debt can be discharged in death, so they load up her card with all sorts of goodies, until they start worrying about being charged with fraud.

Legally, the deceased person's estate is responsible for all legitimate charges on an account, which the credit card company can claim if the estate goes through probate. If there aren't enough funds in the estate to cover the charges or if it's too much of a hassle for it to go after the payment, the credit card company will take a loss. It's hit or miss what they do.

In my experience, any entity my mother regularly paid through electronic payments was glad for me to pay it off or keep paying on the same schedule but with a different card, so I covered all the bases and kept paying the carrying costs of her condo.

Getting money back that my mom was owed was a much harder process. I called her pension administrator and found out that her last payment, which never showed up because her bank account was locked, was for the current month, not the prior month. Since she died on July 1, she was not due a pension payment for July, so we were all square. They directed me to mail in the death certificate to complete the process and said they would send me another form to file separately for any death benefit we might be due. When we finally sorted that all out, the amount of our inheritance for her work as a teacher, which encompassed almost all of her adult life, was $28.50. To get it, my brother and I either had to send in eight pages of notarized forms, which would have cost us $8, or wait for letters of administration from probate. We waited and each got our check, because my mother would have vindictively wanted them to go through the hassle of doing the paperwork.

My mother's missing last Social Security payment was a much more complicated problem, and figuring out what happened to it and if we could get it required a deep dive into the administrative rules. There was no number to call for easy answers, because Social Security wouldn't talk to me about it without my filing forms first.

We were sort of an unusual case, because my mom was due a payment she didn't get. Most families face the opposite situation, which is that the deceased person gets a payment that wasn't due and the Social Security Administration claws it back from their bank account. It can access the account to do that even if the family can't. One day you think you have $1,400 or so in the person's account from the payment, and the next day it's gone without any recourse.

The explanation lies in the way that Social Security handles payments for the last month of a person's life. Unlike any other payment you might have where the bill is prorated if you stop service in the middle of a month, Social Security doesn't do that. The amount that lands in a recipient's account is for the month prior. So you receive the payment for June in July. The rules state that you have to live the whole month in order to collect the benefit for that month, even if you die at 11:58 P.M. on the thirty-first of the month.

Many people who die at the end of the month and are due their next payment at the beginning of the following month get a payment that they technically did not earn, but the paperwork didn't catch up yet. As soon as Social Security or the bank spots the error, they go into the account and send the money back if you haven't already returned it—which was what Madeleine Smithberg's family did after her mother died. "You have to give that money right back. Doesn't that seem a little bit callous?" Smithberg asked.

It can catch a family unaware if they were looking at the bank balance and figuring out how to pay bills. Devin Carroll, a financial planner who runs a Facebook group about Social Security, told me that it makes people angry, to say the least, and he often sees complaints and outrage over what people see as a seizure of their money. "'That was our money,' they say. The whole issue of the payment in arrears is somewhat misunderstood. When you compound it with not receiving benefits in the month of death, it does cause confusion," Carroll told me for my story in MarketWatch.[5]

The system works this way because, well, that was how it was set up. It would be so costly to change it that legislators have not acted, despite numerous proposals over the years. The Social Security Administration estimates that it would cost $1.6 billion per year to pay for the full month of death and $800 million to prorate payment up to the date of death.[6]

My mom did earn her June payment, which should have been delivered in July, but by then her bank account was already frozen. I took to the internet and experts to find out what to do. Naturally, there is a form to fill out for this. Form SSA-1724, Claim for Amounts Due in the Case of Deceased Beneficiary, is simple enough, but mailing it off to your nearest Social Security office feels like sending a paper airplane into a giant black hole.[7] It's easiest for a surviving spouse to fill it out, but there are slots for other living relatives, and if none is available or listed, an estate representative with proper probate authorization can fill it out. It even has an input for direct deposit information.

I sent off the form and expected nothing in return, as the experts I consulted advised me to keep my expectations low. About twelve weeks later, my brother got a check for his half in the mail, and the next day, my half was deposited into my account. It felt like a sweet victory. The first thing I did was email the probate attorney, ostensibly to update her but mostly because I wanted her to be proud of me, as my mom would have been. "That is wonderful!" she responded. "I am proud of you, too. ☺ I am still waiting after almost 2 years for another estate I am working on. So you did well."

DO NOW

Look over the checklist on page 259 to see what needs to be done when somebody dies, and decide if you'll be prepared when the time comes.

Life Insurance

The best thing about life insurance is that it's usually easy to claim. But there's a big caveat: only if the heirs know about the policy.

I was able to quickly locate my mom's life insurance policy in her files, in a manila folder labeled, appropriately enough, "Life Insurance." It was a $10,000 policy she took out in 1983 that was meant to cover her funeral expenses, which might commonly be done by a nonworking spouse or a lower-earning spouse. The point of it is to have a little extra on hand when a person dies so that nobody has to foot the bill for the funeral out of their own pocket. My mom was paying only $14 per month for her policy, which she got when she was 37, and the death benefit grew to $14,000 by the time we claimed it. If you took out a new policy these days at $25,000, to account for inflation, it would cost around $76 a month for a healthy 60-year-old woman, according to a quote in 2024 from a calculator at Choice Mutual.[1]

Making the claim was maybe the smoothest part of my financial caregiving experience. I simply sent the death certificate to the company with our preferred payment details: mail or direct deposit. The money showed up nineteen days after my mom's death and in plenty of time to pay off my credit card bill for the funeral expenses.

My mom had another policy through AARP for accidental death and dismemberment (AD&D) insurance that cost her $36 per month, but her circumstances didn't apply. That would have been more complicated to claim, because it would have required support documentation such as medical or police reports.

Bigger life insurance policies can have a corollary bigger impact on heirs. My father had a traditional life insurance policy for double what my mom had. She got even more from a life insurance rider on his annuity contract when he died. Without those, my mom might have struggled without my father's benefits and the freelance income he was still earning. The annuity rider was not quite the same as life insurance but served a similar purpose. For my dad, the cost was an additional fee added to his contract—an upsell, basically. The annuity representative said that this type of rider was no longer available, so he was lucky to get it.

Social Security Death Benefits

- If the surviving spouse is at full retirement age (67) or older, they can claim 100 percent of their spouse's benefit instead of their own.
- If the surviving spouse is younger than full retirement age, they receive a reduced percentage.
- Divorced spouses who were married more than ten years can qualify for survivor's benefits, depending on their age and current marital status.
- Minor children are also eligible for Social Security death benefits, awarded as a percentage of the deceased's benefit until they are of age and up to a family maximum, unless they are disabled.

All of this applies, however, only if the deceased was already claiming benefits. If the person was not already claiming, the surviving spouse can claim survivor's benefits as early as age 60. To apply for any of these options, you have to fill out forms with your local Social Security office and wait to get approved.

Source: Social Security Administration[2]

As the primary wage earner in the family, my father got a bigger Social Security benefit check than my mom did. When he died, she had the choice to keep going with her own benefit or switch to a spousal death benefit. In this case, it was a no-brainer because he got so much more than she did, even when adjusted downward by 30 percent because they both claimed their benefits early. Nothing is ever really enough to make up the difference between two benefit checks together, though. The switch to a single benefit can be a big financial shock if you're not aware that that's what will happen and don't plan for it.

As powerful a tool as life insurance can be, it was appropriate that my mom didn't have any life insurance on herself other than the funeral expense policy. She had been retired for more than twenty years and had enough savings to cover her mortgage payments and any other debts there might be. My brother and I were grown and had careers of our own. The point of life insurance is to protect your family from the loss of your income should you die, not to provide a bonus to the family. This is why most people who have life insurance choose term life insurance or get it through their employers, because it's designed to cover your working years with a relatively low premium. So it was a good thing for my dad to have had robust coverage and fine for my mom not to have had much.

The other choices for life insurance are called permanent policies because they stick with you until you die. The subchoice is between whole life, which usually has fixed premiums and builds up cash value according to a set return, and variable life, which has flexible premiums and more investing choices for the cash value portion. Both types are more expensive than term life, and you typically have to pay premiums all your life or the policy lapses.

In 2023, only 52 percent of individuals in the United States had any life insurance at all, down from 60 percent in 2011, according to LIMRA, the life insurance trade group.[3] Despite the Covid pandemic, increased awareness, and financial education campaigns, the number has only decreased in recent times. The most likely culprit is demographics, in that the baby boomer generation is aging and their workplace life insurance goes away when they retire. Term life insurance makes up about 40 percent of the total marketplace.

The older you are when you buy a policy, the more you pay, and premiums go up over time, too. Most insurance companies won't issue new term policies to people over age 90, and they may also limit the policy length for those who are slightly younger.

A financial caregiver stepping into an aging relative's situation might have to guide them through a number of choices. A friend once asked me what to do about his 78-year-old father, who was still working part-time as a consultant and struggling to pay $2,000 a month for a $1 million policy. After he turned 80, it was scheduled to go down to $100 a month for $100,000 in coverage. To my eye, the payments seemed excessive, and the big payout seemed more than they needed at their standard of living, especially considering that he was likely to live through the policy and the $100,000 wouldn't help his wife as much as putting $2,000 a month back into the budget would.

The best thing might have been to seek out a less expensive alternative that would satisfy the man's intent to provide for his wife if he died but not threaten their current lifestyle with a huge bill that was more than their mortgage. A new term policy might have been just as expensive as the policy he already had. But he could perhaps have done a trade—the 1035 exchange—to get a hybrid life insurance policy that also offered long-term care benefits. He would have had to shop around and see the pricing. Another option would have been to switch to a burial policy, which at older ages can still be affordable—although still much more expensive than buying one at age 65. A 78-year-old man would have had to pay around $3,000 a year for a $25,000 policy in 2024, according to the Choice Mutual calculator.

An even bigger issue for financial caregivers is what they don't know about life insurance policies that aren't in the files or listed on account statements. Does the person you're taking care of have more than one life insurance policy? Maybe several of them? If they haven't been careful about recordkeeping and filing, you might not come across the paperwork in a timely fashion. I found my mom's policy, but I never knew if she had others, and I had to search through all her paperwork to make sure I wasn't missing anything. If you end up not finding anything, one way to backstop yourself down the road is to search for unclaimed funds (see chapter 30).

Dana Chitwood thought she knew everything about her parents' finances before they died on the same day in 2023 at age 92, both after long illnesses. Chitwood is a financial educator in Georgia and had been taking care of her parents' money for years, slowly simplifying their financial lives down to virtually no transactions while they were in a nursing home. Still, she had surprises after they died, one of which was finding paperwork for an ancient funeral home insurance policy that her grandmother took out on her mother in the early 1940s, when her mother was 10, for $1,000 in death benefits. "I found this really old beautiful document that had a coupon book for the payments. The company that issued it was sold and sold and sold, but I said, 'I'm not going to go back on this,'" she said. "I really did my research."

Chitwood tracked down the company that currently owned the policy, but it initially told her on the phone that it didn't see any policy with the identifying number on the document. She went online, created an account, and the automated system found it. "They were just wanting me to go away," she said. "I spent two months trying to get them to pay it off. I sent snail mail, made phone calls, sent them her death certificate. It was a $1,000 policy that grew over the years, and it was worth it."

For Fidelity's David Peterson, that underscored the advice he always gives his clients: "When you go into a home after somebody dies, don't just throw everything out. Don't do bulk shredding. You actually need to look at this stuff."

DO NOW

Make sure you have all needed information about life insurance policies and contacts. Verify that premium payments are being made, and read the paperwork to see if there are any special conditions for claiming the money after a death.

Probate

Is probate really that bad? Almost all estate attorneys, financial advisers, and personal finance experts acknowledge the annoyance of the process and preach avoidance. The main reason is the time and expense involved. Probate is a court process to validate the will of a deceased person and approve an administrator or, in the absence of a will, name one from the available heirs.

In all my years of reporting on estate planning topics, I've encountered only one professional who said that the negativity was unwarranted: Bruce Steiner. "I think it's blown out of proportion," he said. "If I were to give a talk about estate planning, probate wouldn't make the top ten list of topics to talk about."

The hardest thing about probate is the waiting. No matter how you come at probate, it takes time, and you're in limbo until you get the courts to process at least the letters of administration that will allow you to act on behalf of the estate. Then you're stuck with dribs and drabs of paperwork until probate is closed. There's usually a flurry of activity for a bit while you deal with creditors and loose ends; then things generally calm down while you wait endlessly for the official closing of the process.

The time lag is particularly onerous when you're trying to probate an estate without a will. When a person dies intestate, as dying without a will is formally known, the court has to first make a decision about who will administer the estate, and in some states it can take a while even to get a hearing. Then once the court decides who will be the administrator and who is in line for inheritance, the process proceeds along the timeline as if a will were in place.

My attorney, Gayle Owens, said the fastest she'd ever seen the probate process take was three months in Florida, and that was for a small-estate summary judgment with a will. Taking care of that required her work as a lawyer, so there was still a cost to the families that filed that way.

> ## Key Probate Statistics
>
> - The average time it takes to complete probate is twenty months, but only 2 percent of respondents to a survey believed that it would take that long. A third of respondents (37 percent) said they weren't sure what the probate timeline is.
> - 56 percent have no idea what the probate process costs; 10 percent believe it will be $1,000 or less, and only 4 percent believe it will cost more than $10,000. Probate costs range between 3 and 7 percent of the total value of the estate.
> - More than half (52 percent) perceived probate as being somewhat or very difficult, highlighting the emotional and procedural complexities involved in settling an estate.
> - Almost half of Americans (48 percent) have some knowledge that the process of inheriting assets is long and complicated.
> - 65 percent would seek help from a probate attorney, underscoring the necessity for professional guidance during the complicated process.
>
> Source: Trust & Will[1]

Trust & Will, an online estate-planning service, said its internal data showed that the average probate case—whether filing with a will or without one—took an average of twenty months. It can take longer in California, which is notoriously backlogged, and more like six to twelve months in a handful of efficient states such as Texas, Alaska, and Colorado. When there's a dispute of any kind, the process can take many years. Prince's intestate probate, which started in 2016 after his death, was still ongoing in 2024 with a new set of court hearings over who would control decisions about his music catalog rights.

For my family, that checking account with $12,000 in it meant it was best for us to go to probate. And to do that, we had to make some decisions. If we went the small-estate settlement route, Owens explained, it would be a once-and-done filing. On the plus side, it would be pretty quick, and we could settle the probate and access the funds within a couple of months. On the downside, if anything else cropped up that we needed to deal with, we'd have to go through the whole thing again for another summary judgment, at extra expense.[2]

Alternatively, we could file for full probate, which would allow us time to sort out the rest of my mom's paperwork and figure out what we didn't know. I had no idea at that point what she might owe to creditors. When I had to make the choice, it was only a few weeks after she had died, and hospital and rehab bills could have continued to roll in for a long period of time to come. Plus, I was in New York then and had brought home only a handful of her papers. Anything could have been lurking in her file cabinets.

Warren Kozak, who took care of his doctor wife when she got cancer, faced a similar issue when she died with an extraneous checking account that could not be easily assigned to him. He and his wife did not have trusts but rather sweetheart wills that said that each of them left everything to the other, and if both of them died, everything would go to their daughter. Kozak didn't think he was going to need probate when his wife died, because he would roll everything into his own name. But that wasn't at all the case. His wife had one account that was in her name only, and they had somehow skipped over either naming beneficiaries or having him joint on the account.[3] "It was a major screw-up, and it cost several thousand dollars," he said. "We wouldn't have had to go through probate otherwise. And probate is a monster."

Another thing that I knew was going to cause problems down the road was my mom's tax refund for the year before she died. I had directed her Florida tax preparer to file an extension for her 2022 taxes in April 2023, when she was in rehab. That wasn't unusual because she usually filed an extension to have more time to do the paperwork. When we were back in her condo for hospice, I didn't want to get caught short if she didn't make the October 15 extension deadline or was much sicker by then. We filed quickly while she was still able, but then she died shortly after. Her refund had not shown up by the time she died, nor several weeks later, and we didn't know if it was going to arrive any minute, addressed to her, or never come at all. If it did show up, I wouldn't be able to cash it without opening an estate account for her, for which I would need the letters of administration. And if it didn't show up, I'd need the probate letters of administration even to ask questions about what to do on the phone.

My Probate Timeline

July 1, 2023	My mom died.
July 14	Engaged estate attorney.
September 15	Probate filing process started.
October 4	Probate petition filed.
October 16	Letters of administration issued.
December 1	Probate inventory due.
December 13	Claim made against the estate by hospital.
January 3, 2024	Objection to claim filed.
February 20	Claim voided by timing out.
August 16	Received tax refund for 2022.
August 17	Filed discharge petition.
August 27	Discharge petition granted.

This is where my lawyer explained the difference to me between the estate and the trust, because I didn't understand why we needed both. Those words, in simple English, were commingled in my brain as meaning virtually the same thing. Legally, however, they were two separate entities.

The Estate of Ann Pinsker was what took the place of Ann Pinsker as a person after her death. Her Social Security number ceased to function, and I had to apply for a new tax ID number to replace it so that I could handle any matters pertaining to her. Any checks that came for Ann Pinsker or the Estate of Ann Pinsker had to go into an account that I opened with that ID. We received quite a few payments once I started to close things down, addressed in various ways, such as prorated refunds from the cable company, the car insurance company, and the long-term care insurance company.

On the other hand, the Ann Pinsker Living Trust had been aligned with her Social Security number while she was living, as she was the grantor and she was the one paying any applicable tax. Upon her death, it became an irrevocable trust that was an entirely new taxable entity to handle the condo and all her other worldly possessions. I had to file to get a tax ID number for it as the trustee of the Trust of Ann Pinsker so I could open a bank account for it. The main reason we opened the account was that we needed an official trust account to accept the funds from the sale of the condo, which was the main asset of the trust. Since the account title included my mother's name, I found that the bank was pretty flexible about accepting any check that had her name on it—except for checks that were written out specifically as "To the estate of Ann Pinsker."

My lawyer tasked me with signing up for the trust tax ID first, saying that it was easy and doing it myself would save fees. I stumbled through it so badly that it made me feel as though I wasn't quite up to that estate admin-istration task. Perhaps it was grief fog. I searched for "tax ID signup," clicked on what looked like an official site, and started to put in our information, and then I was asked for payment information. "Shouldn't this be free?" I asked myself. Well, yes, it should.

There are websites out there waiting to take your money to walk you through processes that should be free. Always go to the official website of whatever entity you're interfacing with, especially a government agency, and never click through from a link you've found somewhere.

I doubled back, went to the IRS.gov website, and clicked through to get to the correct place to file for the numbers. Then I got stuck on how to fill out the form, because I couldn't figure out if I was supposed to be using my in-formation as trustee or my mother's information. Of course I did it wrong, with my mom's information instead of mine, which must happen often be-cause the form that is generated has a cut-off portion at the bottom to mail in if you make a mistake.

Establishing the estate with the courts didn't take much effort on my part, because I paid the probate lawyer to do it. It cost $5,000, but that was less than the amount in the bank account and what might eventually come in from the tax refund and the scattered other payments we needed to deposit. It made sense financially for us to file for traditional probate versus doing the small-estate filing, so we forged ahead.

If less money had been involved, we might have skipped probate alto-gether and forgone the inheritance. Why pay $5,000 to retrieve $4,000? We could have waited to try to recover whatever was left over as unclaimed funds down the road. We could also have tried to go forward with the small-estate administration on our own, but I simply didn't have the patience.

If you do skip probate because it seems easier, you should know that it's possible you may get jammed up later. Some financial institutions and gov-ernment agencies, such as the IRS, expect you to have gone through probate to obtain official letters of administration. Jenny Rozelle said when she gets an estate to administer, she first tries to figure out whether or not it needs to go to probate. Since Indiana's limit is up to $100,000 for small estates, it's more common to do the shorter process than it is in states where the threshold is lower. When she decides not to proceed with filing probate, she then sometimes runs into problems with banks, which won't give any information to her or the heirs without letters of administration.

"I'm not going to open probate just so the bank can tell me if there's a beneficiary listed on a closed account. Same with a safe deposit box," she said. She described a case she had handled where she approached the bank in a friendly manner and asked it to provide access to a safe deposit box without probate. She told the bank she didn't want to have to charge the family more to get access to the box. "Most of the time, my pleading does not work, but it has sometimes, especially at smaller community banks that don't have the massive legal departments."

Adam Schneider's experience in California as a lawyer has been completely different. California's overall small-estate limit was much higher, $184,000 when we spoke in 2024, but it had a lower cap, $61,500, on real property. You can't really find any property in the state that is under that amount, so everyone with property essentially has to go through probate if they don't have a trust. The only cases he has that don't have to go to probate are people who do not own homes. "I don't sell trusts to people who don't need them," he said. "If you're in a nursing home, your house is already sold, and you have $150,000 in the bank, just make sure beneficiaries are up to date and carry on."

There are some cases where probate was not done right initially, and you have to fix it after the fact. When I talked to my longtime friend and former colleague Lynnette Khalfani-Cox and her husband, Earl Cox, about their estate-planning troubles, that was at the core of their experience. Lynnette and Earl are partners in a financial education company, and Lynnette has written many books on personal finance, including the bestseller *Zero Debt: The Ultimate Guide to Financial Freedom*[4] and the more recent *Bounce Back: The Ultimate Guide to Financial Resilience*,[5] with Earl serving as her agent. They owned a house in New Jersey that Earl inherited with his mother from an aunt, and then he subsequently bought out his mother's share and retitled the house in both his and Lynnette's names. Earl's mom died in 2018, and when Earl and Lynnette went to sell the house a few years later, the title company said there was a problem because they didn't own the house outright; it was still held jointly by Earl's mother.

"I had made a deal with my mother to take full possession, but it wasn't recorded properly," Earl said. They had to track down the lawyer who handled the original transaction when Earl bought out his mother's share of the house to figure out what happened. Fixing the issue came down to needing to file a quit-claim deed signed by his mother, which is a document that disclaims any ownership rights. Obviously, his mother could no longer sign documents years after her death. So then they had to file what is known as ancillary probate, which is like an add-on probate when the deceased is in another state, because his mother was living in Pennsylvania by the time she died. "That was a total nightmare," said Lynnette. "This is in the middle of trying to sell the house. We had accepted a cash offer, and it should have closed in ten days, but it took sixty days or more. It was very frustrating."

Another thing that jams people up in probate, especially when there is no will, is fights over who will be the administrator and who counts as relatives in line to inherit. In most cases, the order is spouses, then children, and then grandchildren. If there are none of those, the next of kin would be living parents of the deceased, then siblings and cousins. In Prince's famous case, for instance, he had no spouse, no children, and no living parents. His estate ended up going to six siblings—one full and five half siblings.[6]

Things can get hairy among heirs in a probate fight. When one administrator wins out, there is sometimes a fight down the road where others challenge them, demanding an accounting of monies spent on the estate and who gets what. This is what has long jammed up settling the singer Tony Bennett's estate, with two of his children suing the third, who was named administrator.[7]

I was fed up enough with a few months of the probate process. We started the process in the same month as her death, and it took from July until the middle of October to get the letters of administration. It sounds almost grandiose to call the piece of paper from the court such a big name as "letters of administration." It was three paragraphs of text with a stamp from a judge and an electronic signature that looked like a squiggle. I presented it at an in-person appointment at a branch of her regional bank that happened to be in the financial district of New York and was able to close out that last bank account. If I lived in a place where there was no branch available, it would have been more complicated. I also scanned the letters of administration and attached it willy-nilly to correspondence to anyone who asked for it to close lingering accounts.

The rest of probate went smoothly for me, although it was a constant annoyance, until we came to the creditor portion. My mom was not famous or rich, but she still had to contend with people coming after her for money.

The lawyer put out the requisite notices in the fall, and in December, right before the closing deadline, we heard back from my mom's hospital system, saying she owed it $10,770. The claim was signed by the correspondence representative of the hospital system with her email address. I had no idea what that sum might have been for, and I had not found any unpaid bills in my mom's papers for amounts of that sort. What I had seen previously were mix-ups with the insurance billing because of the car accident she had at the start of Covid, where some of her visits were coded to the car insurance of the person who hit her. I had already cleared up two such bills, for $800 and $155.

To save on lawyer fees, I contacted the representative myself via email. I was not going to pay that kind of money blindly. I had been through it too many times with my own medical billing. I didn't hear back, so I put on my reporter hat to track the woman down. I'm very good at finding people because I have to verify sources all the time before I can use any of their material in my stories. But I could not find any trace of the person's existence or any sign of the department where she worked. I started to think we were getting scammed.

I contacted the billing department at the hospital, and it said it had a zero balance listed for my mom and sent me on to another department at the hospital. After several tries, I was able to find the department that thought my mom owed it money. It wasn't a scam, but it wasn't really legit, either. It immediately cut the bill in half, because most of it was too old, then sent me an itemized list of lingering charges from 2022 that I could see right away were billed to and rejected by the car insurance company. I sent the billing department my mom's Medicare supplement information and the people there ran it through and confirmed over email that she had a zero balance. After that, they went silent and would not respond to a request to file the paperwork to rescind their claim on my mom's estate. That made extra work for my lawyer, who had to submit a filing to object to their claim. The whole runaround took about two months to settle, but in the end we didn't have to pay a dime.

DO NOW

Look up the probate rules for the appropriate states, and figure out what you will need to do to file. If you don't already have an estate attorney in that area, use the resources on page 254 to find one. Then set up a family discussion about inheritance to avoid fights down the road.

28

Settling Property

My parents were beach people. My mom grew up a block from the ocean in Margate, New Jersey, and her first date with my dad was a few miles down in Atlantic City. It was a blind date, and they went bowling with a group. Afterward, they went for a walk alone on the beach, where my dad picked up a shell and wrote their initials together on it with a heart; apocryphally, that was after he heard that my grandparents owned the Savadove & Getson kosher catering business. "You don't know this yet, but you're going to marry me," he supposedly said.

Money was tight on an English professor's salary, but we lived in a house on the Franklin & Marshall campus that was subsidized by the college. At the first chance, my parents bought a place in Ventnor, New Jersey, the town sandwiched between Margate and Atlantic City on the Jersey shore. The 1974 mortgage of $19,300 at 9.5 percent interest was listed in my dad's name, with my mom as his wife, and was almost fully financed—one of the earliest examples of my mom overleveraging herself. They were able to upgrade in 2003, moving two blocks closer to the beach, and that was the place my mom sold in 2016 after my dad got sick. They bought their condo in Fort Lauderdale in 1998 when my father started phased retirement. He would teach the fall semester, and then they would go down to Florida until the summer. My father liked Ventnor, but he loved that condo more than anything, the balcony in particular. He could look out over the water as he read his books—although he wasn't allowed to smoke a pipe out there. He went to the pool every day and became a legend there, because no matter when you went, he was there, tanned to the point of insanity, drifting on a noodle, spouting slightly off-color opinions to anyone who would listen.

My mother threw herself into the building's social and political scene. Just as at home when I was growing up, she was constantly churning out hors d'oeuvres for football games, cooking for potluck brunches, inviting people for every holiday, and organizing New Year's Eve fests in the condo's party room. She joined the board as treasurer, even though she had no formal financial training. She worked until she understood everything that was going on and managed the staff with humanity—arguing for raises, buying pizza, and listening to their life stories.

I loved the house in Ventnor the most, and I mourn the sale of it almost as though it was a member of the family. I miss it as a place where we all got together as a family, had a lot of raucous parties, and relaxed together. Just as when I was growing up, we spent whole summers there when my kids were little. We even enrolled my kids in the summer camp where I'd worked as a teenager so they didn't have to go to one of the dreary school-based summer camps in Brooklyn. Once the Ventnor house was sold, I came to love going to Florida, too, waking at dawn to see turtles hatch and checking out the little area of shops nearby that had a store that sold both jewelry and puppies (until my kids grew old enough to consider the sale of puppies to be immoral).

All of that factored into what we were going to do with my mom's condo. I wanted so much to keep it. It was an emotional decision rather than a financial one. I went through every scenario in my mind to try to make it work. I calculated what it would cost to assume the mortgage, the monthly maintenance fee, the rest of the massive special assessment that was due, the air-conditioning bill, and the cable. There would be flight costs and either a rental car or more fixed costs to keep her car there. And then there was my brother to consider: Would he go in 50/50 for the plan, or would I have to buy him out?

If we were in it together, we could work out a schedule for who would use it when and what we'd do so we could all be there together and the cousins could hang out. But that's when the dream started to unravel. The condo wasn't exactly the Bush compound in Kennebunkport; it was a two-bedroom apartment. There were eight of us, and who knows how many more of us there would eventually be if any of the kids got married and had their own kids. As it was, when I visited my mom with my two, they usually slept in the guest room and I put an air mattress into the laundry nook. And when exactly would we go? All the adults worked full-time, the kids had school, and they were about to grow up and live their own lives. What would happen if my family used it more than my brother, as often happened with the house in New Jersey? Things could get out of hand quickly. Bottom line, I didn't have anywhere close to the money to buy out my brother. I didn't even have enough to cover half the fixed costs of maintaining ownership, not with college tuition payments looming for the next eight or so years.

Real property is one of the hardest things to settle in an estate. It's often the most valuable item on the table and the hardest to split. It can even be difficult for an only child, because of the logistics and financial burden involved. There's often a disconnect between what the person leaving the house thinks will happen and what the heirs want to do with it. This is an important thing to consider well in advance, because the plan a person sets up might impede what the next generation wants to do with the property.

"Do the kids even want the house?" is what Schwab's Susan Hirshman tells clients to ask themselves. She sees a lot of couples who set up complicated estate plans so that their house or a cherished vacation home stays in the family, and when it comes time, their children or grandchildren don't even want it. Sometimes a property will be passed down through several generations and the ownership becomes too diluted to be practical; then you get the revenge of the cousins.

While I was dealing with those questions, my kids got me immersed in watching *The Summer I Turned Pretty* on Netflix, a young adult series that hinges on exactly this sort of estate fight, but it involves half siblings with sore feelings (which differs slightly from the scenario in the book).[1] When Conrad and Jeremiah's mother, Susannah, dies, her beloved summerhouse that is the setting of the story passes to her estranged half sister. Heartless Aunt Julia shows up nearly immediately with her teenager to put the house on the market, and Conrad and Jeremiah can do nothing to stop it, except perhaps take money out of their trust to buy her out. The trust is controlled by their father, who thinks it's best to sell and move on. This is all easier to understand if you're 14.

The gist is that this kind of generational inheritance plan has to be intentional, and it is usually set up to keep assets in the family. If, for instance, Julia and Susannah's father had left the house to them equally and made no other provisions, Susannah's half would have gone to her husband, who was not yet an ex. Presumably, he might have passed it along to his sons, but there's no certainty in that. If he got remarried, his new wife might inherit the house upon his death instead. Either way, Conrad and Jeremiah would most likely have ended up cut out of the house. The only way for them to inherit directly would have been for the trustee to say that Susannah's shares would go to her sons, *per stirpes* (meaning "in equal shares"), with a trustee until they were no longer minors. But then there would have been no plot-line for season two.

Real life is not that much different, just with worse hair. "People say, 'This is for the bloodline,' and I push back hard," said David Handler about couples who come to him for estate planning. "I say to them, 'You're spouses—you're not the same bloodline. It would be horrible if I told you that you couldn't leave things to each other.' And when you paint it that way, sometimes they loosen up."

If a person owns a house and expects their heirs to keep it, it's best to think through all the possible scenarios and try to account for them in a trust. You can't control everything, but you can at least try to prevent fights down the road. This is easiest when there is only one heir in the next generation and you don't have to worry about hurting anyone else's feelings. If there's more than one heir, you have to consider how they will share it. You'll want to make special consideration if any of the heirs has been living there already while others are elsewhere.

If you expect one heir to keep the house, you don't have to worry so much about a trust—especially if they are already living there. A transfer-on-death deed would take care of the job in that circumstance, and a simple will would also do fine because they wouldn't have to worry about the timing of probate.

Eric Bronnenkant faced that sort of situation when his mother died and left him her house in her will. He was only 30 then and was 23 when his dad passed. He was not yet settled into his career as a tax expert for financial firms, but he might not have made any different choices or urged his mother to plan differently if he had known then what he knows now. He needed time after losing both his parents so young, and he didn't want to make any rash decisions, so the fact that probate took a year was fine with him. He was less fine with the fact that it cost about $10,000 in legal fees, but that was the going rate for what he needed, and it covered both probate and the sale of the house. He ended up living in his mother's house while waiting to be named executor, which took about three months. Then he took time to pre-pare the house for sale.

He waited until he owned it legally and then put it on the market. That was in 2007, and the housing market was already starting to crack, so it took a while to sell and he ended up accepting an offer for $20,000 less than he wanted. "I could not risk continuing carrying costs for the home, and also there was the real potential we might not be able to sell at all," he said.

If you're in a hurry to sell or are going to end up selling anyway, three or four months' wait to approve the executor and then another length of time to be able to sell a house might be very hard. Given the choice of how to inherit, most people would prefer an immediate option with no strings at-tached, such as a trust or a transfer-on-death deed.

While the beneficiary deed sounds efficient, there are cautions. First, many confuse the situation and think it's best to be on the deed from the start, much like being joint signers on a bank account. This is usually a bad decision, according to most estate lawyers and financial planners. One of the primary benefits of inheriting property in the United States is that the system affords you a step-up in basis, which means that the inheritor gets the property at the current market value at the time of death.[2] If your par-ents bought a house for $18,000 in 1974 and they passed it to you when it's worth $350,000, your stake going forward is considered to be $350,000. You don't owe tax on the $332,000 difference. If you sell it relatively quickly and the market value does not change significantly, you don't owe tax on the sale. But if you wait ten years and it's worth $750,000 by then, you'd owe tax on the $400,000 gain—minus your personal exclusion if it's your primary residence by then, either $250,000 for a single owner or $500,000 for a mar-ried couple.

If those same parents added their child to the deed prior to their deaths, that child would effectively share their basis in the house, and their por-tion of it would not receive a step-up in basis when the parents died. They would then have tax liability on the gain if they sold it after the parents died, and they could even have tax complications if they kept the house. While the parents are living, the child's stake would be at the risk of cred-itors, could be considered as an asset in the event of a divorce, and would also count toward financial aid calculations if they have children. Another drawback is family fights if there's more than one heir or there are blended families.

With a trust for property, on the other hand, you get immediate transfer of legal, insurable ownership and step-up in basis. The insurable part of that is important, because you can't sell a house without a clear title. When it came to putting my mom's condo on the market, I was glad for her trust, but my probate attorney said it wasn't absolutely necessary in Florida because of a special provision called a homestead exemption that could also have passed the house instantly and avoided probate. Strangely, for an estate attorney, she was not the hugest proponent of trusts.

"In a lot of cases, it's not beneficial," she said. She thought a trust often complicated the family dynamic, burdened the trustee, and confused the heirs. "A lot of couples don't want to discuss finances with the kids, and so they set up a grantor trust without saying anything to them. But does the trustee understand how it works? Do they just have to figure it out?" she asked.

The process often confuses the people creating the trust, too, so much so that they don't properly fund it. "They get this trust package with a two-inch binder and they never fund it because they didn't follow through with the instructions, and then the whole estate is part of probate," Owens said.

In our case, on the other hand, Owens thought it was fine because my brother and I were able to handle the details. It helped to be able to put the condo on the market quickly, because we had a short window during which we could go down to Florida to hire a real estate agent and start to clean out the condo. We were also fighting a changing real estate market that was about to dip and a huge hike in the building's maintenance fees coming in the next calendar year. Florida coastal properties have their own selling season, which starts in September, and we thought our best chance to get a buyer would be if we were ready to show it by then. The final complication was that my mom's building was in the middle of its forty-year inspection; the inspections were especially stringent since the collapse of the Champlain Towers South condo in Surfside, Florida, in 2021. That meant that nobody could get a mortgage and we needed a cash-only buyer. It was a very small needle to thread. A delay in probate would have rendered that quick timeline impossible.

So back to Florida we went in August. My rational financial brain knew that selling was the best decision for us, but my grieving heart was not ready to face her apartment and all her stuff without her being there to greet us. I dreaded walking into the apartment and not seeing her sitting in her recliner, the house smelling like baking chicken and Vicks VapoRub.

But we did it. My brother and I and our significant others interviewed three agents who came to look at the condo who were familiar with the building, and we all liked the same one. We decided on a listing price, and then the task was to clear the condo out so the agent could take pictures and put it on the market. Because of the aging population there, Florida real estate agents are used to this situation, and all of them had a procedure for helping with the clean-out. The easier we could make it for them, the faster they could get it onto the market. One of the agents told us that another apartment in the building took him five months to clear out because the children who inherited it abdicated the responsibility, and the place was a wreck. Another promised to consign all the valuables as part of the process, which she did as one of her side businesses, and we could leave it all with her. What she couldn't sell, she would donate, and if there was still stuff left after that, she'd call a junk removal service. We ended up going with less of a concierge service, confident that we could clean out most of the apartment ourselves. In the end it took a very short time to find a buyer, even one with an all-cash offer.

DO NOW

Use the resources on page 254 to assess the inheritance plan for all properties in question, and figure out which plan would save you the most time and money.

29

Dealing with Stuff

My mom had six meat thermometers. Some of them were unused and still in their packages. She had the kind that had batteries and a digital display and a few that you stuck in that had a knob on top to tell the temperature. That was a little hint of what was in store.

The stuff in my mom's two-bedroom apartment—and the two (or three) storage cages in the bowels of the building—had been consolidated from two other houses over time. When my parents left Lancaster, they moved all their stuff to their summer home in Ventnor, and when my mom sold that house, her handyman packed his van with boxes and took them south. She had the linens, socks, and kitchen equipment of three functioning households. She had enough beach towels to dry the U.S. Olympic swimming team. She had stacks of silver serving platters and mountains of spoons, some of which dated back to my grandparents' catering business.

I've only ever cleaned out my mom's apartment, so maybe that was a normal amount of stuff for an older person who had lived a full life, and that is what you get when you have to empty every drawer, every shelf, and every closet until they are completely clean. Or maybe not. When I got to the closet in her bedroom, which contained enough medical supplies to stock a small pharmacy, I started to think she was a secret hoarder. Her condo in Florida was spotless on the surface, the tile floor uncluttered and not a lot of knickknacks. You would never have guessed what was right below the surface.

The legendary comedian George Carlin had a famous routine about stuff—something my dad had shown me from time to time over the years. "That's the whole meaning of life, isn't it—trying to find a place for your stuff," he ranted.[1] That stuck in my head the whole time I was packing boxes.

When it comes to dealing with a deceased person's stuff, it's obviously not only about logistics. There are memories in every goddamn set of toenail clippers (and my mom had twelve of them for some reason). It's a minefield of emotions, good and bad and very, very sad. It's also something that's hard to hire somebody to do, at least unsupervised, until some close-enough family member has gone through the stuff to retrieve any important paperwork and valuable items. And then there's the question of who is going to take what.

My main problem with my mom's stuff was that the task was gargantuan and I didn't know how we were going to manage to do it. It was mid-August by that point, and my brother and I each had limited time to work on the apartment. We planned trips that overlapped by a few days. He and his wife were going to pack what he wanted into my mom's car and drive it north, and then my boyfriend and I were going to stay and figure out the rest of what we needed to do in terms of selling what we could, donating to charity, and hiring a junk company for whatever was left. I was planning to hire movers to take what I wanted back to Brooklyn.

I priced getting somebody to help, and there was no shortage of people to call, but most wanted $40-plus an hour, plus extra for packing supplies. I couldn't fathom paying that or having a stranger around for that amount of time, so we toughed it out on our own.

First on my list was getting rid of all the medications, some of it narcotics and some of it long-expired allergy meds. My mom never threw out any half-used prescription, it seemed. I grabbed pill bottles by the handful in her bathroom and stuffed them into a trash bag to take them to a chain drug store that had a proper receptacle for them. The cashier told me I had to first peel off the labels or cross my mom's name off each one before putting it through the slot. So I sat on the floor and altered more than a hundred little bottles with a Sharpie they gave me.

My brother went through the condo first and found only a few things he wanted. It was so little that I said yes to him for all of it. I don't think we were the norm in this situation. Splitting up the stuff is a big problem for most people. There are fights over dishes and doll collections, jewelry and paper holiday decorations. Siblings who had no problem splitting up houses and investment accounts can get down and dirty about photo albums.

Our family had long used the "oldest daughter" inheritance trope to forestall bad feelings. The one thing of real value we had was an ornate pair of fifteen-inch-tall silver candlesticks. I've found a few examples of them on-line, and they aren't actually of significant monetary value, but they have great family historical meaning as a connection to the past. And they are beautiful.

They were fabricated in the mid-1800s and came over from Russia with my great-great-grandmother Fannie. She left the candlesticks to her daughter, who left them to my grandmother Edith rather than Edith's younger sister, Ethel. My grandmother and her sister bickered over everything their whole lives, so I think their mother knew better than to leave it to them to decide things. Despite the fighting, Edith and Ethel talked to each other every day on the phone and never let their disputes interrupt that.

After my grandmother died, there were many potential inheritors of the candlesticks who had an equal claim besides my mother: my great-aunt Ethel, who was still alive but had dementia, my mother's three first cousins, and the family of my late uncle. My mom got the candlesticks because she was the oldest daughter.

After my mom died, there were even more people in the family tree who could have claimed the candlesticks, but they are sitting in my dining room because I was my mom's eldest daughter. My brother assumed that I would take them, because that was what my mom had said to do, even though she did not specify any split of property in her will or in her trust. She left it all for us to decide, which is common but can make things hard.

What works best for deciding who gets what is, of course, planning ahead. If the deceased takes inventory of their valuable items and decides ahead of time who will get what, it will eliminate most family drama. You can delineate these bequests in a will or in a trust, but either way, the designated administrator becomes responsible for distributing the gifts and can be held accountable if items go missing. The attorney Bruce Steiner had one client who was so detailed that they put pictures of all the valuable items into their will. They wrote that they left the items pictured in pages 1 to 9 to Child A, the items on pages 10 to 18 to Child B, and so forth.

I spoke to a woman at a conference whose aunt placed Post-it notes on all her valuable items stating what she paid for each and whom it should go to after she died. Another person in her family put different-colored sticker dots on items before she died so her family would know who would get what, and every time that woman visited, her aunt asked her what she wanted and offered to put a sticker on it for her. "Let's stop all this morbid talk," the woman implored her, but later she realized how helpful it would be.

Some families use the sticker method after somebody dies and they are cleaning out their house. Each family member is given a different color sticker, and they do a walk-through where everyone can put their mark on the things they want. They collect the items that have more than one sticker and do a trade or flip a coin to decide who gets what. Another way is to sort items by type, such as paintings, necklaces, and figurines, and then take turns picking in each category. Families can get as elaborate as they want with points or an auction to gamify the system.

Steiner once advised a pair of siblings who were fighting over seven sets of dishes they both wanted. One child was due to get 55 percent of the estate and the other 45 percent. They ended up taking turns picking, with the one getting the bigger share going first. Another set of siblings in a different case wanted a statue, and the group had to decide whether to have a private auction among themselves or a public one where anyone could bid. "I've seen wills that provide for alternating picks—child A gets first pick, then B and C, and then the order is reversed. As long as you don't have one item of vast value, that can reasonably work," Steiner said. "Or some say that the executors can decide, but if both want the same thing and can't agree, then you're stuck with the same problem."

Whatever way works to split things up without bad feelings is going to be the best way, and the worst way is going to end up in court. Mom and Dad are not going to reach out from beyond the grave to smack sense into people. You have to think really carefully whether a court case is worth it to settle whatever disputes you are having over stuff.

Keeping track of everything is a big part of the battle. I had planned to create a video inventory of my mom's condo and have her narrate the history of the important items. I wanted to do that when I visited with my kids in January, but that was when she collapsed three hours into our visit. I also wanted to tape her while she was going through the old family albums, especially the sepia-toned photos from the early 1900s, and have her document who everyone was. I thought I'd do that when she came home for hospice, but those first few days home were hectic as we set everything up. It's a big regret of mine that we never got to do that. It was one of the rare things we let go, thinking we'd have time.

There are all sorts of technological ways to document a person's history, and while some of the prompts may seem cheesy, you won't regret it when the person is gone. If you can get a loved one to sit down and tell their story, leave a little bit of family history behind, it's priceless. As a bonus, it's easily shared.

That's why I was fine with letting my brother take all the family photos, because he promised to digitize them so we could share them. I didn't need the original albums as long as I'd eventually get to look at them in whatever format I chose.

I had joked most of my adult life that the only inheritance I wanted from my mother was her magic cookie sheets. She had six black-and-white-speckled cookie sheets with no brand markings that she picked up at some point along the way but couldn't remember where. They were the best cookie sheets I have ever encountered. No matter what she made on them, they did not get dirty or worn in any way. Even after she made sugar-coated nuts for holiday gifts and burned a batch here or there, the cookie sheets looked like new. She produced massive amounts of treats on those six pans. My brother did not object.

Other than that, my dad had books and my mom had recipes. They were rich in paper. When I started to pack boxes, I realized that I wanted all of the books and had no place to keep them in Brooklyn. But how could I leave behind my dad's teaching copy of *The Great Gatsby* and a dozen other classics with his handwritten notes and Post-its everywhere? They all still smelled like pipe smoke. He had many signed volumes from authors he knew. My mom was a legendary cook, and her recipes were like a history of modern American cooking. She was always clipping recipes she wanted to try and altering them to perfection.

The boxes started to stack up. I called moving companies and found that the minimum amount we could ship to Brooklyn was a quarter truck, for a ridiculous sum of money. But that meant I didn't have to edit my choices so much. I could take a few pieces of furniture—I wanted my mom's power recliners and her new-ish bedroom TV—and about thirty boxes. We used linens and beach towels as packing material, and I roamed around the house picking what I wanted. I took one meat thermometer. I took a lot of papers, too, because I didn't have time to sort through them.

We had no idea what was important and what was not. I picked up one knickknack from a display shelf that looked biblical, like a tablet of the Ten Commandments, and asked my brother, "Do you remember this? Is it from our trip to Israel?" He shrugged. I rotated it in my hands and noticed a sticker on the bottom from Home Goods. It went into the giveaway pile. My boyfriend became an expert at taking pictures of various items and searching for them in Google Lens to see if they were worth anything. Some things were identifiable, but others were not. My parents had a lot of things they picked up on their travels, such as Native American pottery from when we lived in Albuquerque and Oklahoma, Lladró figurines from their year in Spain, Delft pottery from when we lived in Belgium, but it was all mixed together on shelves with things from discount stores, such as a Maltese falcon replica from Target.

The china cabinet was also a mishmash, with some of my mom's treasures and some from my grandparents' catering business. Much of it was a silver color, and some looked like crystal, but I had no idea what was worth anything and what was not. Same with the jewelry. My brother and I could agree on that front: Neither of us wanted any of it, but we didn't want to throw it away.

The only way to emotionally justify not taking it was to sell it.

There are plenty of options for doing this. You'll want to stick at the local level for ordinary items, but you might want to search online nationwide for specialty items. I asked around for referrals, and a family friend connected us with an estate sale expert who helped him after his mother died. The guy was able to come to the apartment on our short timeline and give us an assessment of what was valuable and what it might be worth. He swung through the apartment and picked through my parents' stuff as though it were a yard sale, making a small pile of what he thought he could sell. He said no to the fancy dishes—my mom had two sets of china, because they kept kosher when they were first married. "Nobody wants those anymore," he said curtly. He suggested we try to sell them ourselves online. He tapped on serving dishes and inspected spoons. He dismissed most of the silver items we had as silver plate, not valuable anymore. A few pieces were actual silver, including a full set of silverware. There were some specialty items of interest, such as a hair comb with a silver cover, a giant engraved platter, a Japanese teapot, some coins, and an antique tea set, that he said he could auction. There was also an ornate Japanese carved chair that used to sit in my grandparent's foyer when I was growing up. We didn't know when they bought it or where it came from, and nobody in the family I called could remember, either. I thought it was hideous, which made me think that it was probably worth some money.

All told, he thought there might be about $1,200 worth of stuff, which he would take on 25 percent consignment. He'd auction it and then send us a check. He gave us a contract and a signed receipt and left with a box of stuff.

I was frazzled and exhausted at that point and didn't think much more about it. It would go on to plague me for months. The guy did as he said and put the stuff up for auction the next month, and I was able to track the bids and what sold. But after that, crickets.

I waited thirty days from the close of the auction and sent an email to ask when we'd receive payment. Nothing. I texted. Every time I made contact, the guy would tell me that the check was in the mail, but I received nothing. A couple of months in, I texted and emailed again, and he sent me to his payment person. She said she had been on leave and would get to it right away. She didn't. I called, texted, and emailed more.

By January, four months after the auction, I ran the scenario by the probate lawyer to see if she could send a stern letter to them, but she thought I'd be better off filing a complaint with the Better Business Bureau. So I warned the proprietor that that was my plan to see if that would shake loose a check, but he didn't respond. Then I filed. It's easy to do, but I had low expectations of it working. You have to fill out a form at BBB.org and give the details of the situation and the remedy you want. I had receipts and a clear solution: The auction guy owed me the money.

I had filed a BBB complaint once before to get a refund for a product that never arrived, and it worked. It helps as a way to get the attention of a legitimate business that cares about its reputation, because the BBB will contact the business owners and ask them what they're going to do. If they can't be shamed or prodded into action, it doesn't do much good.

It worked again for me, because the complaint got the attention of the payment processor, who called to say she sent the payment to my mother's old address months before, despite my having given them my correct address many times, including during the intake process. They had never let me know they sent the check, or I would have been able to check with the building's mail room. She then issued a new check to the right address, and we were done. The moral of this story is to be careful when selling valuables. Take pictures. Establish a clear chain of custody of the items. Make sure to stay in communication, and don't give up if the seller owes you money.

Not everything that falls into the category of "stuff" is tangible these days. While you are emptying closets, you also have to think about what to do with social media accounts, the deceased's phone, whatever is on the hard drives of their computers, and any legacy storage devices they may have. My mom had floppy discs, for example, and we had no device that could read them. Keep them, toss them, get them converted? We boxed them and took them home, but we may never get around to sorting through them. It may be a task I leave for my children, who will likely decide to toss them.

The most important thing to secure is the person's phone. You need it for their contacts, photos, emails, texts, and whatever apps they were using so you can have a sense of accounts you need to close or change the logins for. If you don't know the passcode to open the phone, you could be locked out. Even the FBI has trouble breaking into phones, especially iPhones. There's an easy solution, though, if you catch it early enough—for your parents, older relatives, children, and yourself. You need to go into the settings of the phone and name a legacy contact, which is kind of like naming a beneficiary to a financial account. It does not give the person access to the phone while you're alive, only after you die and with proper documentation. Do it now.

How to Name a Legacy Contact on a Phone

Apple

1. Go to Settings.
2. Tap your name.
3. Tap "Password & Security."
4. Tap "Legacy Contact."
5. Tap "Add Legacy Contact."
6. Authenticate with Face ID, Touch ID, or your device passcode.
7. Choose a contact from your contacts or a member of your iCloud Family Sharing group.
8. Print encrypted access key and store it with your important documents.

Android Phone

1. Open the Settings app.
2. Scroll down and tap "Digital Wellbeing & Parental Controls."
3. Tap "Legacy Contact" and then "Add Legacy Contact."
4. Choose the person you want to designate as your Legacy Contact.
5. Grant them the necessary permissions, such as managing your accounts or accessing your files.
6. Confirm your selection and inform your Legacy Contact about their new responsibility.

Note: Exact directions may vary by phone type and may change over time.

Sources: Apple,[2] Google[3]

Online accounts take some work. Most everything these days has two-factor authorization, which is another reason why the phone is so important. I sat for a long time at my mother's computer with her phone and went through her digital existence. One by one, I changed the email address on the accounts to mine and the password to something new that I kept track of on a list, or I closed the accounts if they were no longer needed. It was tedious and time consuming but needed to be done. For social media, you often have a choice of keeping the account open as is, turning it into a legacy page, or deleting it.

Once my brother and I had removed all the physical items that we wanted from my mom's apartment, we were left with the task of emptying the house for staging. That was my cue to call in help. My mom's aides came and took away carloads of stuff to donate to their churches. Some of the building's staff did a walk-through and took things off our hands. The clothes and kitchen items started to dwindle, but there was still so much stuff. My boyfriend and I started bagging trash and taking down giant loads to the dumpsters in the parking garage. After a day of doing that, we noticed that somebody was going through the bags and putting aside salvageable items. Another tenant was dumping a lot of stuff, too—it was a building full of people at the same stage of life as my mom—and my boyfriend took a liking to a large ceramic planter shaped like a frog. I said, hearing my mother's voice as I said it, "We're trying to get rid of things, not get new things," but he persisted and looked it up on Google Lens. It was a rare item, maybe worth some money, so I allowed him to pack it in one of the boxes, and now it sits on the edge of our kitchen island with an aloe vera plant poking out of it like crazy hair. The Maltese falcon found a new life in a curio cabinet in the lobby of my mom's building, unofficially, as we sneaked it in there late at night as a joke. Then we ran out of time and gave up. We called the real estate agency and told them we did the best we could. They took over the rest, arranging for a charity to come for the large items and then a junk service for the rest.

I applaud anyone who tries to do this on their own. If I had time, I might have been able to finish the job, but I'm not even sure I would have wanted to. Once we sorted out all the good stuff, the rest of it made me too sad. I couldn't even bag up the trash without thinking of my mom and missing her, let alone deal with her clothes. I couldn't bear to part with any scrap of paper that had her handwriting on it. It doesn't have to cost extra money to get help. In our case, the real estate agent was able to pitch in as part of their fee. My cousins would have shown up to help in a minute if I had let them. We had other friends and good citizens nearby who would have helped. Most people in a community have ties to religious organizations or groups that specialize in this sort of thing; they bring food and pitch in. Where we came from in Amish country in Lancaster, they'll even build you a barn. It's hard for a lot of people to accept help, but you just have to, and the last bit of the clean-out after somebody dies is one that people understand is sometimes too hard to do on your own.

DO NOW

Using the conversation prompts on page 258, talk to your loved one about what they want to do with their stuff. Set up a plan to record them taking an inventory of their household, detailing each item, and going through family photo books. Then do it; don't wait for a better day.

Special Handling for Special Stuff

Not all inherited stuff is created equal. Sometimes you have to do a lot more than just throw it away or pack it up. You will often come across an item and wonder, "Now, what the heck am I going to do about this?" Here's some of what you might encounter that will need special handling.

Pets

Even though many more people are planning for their pets' care in case something happens to them, the Humane Society estimated that 10 percent of pets still end up being surrendered to shelters after their owner dies.[1] You don't have to follow the example of the billionaire hotel mogul Leona Helmsley, who left $12 million to her dog, but it's best to figure out something. Making a plan can be as simple as adding a sentence to a will that specifies who you want to take care of your pets or writing a set of instructions, or you can go as far as setting up a trust. No matter what route you take, it's best if you talk to the chosen caregiver first, because the catch is that they don't have to do it.

The lawyer Adam Schneider told me that he's starting to see more pet trusts, which have been formalized since the 1980s. With this kind of trust, you can set aside money for the pet's perpetual care and name a guardian and a trustee. He had one client, an older woman with a dog, who had disinherited all her kids. Schneider worried that if she left everything to the dog, the trust could be challenged in court—as Leona Helmsley's was, and her dog's award ended up being reduced and redistributed to disinherited heirs. In the end, Schneider said, his client didn't leave everything to the dog but gave it to a couple who had an unwritten agreement to take the dog.

How much should you plan to leave for a pet? It can be as little or as much as you can afford. For a Reuters story in 2016, I spoke to Rachel Hirschfeld, who developed one of the first formalized pet trusts. At the time, she said the going rate was $25,000, but it will vary greatly based on the age of the pet and the money you have available.[2] What you can do that won't cost a cent is leave some pertinent information about the pet, such as their favorite toys, medical records, and feeding schedule.

Cars

My mom's accident in 2020 totaled her car, and she bought a new one with the insurance payout, even though she probably shouldn't have been driving at all given her health problems. Considering her age, at that point it might have been smarter for her to lease. I told her all of that at the time she was making a decision, but she and my dad had always bought cars and run them into the ground, and she didn't listen to me. So when she died, my brother and I had a fairly new car on our hands. We had two problems: what to do with it and how to transfer the ownership of it.

Contrary to our decision about the condo, keeping the car seemed easier than selling it and a better financial decision, since we'd likely lose money on a sale. I didn't want the car because it was too big for Brooklyn, but my brother decided to take it. That meant driving it from Florida to Pennsylvania and dealing with the DMV, car loan servicer, and insurance company. A car is considered property, so it passed to us in the trust. But a car can also easily pass through a will. If there is no will or probate process, most states have a way for heirs to inherit a car without having to go through probate. Whatever way you do it, inheriting a car is not as simple as walking off with a bedside lamp and a stack of photo albums. You'll have a lot of paperwork to complete.

The first thing to do, especially if you need to drive anywhere in the short term, is deal with the car insurance by calling the current carrier and your carrier, if they are different, and work out the transfer. You'll most likely need to show the death certificate and some proof of authority to transfer, such as trust documents, will, and letters of administration or an affidavit of some sort. You'll need the same set of documents to take over the car loan, if there is one, or pay off the balance. With the DMV, you can usually register the title in your own locale, if it's different, but this varies by state.

Artworks

You don't want to be the family that gives away the Picasso to the local thrift store, but what about the works of lesser known or even unknown artists? My grandmother's art either is long gone because my mom threw it away or is sitting in an abandoned storage locker in her old condo building. She was only a hobby artist, but I would still like to have those pieces if I could put my hands on them.

When my friend Juliette Posner's stepmother died unexpectedly while her father was in a nursing home, she had to clear out their house, and she found a trove of art there. Her father never gained much acclaim, but he had shows and was part of a circle of artists in Washington, D.C., in his time. She didn't know what to do with the art, but she knew she couldn't throw it away. So she FedExed all of it to herself in New York and then sorted through it. Most of it was stuffed haphazardly into portfolios and in pretty bad shape, smelling of stale cigarette smoke and decay. It was a mix of mediums: oils, pastels, inks, some unfinished. Much of it was portraiture. Nothing seemed salable. "Who wants to buy a picture of somebody else's grandmother?" Juliette asked. "If it had been more oils and landscapes, it might have been easier to sell."

Instead, she thought about what her dad might want, and that was for people to be able to see it. An artist friend suggested having a show, so she mounted one and also created a website showing all the art and detailing as much of the story behind each piece as she could. Her dad was still alive at the time and conveyed his joy about that to her. When he passed, she still had the legacy of the website and the portfolios stuffed in the closet of her apartment.

"If you choose to keep art, it has to be climate controlled; you can't just take it wherever and hope it will be okay," she said. If you can authenticate any pieces, you'll also want to get them appraised, but this can be a tricky process with lesser known artists—and they're more likely than not to have little salable value.

Special Collections

I put out a call on social media to see what people had been left with that they didn't know how to handle, and most of the responses I got back were of collections of items that were too cherished to throw out, too complicated to sell, and too cumbersome to keep. Marisa was advance worrying about a collection of intricate model ships; Melanie had to deal with her mom's collection of figurines; Chelsea inherited a large record collection, plus an old postcard collection and a myriad of other items from a variety of relatives over the years. Another family inherited a large collection of irradiated glass, while still others had coins, precious metals, and stamps.

Some people are willing to part with the things they inherit, and some feel responsible for at least finding them a good home or making some money by selling them. It's all up to your energy level. Kat Tretina, a freelance finance writer, inherited her aunt's jewelry collection of more than eight hundred pieces and had to turn into an expert to figure out what to do with it. She tried to sell one piece that was appraised for $14,500, but the highest offer was only $600, so she decided to keep it—and the rest—for now, even though it has cost her for appraisals and insurance, plus storage to keep it all in a temperature-controlled environment. "It's a big responsibility. I feel like a museum curator," she said. "And it's tricky trying to figure out how to share it with folks while honoring her wishes."

I spoke to another woman who had a similar situation with a collection she had to master, but her items eventually turned out to be worth several million dollars. As World War II was starting, her grandparents smuggled a trove of rare documents out of Europe in false-bottom suitcases. They passed to her father and then her. Her reaction to her inheritance: "What the f%$& do I do with these?" she said.

She decided to try to sell them. First she had to catalog the items, which had been sitting in a bank vault at great expense for fifty years. She went through the boxes and put all the papers into sleeves that filled about forty three-ring binders. Around 2007, she started selling pieces through auction houses. With each sale, she had to declare the full amount as income, because there was no way to establish her basis in the inheritance and it had never been included on any family member's estate tax forms. In the end, parts of the collection remained unsold, and she is still deciding what to do with them. For now, the remains sit in boxes in her apartment, uninsured but at least climate controlled. "My father didn't share my grandparents' passion for these things, and neither did I," she said. "It's a lesson for everyone: The next generation doesn't want your stuff. They want cash. If my grandparents had put those same assets in the stock market, we'd have made much more over the years."

My former colleague Arlene Getz, an editor and writer, had to find a new home for her pilot husband, Robert Schapiro's, elaborate, enormous remote control planes and boats and handmade furniture after he died. She contacted some of his old friends and found an aviation museum to take some of the models, and she gave some away as toys. The rest of the collection and most of the bulky furniture have been in a storage unit in New Jersey for years. Robert also left the draft of a memoir about his flying adventures around the world, which she was determined to publish. That took several years, but finally, in 2021, she was able to find a publisher for *Secrets from the Cockpit: Pilots Behaving Badly and Other Flying Stories,* which became a bestseller in South Africa, where they are originally from.[3] "It's a legacy for my son and my granddaughter," she told me. "It felt good to get it done."

Guns

Depending on where in the United States you live, inheriting a gun is akin to being left either an old ring or a ticking time bomb that could get you arrested if not properly handled.

Guns are technically personal property and pass through a will or a trust the same way as any other item does. The laws in the locality where the gun owner lives prevail. In New York, one of the strictest states, the executor or trustee has fifteen days from the death of a licensed gun owner to turn over the gun to the police or destroy it, and there are rules for who can then inherit the gun; they also have to be licensed and able to receive the gun.

In most other states, the process is easier, and the recipient doesn't have to be licensed in order to receive their inheritance, nor is there any requirement to turn over the guns to anyone. If you inherit a gun or a gun collection, you can keep it or sell it. If you have a lot of guns and they are valuable, you can use a National Firearms gun trust if the firearms in question fall under the National Firearms Act (NFA) and the Gun Control Act of 1968.[4] This will avoid probate and, in some cases, transfer taxes. "We'll specify guns on a personal property list, but rarely have I ever seen the probate court stop a distribution," said estate attorney Kent Endacott, who is based in Nebraska and Iowa. "We deal with tangible personal property and guns in the same way, and then we distribute them to the heirs or sell them at auction."

None of this accounts for the gun you may find in a closet in a relative's house that might have a shady or unknown past and you don't know what to do with it. This is the type of story that you don't hear much about because nobody wants to get into trouble, but once you broach the subject, you find out that many people have a gun story from cleaning out Grandpa's house. If you find a gun and don't want it, and you don't want to get into trouble for dealing with it, the best thing to do is surrender it to your local police department or sheriff's office. "If you don't care about preserving it in the family, I would just give it to the authorities," said Endacott.

Cryptocurrency and Other Digital Currency

If you thought a safe deposit box was hard to get into without the proper credentials, try gaining access to cryptocurrency without the keys. Even crypto held by a custodian will likely not have a beneficiary designation as an investment account would, at least not yet. This is a developing field, so improvements could come, but the companies that currently offer solutions may or may not be around in a few years. People's experience with this will vary by whether the crypto is held by a custodian or in cold storage. Legally, crypto is considered to be property, not a security, so inheritance rules are the same as for jewelry or a couch. To gain access at an online crypto broker, you should be able to present the same kind of documents you would at any other company to make a claim: death certificate, will or trust, letters of administration, and proper identification.

But for directly held coins? The point of self-custodied cryptocurrency is that your investment is secure because you need a digital key in order to control it and you are the only one who has it. The complication is that crypto is like a cashier's check or a cash bearer bond in that whoever has possession of it can claim ownership, which makes it hard to designate a person to take it over in the event of the owner's death. Any person who has the keys can take the crypto whenever they want, which puts the onus on crypto holders to have some sort of secure succession plan in place for their directly held assets, such as having a copy of the keys or PINs available in a protected fashion. Crypto owners are not typically a population that is keen on doing these sorts of things because it opens them up to theft. You wouldn't want to list the keys in a will or even in supplemental documents, for instance. A will would be subject to probate and therefore public. A trust would be more private, but you still wouldn't want to list the access information directly in the documents. You'd have to take the heirs on a sort of treasure hunt that could take place only after you die and hope that they can follow your directions and are technologically adept enough to handle the task. But still, it's a hard sell. When I interviewed a crypto investor about his plan for his self-held crypto holdings, he said he would wait for a solution to present itself. And if that didn't happen in time? He shrugged. A top Reddit thread on this topic concurred with the sentiment: Better to die with it.[5]

Time-shares

A time-share is truly the inheritance that will never die. When you inherit a time-share, you inherit all the fees and conditions that come with it, and it's a nightmare to get out of. This is one case where you'll want a lawyer, for sure. "It's always a mess when those come up," said Endacott.

If you have a relative who has a time-share they might leave to you, it matters what kind of deal it is. Some time-shares are an interest in real estate, which means that they can put it into a revocable trust. Endacott said that this is the best way to deal with it, because then you don't have to do an ancillary probate in another state. If the time-share is a contract, you could inherit as a beneficiary, or you might need probate for shares passed in a will. If you don't want to continue on with the time-share, do the best you can to get the person to dissolve the time-share before passing it on to you.

This could also be a good time to disclaim an inheritance rather than be left with a mess. You'll want to have an attorney help you file a disclaimer or renunciation of interest, but at least that will be less involved than trying to untangle the whole thing. But signing a disclaimer might shift the burden to another unsuspecting relative. The attorney Howard Krooks said that if you disclaim a time-share, it passes pursuant to the next person in line and so forth, until nobody is left in the family line, and then it passes to the laws of intestacy as if there were no will or trust involved. If the estate administrator gets to the end of the line and nobody is left, Krooks presumed, the time-share would revert back to the company or possibly be turned over to the state as unclaimed funds, but it would depend on the terms of the contract, which is why you'd want a lawyer involved from the beginning.

Businesses and Farms

My deceased father made $7.99 in royalties the year my mother died, and in order to claim them to be faithful to his intellectual legacy, I had to look through my parents' old tax returns to track down the business office of the publisher, then file tax paperwork. That's nothing compared to what you have to go through to take over an operating business or farm. That is something the business owner should be thinking about and planning contingencies around from the moment they file for their first business license. The risk of death or incapacity starts at the beginning and never ends. Still, many people avoid doing so, and much of it comes down to the vexing question of whom to leave it to, like a real-life version of *Succession*.

The scenario that Kent Endacott sees most on family farms is that one sibling has stayed on the land and wants to keep farming, while the others have gone to bigger cities and started other careers. The matriarch and patriarch get stuck in the debate between what is fair and what is equitable: Do they leave the farm to one child and other assets to the rest, even if their values are not quite equal, or do they split the farm into equal shares? How does the one who wants to keep the farm come up with enough cash to buy the other siblings out?

"There are some that are really careful with it, and they come up with other liquidity planning for the siblings who aren't farming, like life insurance trusts," Endacott said. "Sometimes they'll split it into equal shares, but the farmer sibling will get the right to buy out the other siblings over time at an applicable rate."

In Endacott's view, a family business in the city that makes widgets is the same as a family farm. "If people slow down and do some planning, it really pays off," he said. They can figure out tax-planning elections, pick successors, and detail buy/sell agreements, which outline how the business can be transferred. Even though it's a complication for the family to figure out what comes next, the tax savings of making a plan would be worth it.

Charitable Legacies

Not every family is going to face the decision of who will take over a charitable foundation, but many want to have a charitable legacy to carry forward, whether it's making cookies for an annual bake sale or continuing a planned donation. Many people also intend to leave money to charity, and sometimes they task their children or other heirs with doing so. If you make a plan for this ahead of time, you can both save on taxes and make sure that your intentions are fulfilled.

When she first started her practice, financial planner Carolyn McClanahan had a client who inherited a great deal of money from a mess of an estate—the probate cost $60,000 in attorney fees alone. Out of that, she and the client created a revocable trust and the family became philanthropists. The matriarch even left money for her children to donate to charity after she died. "For a five-million-dollar estate, the trust administration fees were a little over a thousand dollars (and no estate taxes due), and her kids said, 'This is a miracle.' I said, 'No, it's just about setting it up right.' They've given over a million to charity since she died," McClanahan said.

What's important to keep in mind always is the point that there's no default charitable option. If a person dies without a will, the state will split up their assets among the identifiable heirs. If none is found, their assets go to the state as unclaimed funds. If you want to give to charity, you have to make a provision in a will or trust that delineates a specific bequest, a dollar amount, or a percentage of an account to go to a charity or it won't happen. The same goes for passing along the responsibility for this to your heirs to complete for you.

Things You Don't Know About

When I was looking for unclaimed funds for my parents on the websites for Florida, Pennsylvania, and New Jersey, I found $300 worth of entries for myself. I clicked through a few electronic forms, and a few weeks later, checks arrived. Claiming money due to my deceased parents required much more effort, including notarizing documents and sending off the death certificate and letters of administration. And that was for a few hundred dollars.

The biggest unknown I dealt with when closing the estate was when we were trying to finalize the sale of my mother's condo. The title agent called me and said that there was an open home equity line of credit on the apartment that we'd need to settle before we could close. What home equity line of credit? I had no clue. She had no clue. My mother had never mentioned it, and there were no account statements in her files. I pulled apart the boxes I had moved back from Florida, but still nothing. I searched her email, looking for keywords such as *home equity* and *refinance* and finally found something that might pertain that had an account number attached, and the mystery started to unravel.

It turned out that when my father first got sick, my mom was worried that she would not be able to put her hands on the funds she would need for his care because they were locked up in his annuity and he was not able to authorize withdrawals at that point. So she took out a home equity line of credit on the condo in case she needed it. But then she was able to get what she needed with a power of attorney document, so she never took any money out of the line of credit and the balance was zero. She had probably long forgotten about it.

The account number I found was no good, though, because the bank had changed ownership and a new number was assigned. I was able to call the new entity and use my trust documents to settle it. It cost $10 to close the empty account, which we were able to pay out of closing costs, and two full days of my life tracking down documents.

Instead of problems, some people find treasure. This is why you can't just shred documents in bulk or let leads go cold. When you are the administrator of an estate, you're a detective, and you have to follow the clues where they lead.

Long into taking care of her mother, Cameron Huddleston came upon a notice that an account with $50,000 was about to be turned over to the state as unclaimed funds. At that point, her mother had transitioned from living with her to living in an assisted living facility and Huddleston was completely in charge of her finances and had all the mail delivered to her. She thought that all of her mother's accounts had been transferred to one brokerage, but she had missed that one account, which her mother had inherited from another family member long before. "I had not seen any statements about this account," Huddleston said. "I didn't know it existed."

She called the financial institution and tried to get it transferred under her power of attorney, but the people there said that wasn't good enough. That was when she encountered the dreaded need for a medallion stamp to verify her identity and her authority to act on behalf of her mother. The investment firm holding the account wouldn't do it. Her mom's bank wouldn't touch it because it was not its account. Her own bank wouldn't do it. She turned to her uncle, who worked at a brokerage firm, and he found somebody who had medallion authority. "I had to drive to Nashville to get that document stamped, and then I sent it to the investment firm. When I cashed it out, I put the money in a savings account and it covered a year of caregiving costs. I said, 'I've had enough of jumping through hoops. This money will be much more accessible for my mom's needs.'"

When CPA Jeanne Wiener went on her scavenger hunt after her father's death, she was looking for booby traps such as unpaid debts but found the opposite. Before her father died, he told her that he had a deferred compensation plan that would leave his wife a lump sum when he died that he ballparked at under $100,000. When Wiener went looking for the paperwork after he died, she realized that it was a monthly payout for ten years that was for much more than he thought. What if she had not gone looking for it? Her job as a trustee led her to develop a binder for her clients and her extended family. "You need to leave an information legacy," she said.

A few years later, when a relative of her husband's was in the hospital and Wiener was listening to her husband and his siblings trying to sort out end-of-life issues, they were asking a lot of questions and none of them knew the answers. What was up with their finances? Did they have a prepaid funeral? "I raised my hand. I had that information, because my mother-in-law had filled out the binder," she said.

What happens when you don't find these accounts? The money is eventually turned over to the state's escheatment fund, and you have a designated time period during which to claim it, which can range from five years, as in Ohio, to indefinite, as in Florida. Each state has its own website, and you can also check nationally at the National Association of Unclaimed Property Administrators (https://unclaimed.org). You have to periodically look in case new entries appear, and then you have to follow the instructions to claim any funds, which may involve paperwork. If you don't do this, the funds will be turned over to the state when the statute of limitations runs out or will lie dormant if there isn't one.

DO NOW

Have anything that needs to be appraised done as soon as possible and insured, if need be. Using the template on page 258, make a household inventory, list all specialty items that need to be dealt with, and determine who will be responsible for seeing each of them through.

The Final Tax Return

When I was growing up, we were audited three times. Three times. While my father was probably responsible for me wanting to become a writer, I think my mom's endless battle with the IRS was why I ended up going into financial journalism. She fought a good fight with it. She had no formal financial training, but she was fueled by righteous indignation. Every year at tax time, she took over the dining room table and pulled out shoeboxes filled with receipts. She sorted and crunched numbers and then would eventually pack up the whole shebang and take it off to Mr. Mester, her certified public accountant. The reason the government picked on my mom was because of all the sabbaticals my father took from his teaching job. Every few years, my parents would pack us up and we'd go somewhere on a grant: New Mexico, Oklahoma, California, Belgium, Spain, New York. My father's income would dip, and my mom would write off his trip expenses against whatever stipend he got. The IRS saw that as a red flag and always wanted more explanation, which then turned into an audit.

My mom was no tax cheat. Her biggest financial sin was overleveraging herself. She was always robbing Peter to pay Paul, as the saying goes. Back in the day, that might even have gone as far as innocuous check kiting, which is when you write a check you know you can't cover, and float it with another check, and keep doing that until you eventually get the money in the bank to cover the funds (or not, if you're being criminal about it). In the 1970s, when interstate check settlement was slow, that was the best she could do to keep us afloat. When we went to New Mexico in 1978, my father had his sabbatical pay deposited in a local bank in Lancaster, and his grant pay was deposited in Albuquerque. My mom would have to string along a chain of checks in between to pay for groceries and our other bills. She kept track of everything down to the penny, though. The year we went to Belgium, she even kept a notebook with the daily exchange rate and what we spent that day. We went everywhere that year, all over Europe, plus Russia, Greece, and Israel. The next year when she was audited, my mom and Mr. Mester went to the meeting with the IRS and she pulled out her little notebook and had an answer for every question they asked. The government ended up owing her money.

I couldn't let her down on the tax front, but taking care of filing her returns after she died was like playing in the Super Bowl of estate administration. It brought together all that I had learned up to that point, from knowing her income to how to access her mortgage statement.

Tax time for me came after a lull in the paperwork, and I dreaded jumping back into the mess. In January, statements started to arrive from Social Security, the long-term care insurance company, and all sorts of other places. I went back into organizing mode, taking over my own dining room table for all the stacks of paper. I started out not even sure I had to file for my mom, and then I learned that I would have to file at least two returns for her and possibly three. That year, I was responsible for three other returns as well: one for me and one for each of my working teen children. Keeping track of the information I needed for five or six returns was, as I had learned to say, "a lot."

Whenever I thought about how hard it was for me, I kept turning to a TikTok video that became popular around that time by the Wollners, two young adult sisters whose mom had died of cancer the year before. In "Confessions to Our Dead Mom," number one was "We didn't know we had to file your taxes."[1]

"Nope," chimed in the other, giggling, in what became their viral signature.

How could they be expected to know all of that complicated stuff? The IRS instruction manual on how to file returns for deceased individuals is fifty-one pages long, and it doesn't even cover everything you need to know in a practical sense.[2] It seems ludicrous that we have a system in this country that puts the burden of this on families, who may or may not be cut out for complicated financial tasks. It solidified my resolve to try to help people going through this, at least once I got a handle on my own situation.[3]

What the Wollner sisters didn't realize at first is that the government generally expects to receive a tax return from every taxpayer every year, even if a person died at some point during the year. You have to file a regular Form 1040 for the part of the year that they were alive, and then you have to figure out if you need to file an estate return for the part of the year they were dead, plus possibly a trust return for that part of the year and even for subsequent years if a trust remains open and has income to report.

Return number one for my mom was for six months of 2023. Technically, not every deceased person has to file a Form 1040 for the portion of the year they were living, and the question of whether or not to file can be extremely vexing to the person who has to do this task. As a financial professional, Dana Chitwood thought she had all of her parents' finances handled so well until she came to their final tax return. Her parents were the ones who died on the same day at the age of 92—not in an accident, but because they were together all their lives and went out together, too. They weren't going to need trust or estate returns, because they no longer owned any real estate before they died, and she had simplified their assets to be all beneficiary accounts. They were alive for only thirty-nine days of the tax-filing year so had received hardly any income from Social Security or investments.

Chitwood figured she could handle the job herself instead of paying an accountant $400. Her stumbling block stemmed from the fact that her parents died in the same tax year. All of the tax-filing rules seem to pertain to only one spouse dying at a time. Chitwood couldn't figure out whether she was supposed to file a last Form 1040 for them together as a deceased married couple or separately and how she should do that in a practical sense: paper file by mail or submit an electronic return. She had been knocking her head against the tax-filing issue for hours, her sofa covered in papers, and was near tears when I spoke to her. "I love doing taxes, but this is awful," she said. "I have a master's in financial counseling, and I've taken a graduate-level course in income tax. This is intimidating to me. I should have been able to get an easy answer about whether I needed to file."

Her CPA said that yes, she should file, but when she searched online, the articles she read seemed to indicate no. She was confused by the way the do-it-yourself tax software dealt with the issue. She called the IRS and was disconnected multiple times.

When I wrote a story about this for MarketWatch, I spoke to Owen Arnoff, a specially certified accountant with the IRS called an enrolled agent. He said that the question of whether or not to file comes down to income. In the case of a married couple where both spouses died on the same day, you'd add up their income and divide by two to see if either was over the filing threshold—which in 2023 would have been $15,350 for a person over age 65.

Many people file a final Form 1040 even if the deceased person was under that limit, the biggest incentive being that they might get a refund, especially if the deceased had high medical expenses. Some like to file to close the loop on the paperwork, writing FINAL on the top of the return. To do this, Chitwood could file for them together as a married couple, write FINAL DECEASED and their date of death on the top of the paper return, and mail it in.

My mom had accumulated enough income in her final six months that I definitely needed to file for her, and also because I needed to file the paperwork to generate wage statements for the caregivers (which my mom seemed to have not been doing properly). The IRS sets a dollar limit every year over which you need to give the caregiver a W-2 wage statement and pay the proper employer Medicare and Social Security taxes; it was $2,600 the year my mother died. If you think you're going to do this wrong, ask your tax accountant or hire a household payroll service to help you. This can take some cleanup if you step into a situation where this hasn't been handled properly, which is what I had to do.

I also faced the question of how to file and what forms to file with the return. In most cases, you end up having to paper file the return, which inevitably creates delays. This is not because of the Form 1040 itself but because of the ancillary forms that must be submitted with it. The key ones for families are Form 56, Notice Concerning Fiduciary Relationship, which you need to establish authority to file; and Form 1310, Statement of Person Claiming Refund Due a Deceased Taxpayer.

If there's ever a time to hire a tax professional, this is it. You're going to have questions, and the answers you will find online can be both confusing and contradictory. It's also likely that something will get gummed up along the way, as it did for me and Dana Chitwood, and you'll need somebody who can call the IRS in a professional capacity and get answers for you. You may also get letters in the mail from the IRS after the fact; these are always scary to receive, and anytime it happens, you want a proper representative to help you communicate with the agency.

In my case, I received numerous letters from the IRS about my mom's lost 2022 tax refund and then also for her 2023 return. The letters would come on successive days and look identical except for a case number in the signature line. I had to file the Form 1310 again, for both cases, with what the IRS calls a "wet" signature, meaning that you can tell it's by a pen and not a photocopy, and mail it back. Then, every sixty days or so, I received another batch of correspondence saying that the agency needed another sixty days before they could give me more information, or the refund itself.

What to Look for in a Tax Professional

Anyone can file your taxes; a person doesn't need any special certifications or licenses to claim that they are a tax preparer. But that does not mean you should hire just anyone, especially to file a complicated return. You want to look for somebody with an accredited certification. Your options are:

- Enrolled agent (EA): Has a special certification from the Internal Revenue Service gained either by passing a test or through work experience as a former IRS employee. This is the highest credential that the IRS awards. There are ethical standards, and the EA must complete seventy-two hours of continuing education every three years.
- Certified Public Accountant (CPA): Has earned a professional certification from their state and by passing a test from the American Institute of Certified Public Accountants (AICPA) and the National Association of State Boards of Accountancy (NASBA), completing work, fulfilling education requirements, and completing continuing education courses, which varies by state.

One day, out of the blue, about fourteen months after I had filed her 2022 taxes, the lost refund showed up, with interest. That meant I could close out probate and was nearly done with the paperwork.

When it came to the estate and trust returns, I had an easier time, but it was still an education in tax forms. This is not about paying estate tax per se, unless you're dealing with an estate worth more than the current estate tax exemption. For all those who aren't dealing with tens of millions of dollars, trust and estate returns are for paying tax on the interest or income earned by the estate or trust assets in the tax year, and the threshold for filing is generally $600 (or $100 for a complex trust). If the person who died had a simple revocable living trust with no ongoing provisions to hold money, you might deal with this for only one year as trustee and then distribute the funds and close out the trust.

Because my mom had a trust, very little cash passed through her estate account, and it didn't earn enough interest to merit filing a return. I could file anyway, because if it was going to be the last estate return needed, we could have marked it closed and final. The advantage of doing this is that it shortens the window that the IRS has to audit the estate from three years to eighteen months. In my mom's case, we had to leave the estate open through the end of 2023 because of her stalled 2022 tax refund. It was a catch-22 that my literary-minded father would probably not have found amusing.

Since the trust account held the proceeds of the condo sale and savings account rates were high at the time, we did make more than $600 in interest in the trust account. My longtime tax preparer, Susan Lee, was slightly displeased with this on my behalf. Her rationale was mostly about paperwork efficiency. If I had understood beforehand about the tax implications of growth, I could have opened the trust account at a bank that offered barely any interest and used it as a conduit account to hold the money until my brother and I transferred it to ourselves. No muss, no fuss. We would have stayed under the $600 limit and avoided having to file a tax return and pay the fee for the accountant to prepare it. But of course I didn't ask Susan Lee about that until after the fact, at tax time, when the interest was already accrued and it was too late for us to change things for the tax year in question.

I might have done things the same way anyway. I picked the bank for the trust account out of convenience because it was a national online financial institution and my brother and I could both easily access the account. I also couldn't fathom having money in the bank that wasn't earning peak interest, as I constantly counseled readers to move from big banks offering less than 1 percent interest to high-yield savings accounts offering 5 percent or more. Once I understood the complicated math and saw that we weren't gaining much considering the fees on the other end, I changed it so we wouldn't have to file again for interest earned in the following year. There's no sense paying $700 in tax preparation fees to file for $600 worth of interest earned.

Another advantage to not having to file again was that we wouldn't need to file a Schedule K-1. Most people have never seen a Schedule K-1 before they get involved in a trust situation, unless they're part of a partnership, such as a lawyer or business owner. You need a bit of education to manage it, but filing turned out not as scary as it sounded. For the purpose of a simple trust, a Schedule K-1 is akin to a Form 1099 from a brokerage that lists your taxable gain for the year or a Form W-2 wage statement that documents your work income for the year. If you receive a Schedule K-1 from a trust and it shows income assigned to you, you must file it with your own tax return. It's like a table of contents for what has to go onto your tax return, my accountant explained. A trust or estate can't receive a refund, but you can write off certain expenses. There are plenty of receipts to produce in a year of death, including lawyer fees, funeral costs, even the cost of a headstone. Our trust income ended up zeroing out, and we didn't owe any tax, but we still had to generate and file those Schedule K-1s.

When I talked about that with Susan Lee, who is a CFP® professional along with being an enrolled agent, she made me see that it's okay to not always make the optimal decision or do everything the right way on the first try. "First of all you have to breathe and understand doing this will bring up a lot of feelings," she said. "It causes people to go through all sorts of circles, but things happen. Don't get yourself in a tizzy."

I still think back to the Wollner sisters for this, too. They eventually learned what they needed to do to handle things after their mom died. They didn't need to get things together all at once and overwhelm themselves. The IRS or other government and financial entities might become irked if you don't do things in the expected timeline, but as long as you get them done eventually, it'll all work out.

DO NOW

Connect with your loved one's tax preparer, if there is one, and your own, if you have one. If you don't, use the resources on page 261 to find one in your area. Then start as early as you can to file the necessary paperwork to be a personal representative.

32

Legacy

While going through my mom's papers, I found a notebook in which she kept her budgets over the years, with detailed ones starting in September 1974, when I was about to turn three. Money was tight then, and she kept track of everything she spent, down to $11.06 for dairy delivery, $25 for my nursery school tuition, and $23 for the dentist, for a total monthly budget of $714. There was no line item for savings.

In later years, she still kept receipts for everything she bought, but her ledgers started to tally up retirement accounts instead of expenses, and she started to project out into the future. My mom and dad's income slowly crawled upward, thanks to side hustles and second jobs, and they managed to have a pretty good life in retirement. Of course, their idea of luxury was having the time to read, maybe eat out a few times a month, and stream a movie anytime they wished. The savings were so they would have enough to take care of themselves, which they would have had.

The only reason I was left with any of their money was that they died relatively young—both at age 76, five years apart. At first, the way I experienced it was that every dollar I received represented a day that they didn't live. It's a hard way to look at it, but grief does weird things to your brain. I talked it out with Madeleine Smithberg—another woman I realized I was looking to for wisdom because my mother wasn't there to provide it—because she was on the other end of the spectrum as her mother lived a long life and ran her savings down to zero. "Other parents pass, and you get a little chunk of change," she said, shrugging. "It didn't bother me, I was just happy that my father put plans in place to have my mom get the care she needed."

Smithberg didn't look at caring for her mother as a burden, even financially, but after the fact, she did see that she was very caught up in the moment while it was happening. "Once she passed, the last twelve years evaporated," she said. "I remembered her as she was before. My mom was a giant brain that a body carried around. She had two PhDs and worked to make the world a better place."

Alex Murguia, whose parents ran through their money many years before and relied on him and Medicaid, had similarly sanguine feelings about the prospect of not receiving any inheritance and in fact of having to help with his own money to pay for their care as they age. "Their investments were in our education," he said. "What happens is there's an acceptance stage in it. I do what I can. You appreciate whatever time you have. I'm not ripping my hair out about how to pay for it."

Because of the economics of retirement savings and the high cost of care, most people will not end up with an inheritance of any significance, despite the great wealth transfer going on from the baby boom generation. But even those who don't receive much cash may still get something of value, such as jewelry or other salable items or perhaps a house. No matter what you inherit, you will have to become a steward for that money. You can use it for good, or you can become a jerk. When the estate attorney Jenny Rozelle posted some of her best estate fight stories on social media, it turned into a running viral conversation seen by nearly 5 million people and commented on by hundreds. The stories people told were all over the map but were mostly about people who turned sour over money. One person said he knew people who fought over the inheritance of a couch and another who told a story about a son who tried to cheat his siblings out of a $600,000 estate by having his mom change her will right before she died. There were lots of stories about stepparents inheriting and cutting out the children from the first marriage. More than one person said something along the lines of "I'd rather have my parents back than the money."

"In my world, estate fights and disagreements are caused by resentment that has built up over time or about something that happened years or decades ago that was far bigger, far greater, far worse, and now is the time they're going to make things even," Rozelle said.

Who Gets an Inheritance

The Federal Reserve's Survey of Consumer Finances breaks inheritances down by income level to give a better picture of what most people receive, because the national average of a $46,000 inheritance is so skewed by those inheriting on the high end. More than 50 percent receive less than $10,000—and that includes many people who receive nothing. The next 40 percent receive close to the national average of $46,000. Even the top 10 percent of inheritors are skewed: 9 percent receive about $175,000, and the top 1 percent receive an average of $719,000, which includes those who inherit millions.

Sources: Federal Reserve Board,[1] SmartAsset[2]

My family didn't have any fights, so my biggest challenge was in my own head. I couldn't make the mental shift when the funds I was managing for my mother went from being her money to being my money. All during my mom's illness, I was determined to be as good at handling her affairs as she would have been and maybe even better on some fronts. I wanted to make sure she was well taken care of. I spent money when we needed to and conserved it when we could. I took it all very seriously.

And then when she was gone, half the money that was left was transferred into my account, and I couldn't stop thinking of it as hers. That then broadened out to being hers and my dad's, mostly because of the structural way in which I had to inherit the money.

Nothing in this process is easy, neither emotionally nor logistically. Inheriting money after somebody dies is no different. My brother and I were named as co-beneficiaries on my mom's financial accounts, and I thought it would take one form to get that money transferred. It was much more complicated than that.

I heard stories like this from many other people when I talked to them about transferring funds, even within the same financial company. One man became very frustrated when describing how he had to fight with a brokerage to inherit money from IRAs after his parents both died, even though he was clearly named their beneficiary. The company kept losing his paperwork. He went up the hierarchy to the head of the IRA inheritance division, but after the manager listened to him, she pushed his case back onto her staff, and they still couldn't get it straight. It took weeks to get settled.

My experience took even longer because I was trying to transfer my mom's three annuity contracts into an inherited IRA and it had to be done manually because of the change of account types. I filled out a form supplied by the annuity company that verified me as a beneficiary and gave it the account information for the transfer. It processed the request and set aside the year-of-death required minimum distribution and the taxes on it, but then it got all jammed up in transit to my brokerage firm.

After a couple of weeks, the two smaller accounts made it over and could be merged into one inherited IRA, but the third, which was the bulk of the money, seemed to be lost forever and showed as red on the brokerage's tracker with no other explanation. I worked my way through the phone tree and called so many times that I got to know the people on the other end. "Ryan, it's me again," I'd say in a message. "I'm still trying to get my mom's money ported over." We eventually figured out that the problem was that what I'd thought of as my mother's money was actually technically my father's money. Even though he was long dead and my mom had inherited his money, he was still considered the originator of the account, and that mattered somehow to the computer systems at my brokerage firm that had to figure out the tax implications of the account passing to me. Once I set it up to come over as his money, it made it through after another two weeks.

Because they were inherited accounts, they had to stay separate from my own retirement accounts, so every time I looked at my balance—which was way more than I professionally recommend for other people—I saw the account nicknames, "Mom's IRA" and "Dad's IRA," and still saw it as their money. The reason such accounts need to be kept separate from your own funds is that inherited IRAs have special rules and the brokerage will keep them walled off from each other to keep track.

If you inherit a spouse's IRA or any other kind of tax-deferred retirement account such as a 401(k), 403(b), or 457, you can bring it into your own account and it will count as your money and follow your schedule for taking required minimum distributions (RMDs). My mother obviously didn't do that; she kept the account she inherited from my father as a separate account. There are reasons to do this for tax or accounting purposes, but my mom most likely did so by mistake.

If you inherit a tax-deferred retirement account as a nonspouse, in most circumstances you have ten years to empty the account, and you now have to take at least required minimum distributions out every year (although the rules keep shifting, so ask before you take money out). You calculate the required distribution amount based on a formula that the IRS supplies, and it's best to get help to do that, at least from the online calculator of the account custodian. If you make a mistake and take too little or none at all, you'll be subject to penalties and fees of 25 percent, or 10 percent if you remedy the situation quickly. It's also important to note that minor children can't directly inherit an IRA; they need an adult trustee to be named as the recipient until they reach their majority.

When you inherit, it's your choice how to go about transferring everything out of the inherited IRA account into a taxable account such as a brokerage account, money market account, or bank account over the course of ten years, but a key thing to figure into your decision is that whatever you take out of the account as a distribution will add to your taxable income for the year. Some people take only the minimum for as long as possible so that the principal has as much time to grow tax deferred as possible. But Ed Slott, one of the nation's top IRA strategists, implores people to work out some sort of even withdrawal schedule over the ten years that will smooth out their tax burden.[3] The less you take in the beginning, the more you will have to take later, and his reasoning is that you will end up paying the same or more in taxes if you wait.

The tax burden pertains only to inherited accounts from traditional IRAs. If you inherit a Roth IRA as a nonspouse, you also have to transfer everything out by the end of ten years, but you don't have to pay any taxes on the withdrawals. The whole idea of a Roth account is that the owner pays the income tax up front and deposits only the after-tax money, which can then grow tax free. If you inherit an account such as this, it can grow tax deferred for ten years, and then you can transfer it to a brokerage account, where any further growth will be taxed.

If you inherit a taxable brokerage account, bank account, or any other type of cash-based financial account, the inheritance is a straight-up cash transaction. When you are named as a beneficiary, you fill out some paperwork, send off the death certificate, and then the financial institution will either cut you a check or ask for direct deposit instructions. With investment holdings such as stocks and bonds, you can ask for them to be moved into your account in kind, which means that they will be moved over as is and you don't have to buy or sell anything. You can also sometimes do this with an inherited IRA, depending on the investment and account types—but not always. In many cases, you might not want to keep the same investments as the person you're inheriting from. I, for sure, did not want to stay invested in the same kind of annuities that my parents owned, which would not have been right at all for me at my age. Some people inherit accounts that are full of company stock from the place where their loved one worked, and they have no association with that place at all, so they want to sell. If you're dealing with even a twenty-year age difference, the portfolio of the deceased might be way too conservative for the person inheriting.

Whatever money you inherit, moving the money from their account to your account is only step one. Too many people forget that or don't understand it, even when it's their own account.[4] The major brokerage houses have found that a large percentage of people do not invest the funds in IRAs because they think they operate like their workplace 401(k) plans, which often now have default investments for regular contributions. In individual retirement accounts and other accounts under your control, however, the money will sit in cash unless you direct it into investments yourself. Given that interest rates on savings deposits usually fall below the rate of inflation, you will lose ground over time if you don't do something—even just buy Treasury bills or CDs.

When you inherit money, you want to have a plan for it. That can be hard to think about, especially if you don't think of the money as yours. It doesn't matter if the amount you are dealing with is $500 or $500,000, you need to think about the best way to go forward with it. You don't want to end up as an example in one of Jenny Rozelle's social media threads or as a cautionary tale in one of my personal finance stories.

All the same rules apply to the money when it's yours that did when it belonged to your loved one. The most important thing to consider is the sequence of returns risk. If you spend a lot right off the bat, the amount you have left will not grow as fast. Before you go on an expensive trip or buy a house, run the same kind of numbers you ran when you were trying to figure out how long the money of your loved one would last. Then you can figure out how much you can reasonably spend while the rest grows. At that point, you can determine what kind of growth rate you will need to sustain the level of spending you want and pick investments that will get you there.

If you prefer to be conservative and earn 3 or 4 percent interest, you might think about safer investments such as Treasury bills, CDs, or even a high-yield savings account, depending on the best rate available when you are investing and your timeline. If you're seeking longer-term growth at a higher rate, you might want to consider index funds, which have low fees and offer you diversity in the stock market. Unless you are an experienced investor, you will probably want to stay away from individual stocks or more complex investments, such as cryptocurrency, stock options, or real estate partnerships.

If you want help with the investments, it's best to look for an adviser who is a fiduciary, which means they will look out for your best interest and not make decisions based on what they will get in commissions. That may mean breaking up whatever financial relationship your loved one had going. Don't worry about causing hurt feelings in this circumstance and do what's best for you. If you're not feeling the right connection, it's the same as changing estate lawyers or doctors; you have to cut the cord and make a new arrangement.

As a CFP® professional, obviously I favor looking for somebody with that kind of credential or a comparable one, such as a Chartered Financial Analyst (CFA), because with these professionals, you will get holistic planning and not just investment advice. But it's also important to consider fees, and for that, my best advice is to engage a fee-only financial planner, which you can find through an internet search. You can set up a onetime project with them to help you get started and manage everything yourself going forward.

The route I took with my inherited money was like that, and I settled on a mix of index funds and CDs, because I don't like to choose individual stocks. Most of the money was earmarked for my kids' college educations, as my parents would have wanted it to be, so I didn't have a long time horizon before it would be needed. Beyond that, I'm still not sure what other kind of legacy the money will yield. I am still thinking about what charitable contribution would be meaningful and how I want to handle the rest of my financial life.

The money my parents left me was dwarfed by the emotional legacy they gave me, which I think is pretty common. It was mostly for the good, although I did learn "teacher voice" from my mother, which my kids say is scary, and I can curse like a sailor thanks to my father.

Someday, maybe when the ten years is up and all their money has filtered into my own accounts and is commingled, I'll think of their money as my money, but I can't quite yet. I think that what's more likely to happen is that for the rest of my life, anything nice or good that I decide to spend money on will come from "Bubbe money." If I buy myself a pair of shoes or help my kids or start a scholarship fund, it'll be a gift from my mother. All she ever wanted was for her resources to be used for good purposes and to make us happy. I think that is ultimately what my mom would have wanted me to do with her money.

> **DO NOW**
>
> Think about all you've learned about estate planning and administration and feel at peace that you've got this all under control. Make plans, execute them, and spend the rest of your time enjoying your loved ones.

Acknowledgments

My father would say that it's a cliché to start an acknowledgments section by thanking your parents, but this book is about them, so it's what I have to do. I could not have written a decent sentence in my life if it hadn't been for both of them—the good-cop and bad-cop editors of my youth. I also would not have been able to do any of this—the writing or the caregiving—without my brother, who was there every step of the way but is much more private than I am, so he figures into this story as little as possible on purpose.

My mom's aides are also very private, but they are my heroes, and I hope they know how much my mom appreciated them, even if she ran out of time to tell them herself. We all need to put more value on the impossible, essential work that caregivers do, whether they are family members or paid helpers. God bless them.

While I was helping to take care of my mom and then writing, Brian, Eli, and Abigail took care of me, and they did a very good job. Their love and patience sustained me, such as Brian tackling a sinkful of dishes while I wrote this very paragraph. I was also buoyed by a great support network of family and friends. They're too many to name and it's too easy to leave an essential person out, so I won't try to name everyone. You know who you are and that I love you.

Thank you to my agent, Ann Leslie Tuttle, and the team at Crown Currency, especially Leah Trouwborst and Madhulika Sikka, for believing in this project and shepherding it through all its phases.

I owe a great debt to my early readers, who helped me shape the book: Nan, Meg, Jody, David, Joyce, Brian, Eli, Gayle, John, Stacie, Jennifer, Juliette, Amanda, Rita, and Gwen. My Reuters and MarketWatch editors, Lauren Young and Angela Moore, live in my head and I hear them talking to me while I write. But they also gave me essential feedback in real life, so do not worry that I am delusional. The incomparable Jody Prusan lent me her voice and her acting expertise for the audiobook, and our mothers would be so proud.

The Highlights Foundation provided me a quiet refuge at a literal cabin in the woods when I needed to pound out the last pages.

Finally, I want to thank everyone who took the time to talk to me either for this book specifically or for any of the other caregiving stories that I've worked on over the years that fed my knowledge. It's not an easy topic to talk about, but so many people were open and honest with me. Our collective purpose was to help other people get through this, and I hope we did.

Resource Guide

Prepare these worksheets and documents for each loved one and keep them in a place the financial caregiver can access. That can be a binder, a physical folder, a storage box, a "Death" folder on a computer hard drive, or a secure online storage option—anywhere but a safe deposit box.

This guide is meant to be a starting place, but will not encompass everything you might need, especially if you encounter special circumstances. Also note that links often change, companies go out of business, and government departments can be dissolved.

Medical Emergency Necessities

Map of who matters to you,
whether they are family members or not:

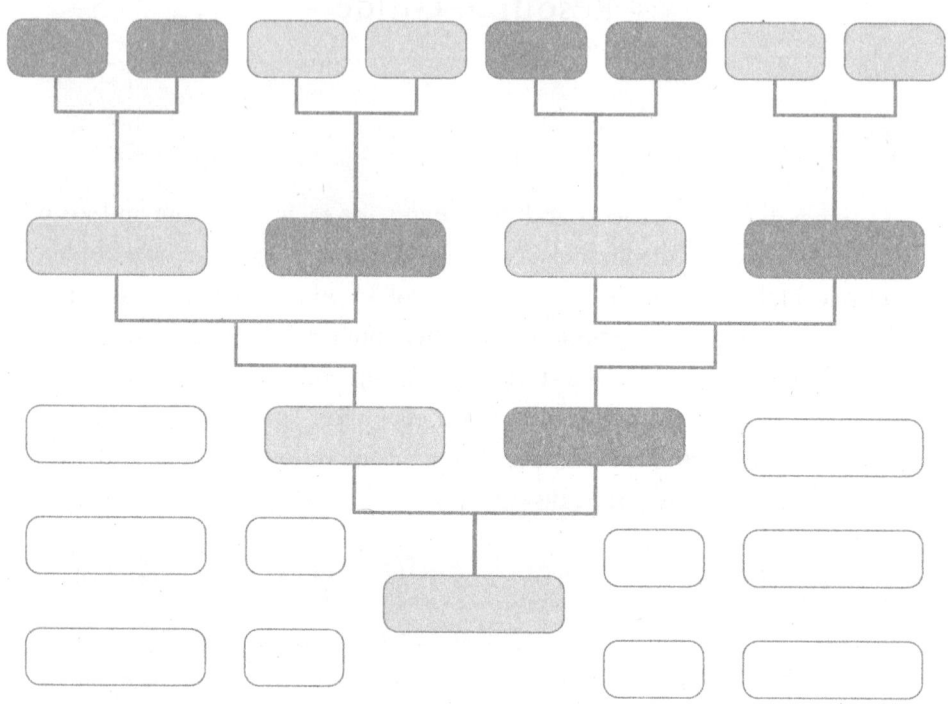

Emergency call list:

Name _____

Number _____ Relationship _____

Name _____

Number _____ Relationship _____

Neighbor name _____

Number _____

Religious leader name _____

Number _____

Primary care doctor name _____

Number _____

Closest hospital:

Name _____

Address _____

Number _____

Preferred hospital, if different:

Name _____

Address _____

Number _____

Emergency plan instruction example:

If I have a medical emergency, please take me to the nearest hospital.

If it is not urgent, please take me to my preferred hospital.

Copies of documents to attach:

- ❑ Copy of driver's license (both sides)
- ❑ Copy of insurance card (both sides)
- ❑ Healthcare proxy (signed and notarized)
- ❑ Living will (signed and notarized)

- ❏ HIPAA authorization (signed and notarized)
- ❏ Copy of any official Do Not Resuscitate (DNR) order signed by a doctor; this should be easily accessible in an emergency, such as on the fridge with a magnet
- ❏ Last will and testament
- ❏ Any applicable trust documents

Emergency Medical Information Cheat Sheet

Name _____

Date of birth _____

Address _____

Home phone _____

Cell _____

Emergency contact _____

Caregiver _____

Primary care doctor name _____

Insurance _____

Medications:

Name of Medication	Dosage/Frequency	Condition

Name of Medication	Dosage/Frequency	Condition

Surgeries/prior hospitalizations by date:

Major illnesses:

Important family history:

_____

_____

_____

_____

_____

_____

Vaccinations:

_____

_____

_____

_____

_____

List of all relevant doctors with phone and address:

_____

_____

_____

_____

_____

_____

Family Meeting Agenda to Discuss a Care Plan

List of attendees (suggested: immediate family,
person being cared for, mediator):

Name _____

Relationship _____ Location _____

Availability _____

Name _____

Relationship _____ Location _____

Availability _____

Name _____

Relationship _____ Location _____

Availability _____

People to consult (suggested: paid caregivers,
primary care doctor, financial planner, tax preparer):

Name _____

Relationship _____ Location _____

Availability _____

Name _____

Relationship _____ Location _____

Availability _____

Meeting scribe (select attendee) name _____

Date of meeting _____

Agenda items:

1. _____

_____

_____

2. _____

_____

_____

3. _____

_____

_____

4. _____

_____

_____

5. _____

_____

_____

Suggested topics:

Where can the person best be cared for?

_____

_____

_____

_____

_____

_____

_____

What care do they need?

_____

_____

_____

_____

_____

_____

Who can do the care?

_____

_____

_____

_____

_____

_____

_____

What will it cost?

_____

_____

_____

_____

_____

_____

What would trigger a different level of care?

_____

_____

_____

_____

_____

_____

What is the decision-making process going forward?

_____

_____

_____

_____

_____

_____

_____

Care schedule:

Create a spreadsheet with the days of the week and the hours you need coverage. Fill in the caregiver and the hours, and color code as needed. You may need to expand this chart if your caregivers have variable hours.

Day of Week	Date	Daytime Shift (or by Hour)	Overnight Shift (or by Hour)
Monday		Caregiver 1	Caregiver 2
Tuesday			
Wednesday			
Thursday			
Friday			
Saturday		Caregiver 3	Caregiver 4
Sunday			

To-do list with tasks assigned and due dates:

- ❑ Laundry
- ❑ Grocery shopping
- ❑ Doctors' appointments
- ❑ Paying bills
- ❑ Bathing
- ❑ Sorting and resupplying medication
- ❑ Meal prep

Call list for whom you need to contact if you need to
leave work for any period of time for caregiving:

☐ Supervisor

☐ Human Resources

☐ Close family members

☐ Caregiver for your own children

☐ Caregiver for pets (if different)

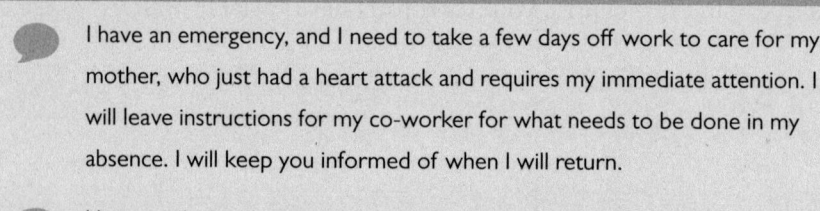

Conversation Prompts for Taking Leave

I have an emergency, and I need to take a few days off work to care for my mother, who just had a heart attack and requires my immediate attention. I will leave instructions for my co-worker for what needs to be done in my absence. I will keep you informed of when I will return.

I have to deal with a sick relative. Can we discuss ways I can work remotely and still contribute to the team while I deal with this situation?

I am needed at home and need to take a leave. I want to come back to my job as soon as I can. Can we start a process with human resources for that?

ELDERCARE AT-HOME RESOURCES

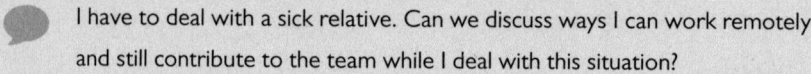

- National Council on Aging (NCOA): https://www.ncoa.org/caregivers/benefits/caregiver-support
- AARP: https://www.aarp.org/caregiving
- Caregiver Action Network: https://www.caregiveraction.org
- Rosalynn Carter Institute for Caregivers: https://rosalynncarter.org
- National Alliance for Caregiving (NAC): https://www.caregiving.org

LONG-TERM CARE INSURANCE RESOURCES

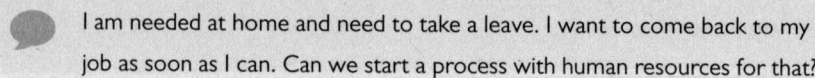

- State insurance departments—list for all fifty states: https://content.naic.org/state-insurance-departments

- AARP: https://www.aarp.org/caregiving/long-term-care
- Medicare: https://www.medicare.gov/coverage/long-term-care
- American Association for Long-Term Care Insurance: https://www.aaltci.org/long-term-care-insurance

Glossary of Key Contract Terms for Long-Term Care Insurance

- **Daily benefit amount:** This is the amount the insurer will pay per day.

- **Elimination period:** This is the length of time you have to wait before the claim will pay; it is typically 90 or 180 days, but some policies may have no wait time.

- **Inflation protection benefit:** You can raise the coverage level over time, either automatically or by paying extra.

- **Lapse:** Your policy will be canceled if you do not pay the premiums due.

- **Lifetime maximum:** The policy will likely have a total dollar cap and a number of covered care days.

- **Waiver of premium:** After you go on claim, the premium is waived while you are on claim.

RESOURCES FOR SENIOR LIVING OPTIONS

- A Place for Mom: https://www.aplaceformom.com
- Caring.com: https://www.caring.com
- U.S. Department of Housing and Urban Development Information for Senior Citizens: https://www.hud.gov/topics/information_for_senior_citizens
- Ask a local hospital for their list; it will most likely be a sheet of paper or a packet with a list of facilities. It may contain star ratings from the Medicare comparison tool (https://www.medicare.gov/care-compare), but you'll still need to do your own assessment.

GOVERNMENT AGENCY CONTACTS

- Internal Revenue Service (IRS): https://www.irs.gov
- Medicare: https://www.medicare.gov

- Social Security Administration: https://www.ssa.gov
- Department of Veterans Affairs: https://www.va.gov

MEDICARE HELP

- State Health Insurance Assistance Program (SHIP) (listing by state): https://www.shiphelp.org/about-medicare/regional-ship-location
- Medicare Rights Center: https://www.medicarerights.org
- Boomer Benefits: https://boomerbenefits.com

SOCIAL SECURITY HELP

- The Senior Citizens League (TSCL): https://seniorsleague.org
- Social Security Intelligence Member's Group (Facebook group): https://www.facebook.com/groups/428684237572614
- Consumer Financial Protection Bureau (CFPB) Planning Your Social Security Claiming Age: https://www.consumerfinance.gov/consumer-tools/retirement/before-you-claim
- AARP Social Security Calculator: https://www.aarp.org/social-security/benefits-calculator
- Social Security Works: https://socialsecurityworks.org

MEDICARE APPEAL QIO INFORMATION

To find information on your appeal:

- Contact the Quality Improvement Organization for your location: https://qioprogram.org/appeals
- Contact Medicare: https://www.medicare.gov/providers-services/claims-appeals-complaints/appeals/fast-appeals
- Contact your facility social worker

Medicaid Help

Checklist for documentation needed for Medicaid:

❑ Wages and salary pay stubs or payroll records

❑ Interest and other investment income statements

❏ Proof of rent payment

❏ Self-employment tax returns or earnings statements

❏ Unemployment benefit statements

❏ Pension statements

❏ Social Security statements

❏ Workers' compensation statements

❏ Letters for child support and alimony payments

❏ Veterans' benefit statements

HOSPICE RESOURCES

- Hospice Foundation of America (HFA): https://hospicefoundation.org
- International End of Life Doula Organization (INELDA): https://inelda.org/about-doulas/what-is-a-doula
- ProPublica: https://www.propublica.org/article/hospice-healthcare-aseracare-medicare
- Joan Didion's book *The Year of Magical Thinking*

CEMETERY RESOURCES

- Neptune Society: https://neptunesociety.com
- International Cemetery, Cremation & Funeral Association (ICCFA): https://iccfa.com/resources
- International End of Life Doula Association (INELDA): https://inelda.org

Checklist for cemetery folder (or equivalent):

❏ Contact number for preferred funeral home or burial facility

❏ Contract for burial plot

❏ Prepaid receipt for any funeral or other arrangements made in advance

❏ Prior receipts from past funerals to use as a guide

Conversation Prompts for Burial Plans

- Ask: "Do you know where you want to be buried or if you want to be cremated?"

- Talk about what you want done for yourself: "I've been thinking that I don't want to be buried and I'd rather be cremated. What do you think about that?"

- Ask about or talk about previous family funerals and discuss the pros and cons: "Remember when we went to Uncle Joe's funeral? I really liked that they had somebody sing at the service. Would you want something like that? What song would you pick?"

Financial Planning

List of accounts and access:

Check title and beneficiary designation of each and trusted contacts added.

INSTITUTION			
	Account Number		Balance
Main Bank			
	Beneficiaries	Joint Owners	Passwords
	Account Number		Balance
Brokerage			
	Beneficiaries	Joint Owners	Passwords

INSTITUTION			
	Account Number		**Balance**
Credit Card 1			
	Beneficiaries	**Joint Owners**	**Passwords**
	Account Number		**Balance**
Life Insurance			
	Beneficiaries	**Joint Owners**	**Passwords**
	Account Number		**Balance**
Long-Term Care Insurance			
	Beneficiaries	**Joint Owners**	**Passwords**
	Account Number		**Balance**
Auto Loan(s)			
	Beneficiaries	**Joint Owners**	**Passwords**
	Account Number		**Balance**
Mortgage			
	Beneficiaries	**Joint Owners**	**Passwords**

List of bills paid or access to statements
(need account logins, passwords, and payment dates):

TYPE			
	Account Number		Due Date
Credit Cards			
	Joint Signers	Password	Average Payment
	Account Number		Due Date
Car Insurance			
	Joint Signers	Password	Average Payment
	Account Number		Due Date
Rent or Mortgage			
	Joint Signers	Password	Average Payment
	Account Number		Due Date
Home or Renter's Insurance			
	Joint Signers	Password	Average Payment
	Account Number		Due Date
Utilities			
	Joint Signers	Password	Average Payment

Budget worksheet:

Income:

Income	Monthly	Yearly
Social Security		
Pension		
RMD		
Other Income (Rentals, etc.)		

Liabilities:

Liability	Monthly	Yearly	Special
Rent or Mortgage			
Car Payment			
Credit Card			

Utilities:

Group bank account charges (checks to caregivers, autobills, cash from ATM)

Other bills (if yearly, divide)

Calculation: How long will the money last?

Step 1: Add up your current monthly expenses; this is your burn rate.

Step 2: Calculate current income (Social Security, pensions, annuities, investment income, etc.).

Step 3: Subtract your monthly expenses from your monthly income. If there is a current shortfall, determine how much needs to be covered monthly.

Step 4: Assess supplemental sources of funds from savings. Use a savings distribution calculator to determine how many months the funds will last at the estimated spending rate.

Step 5: If savings are not sufficient, determine the shortfall amount and see if there are other sources available, such as family members to make up the difference.

Calculate this for future "what if" care scenarios as needed, and then compare costs.

CALCULATOR RESOURCES:

- Savings distribution calculator example: https://www.dinkytown.net/java/savings-distribution-calculator.html
- Genworth cost of care calculator: https://www.genworth.com/aging-and-you/finances/cost-of-care
- AARP retirement calculator: https://www.aarp.org/retirement/retirement-calculator
- Boldin: https://www.boldin.com

FINANCIAL PLANNER RESOURCES FOR FEE-ONLY SERVICES:

- The National Association of Personal Financial Advisors (NAPFA): https://www.napfa.org
- Nectarine: https://hellonectarine.com
- Wealthramp: https://wealthramp.com
- XY Planning Network: https://www.xyplanningnetwork.com
- CFP Board of Standards: https://www.letsmakeaplan.org
- Financial Planning Association (FPA) PlannerSearch: https://www.financialplanningassociation.org/practice-support/plannersearch

REVERSE MORTGAGE RESOURCES:

- Wade Pfau, *Reverse Mortgages: How to Use Reverse Mortgages to Secure Your Retirement* (McLean Asset Management Corporation, 2016)
- Consumer Financial Protection Bureau (CFPB): https://www.consumerfinance.gov/consumer-tools/reverse-mortgages
- U.S. Department of Housing and Urban Development (HUD): https://www.hud.gov/program_offices/housing/sfh/hecm/hecmhome
- National Council on Aging (NCOA): https://www.ncoa.org/article/get-the-facts-on-reverse-mortgages

REQUIRED MINIMUM DISTRIBUTION (RMD)
CALCULATIONS/FORMULAS:

- Securities and Exchange Commission (SEC) Required Minimum Distribution Calculator: https://www.investor.gov/financial-tools-calculators/calculators/required-minimum-distribution-calculator
- IRS Required Minimum Distribution Worksheets: https://www.irs.gov/retirement-plans/plan-participant-employee/required-minimum-distribution-worksheets
- IRS rulebook (with life expectancy tables): https://www.irs.gov/retirement-plans/plan-participant-employee/retirement-topics-required-minimum-distributions-rmds

Family Meeting Agenda to Discuss Financial Planning

List of attendees (suggested: immediate family, person being cared for, mediator):

Name _____

Relationship _____   Location _____

Availability _____

Name _____

Relationship _____   Location _____

Availability _____

Name _____

Relationship _____   Location _____

Availability _____

People to consult (suggested: paid caregivers,
primary care doctor, financial planner, tax preparer):

Name _____

Relationship _____   Location _____

Availability _____

Name _____

Relationship _____   Location _____

Availability _____

Meeting scribe (select attendee) name _____

Date of meeting _____

Agenda items:

_____

_____

_____

_____

_____

_____

_____

_____

_____

Take the calculations from above for different scenarios of how long the money will last, and discuss options. Each family member should say what they think on each point. If there is not an immediate unanimous agreement, they should discuss further until each is comfortable.

Example:

Plan 1

Ann goes home and lives with private caregivers at her condo, with hospice covering her medical care.

Duration of cash retirement savings if she recovers and lives another twenty years (but still with caregivers), drawing down $5,000 per month for the next three years until the long-term care benefit is exhausted, then $12,000 per month: roughly 5 years.

Plan 2

Ann stays in the rehab facility as a private-pay patient at $12,000 a month, with private aides. The long-term care policy will pick up part of the cost of the long-term care facility. Medicare's hospice benefit will cover the medical care. The aides will be paid out of pocket, plus there will be housing costs. The monthly burn rate will likely be $20,000.

Duration of cash and retirement savings if she continues in this scenario: 2.5 years.

Plan 3

Ann takes a medical flight to New York at a cost of $20,000 and either enters hospice at a rehab facility near her daughter with full-time aides or moves into a one-bedroom rental apartment with full-time aides. The sale of her condo could generate $150,000 in additional retirement savings.

Duration of cash and retirement savings with a large withdrawal for moving expenses and setup costs: 3 years at current savings, additional 11 months with proceeds from the condo.

Create a flowchart for what you will do with the assets in your estate plan. Consider your home, car, retirement accounts, and cash. If any of the assets requires more than a beneficiary designation or you have other considerations, such as naming a guardian for a minor child, proceed to make an estate plan, either on your own or with an attorney.

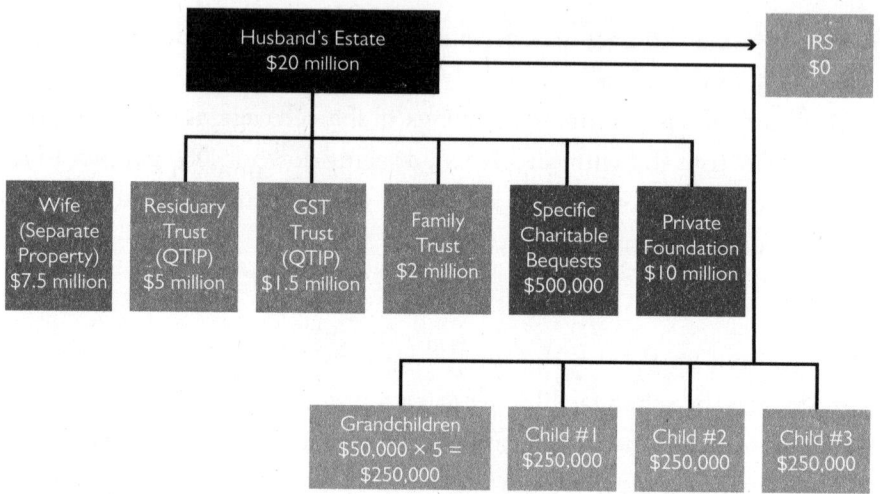

Source: Justin Miller, J.D. LL.M., TEP®, AEP®, CFP®, Partner and National Director of Wealth Planning at Evercore Wealth Management. The information provided is for illustrative/educational purposes only. The material is not intended to constitute legal, tax, investment or financial advice. 2024 All Rights Reserved.

RESOURCES FOR FINDING AN ESTATE LAWYER:

- National Academy of Elder Law Attorneys (NAELA): https://naela.org
- The American College of Trust and Estate Counsel (ACTEC): https://www.actec .org/resource-center/video/how-to-choose-an-estate-planning-attorney
- Avvo: https://www.avvo.com
- FindLaw: https://lawyers.findlaw.com

Checklists for Legal Documents

Power of attorney:

❑ Primary decider

❑ Secondary decider

❑ What accounts do you want those holding the power of attorney to have access to? (bank accounts, safe deposit box)

❑ What decisions do you want them to be able to make? (sell property, invest)

❑ Will you allow payment to the power of attorney agent?

❑ Does your agent know about being chosen and know what to do if you become incapacitated?

❑ Will anyone object to the person you picked and cause legal action?

❑ Where will you keep the power of attorney document for the agent to access if needed?

Healthcare proxy:

❑ Primary decider

❑ Secondary decider

❑ What can your agent access and decide for you?

❑ If you have more than one proxy, is there a tiebreaker in case of disagreement?

❑ Does your agent know their duties and are they prepared to carry them out?

HIPAA:

❑ Primary decider

❑ Secondary decider

WHERE TO GET BASIC ESTATE FORMS:

- IRS list of state government websites: https://www.irs.gov/businesses/small -businesses-self-employed/state-government-websites
- Rocket Lawyer: https://www.rocketlawyer.com
- Nolo: https://www.nolo.com
- LegalZoom: https://www.legalzoom.com
- FreeWill: https://www.freewill.com
- Trust & Will: https://trustandwill.com
- Mama Bear Legal Forms: https://mamabearlegalforms.com

POWER OF ATTORNEY RESOURCES FOR GOVERNMENT AGENCIES:

- IRS About Form 56: https://www.irs.gov/forms-pubs/about-form-56
- Medicare: https://www.cms.gov/medicare/cms-forms/cms-forms/downloads/cms1696.pdf
- Social Security Administration Form SSA-1696: https://www.ssa.gov/forms/ssa-1696.html
- Department of Veterans Affairs (VA) Form 10-0137: https://www.va.gov/find-forms/about-form-10-0137

GUARDIANSHIP RESOURCES:

- Center for Elders and the Courts: https://www.eldersandcourts.org
- Justice in Aging: https://justiceinaging.org
- National Center on Elder Abuse (NCEA): https://ncea.acl.gov/home
- National Center for State Courts (NCSC): https://www.ncsc.org

LIVING WILL RESOURCES:

- Five Wishes: https://www.fivewishes.org
- National Institute on Aging: https://www.nia.nih.gov/health/advance-care-planning/preparing-living-will

Conversation Prompts

I know you may not want to talk about it, but I want to make sure I know what you want if something should go wrong, so can we talk about what kind of measures you want taken if you get really sick?

When Grandma died, she was in the hospital for a long time hooked up to machines. Do you want those kinds of measures taken, or do you want to sign a Do Not Resuscitate order?

I looked at your driver's license and noticed you were (or were not) marked as an organ donor. I'd love to know what you think about that and what you would want done if it comes to making a decision about that someday.

Wills:

❑ Primary executor

❑ Secondary executor

❑ Guardian for minor children

❑ Digital asset plan

❑ Burial instructions

❑ Provisions for pets

❑ Specific bequests of personal items

❑ Make sure there are no beneficiary designations that would conflict with instructions in the will

Trusts:

❑ Primary trustee

❑ Secondary trustee

❑ What assets are expected to be in the trust

❑ Update title of all assets to the trust

❑ Decide what the trustees will be allowed to do with the assets (sell, invest).

❑ Craft discretionary or spendthrift provisions.

❑ Map out division of assets based on your needs.

Comparison chart for inheriting property:

	Upfront Cost Estimate	Upfront Time	After Cost	After Time
Will	$500	1 hour	$5,000	20 months
Trust	$4,000	5 hours	0	0
Transfer Deed	$500	5 hours	0	5 hours
Nothing	0	0	$10,000	20+ months

Conversation Prompts for Planning for Possessions

You sure have a lot of stamps, Grandpa. Do you have a list of them all and know what they are worth? Do you have a plan for them?

Mom, I know how much you love your cat. If something were to happen to you, who would you want to take care of her?

You have so many interesting things in your home. Can you tell me about them?

Household inventory checklist for what needs to be appraised, valued, and who it goes to:

Item	Location	Value	Who Should Get

Checklist for securing assets in the event of a death:

- ❏ Who is closest to the house?
- ❏ What assets need to be addressed?
- ❏ Does property need to be secured?

Checklist for financial caregiver immediately after a death:

- ❏ Forward mail (you may need to go to a post office with ID if you can't do it online).
- ❏ Find copies of needed documents: birth certificate, marriage certificate, VA discharge papers, passport, driver's license.
- ❏ Order 15-plus copies of death certificate (mix of long and short).

Plan funeral and mourning period:

- ❏ Schedule service or memorial with officiant.
- ❏ Invite guests.
- ❏ Make travel arrangements.
- ❏ Plan meal afterward, if needed.

Sample funeral charges:

- ❏ Facilities for chapel service
- ❏ Staff at committal service
- ❏ Refrigeration and sanitary care
- ❏ Washing, dressing, casketing, and cosmetology
- ❏ Casket or urn as selected
- ❏ Cremation (if selected)
- ❏ Removal vehicle
- ❏ Hearse

❑ Limousine

❑ Burial garment

❑ Certified copies of death certificate

❑ Newspaper publishing of obituary

❑ Officiant honorarium

❑ Funeral director charges

❑ Transportation from place of death

Once you have the death certificates:

❑ Contact the life insurance company.

❑ Contact long-term care and other insurance companies.

❑ Take inventory of bank accounts and credit cards and start calling to cancel them.

❑ Go through online accounts and cancel them.

❑ Contact any accounts with beneficiaries and start process to transfer funds.

Probate steps:

1. Look up the state's probate filing rules and thresholds and determine if you need full probate.

2. If you do, hire a lawyer and file for an administrator.

3. Catalog assets and expenses.

4. Wait.

5. Once you have letters of administration, do any necessary paperwork.

6. File final tax returns and distribute assets.

7. Inventory all expenses and close probate.

HOW TO CREATE AN EMPLOYER IDENTIFICATION
NUMBER (EIN) FOR AN ESTATE OR TRUST:

- Go only to the IRS.
- Full instructions: https://www.irs.gov/pub/irs-pdf/p1635.pdf
- Apply here: https://www.irs.gov/businesses/small-businesses-self-employed/apply
  -for-an-employer-identification-number-ein-online

Tax return checklist for deceased and estate trust:

❏ Contact of accountant

❏ Social Security Form 1099

❏ Mortgage interest statement

❏ Pension statements

❏ Distributions from retirement account statements

❏ Medical spending records

❏ Any other income statements

❏ Any other interest/capital gains statements

❏ IRS Form 56

❏ IRS Form 1310

RESOURCES FOR FINDING AN ENROLLED
AGENT OR CPA IN YOUR AREA:

- National Association of Enrolled Agents (NAEA): https://taxexperts.naea.org/
  expertdirectory
- American Institute of CPAs (AICPA): https://us.aicpa.org/forthepublic/findacpa

Notes

Introduction

1. "Survey: 60 percent of Americans Lack Will or Estate Planning," AARP, March 16, 2023, https://www.aarp.org/money/investing/info-2017/half-of-adults-do-not-have-wills.html; Rachel Lustbader, "2024 Wills and Estate Planning Study," Caring, July 30, 2024, https://www.caring.com/caregivers/estate-planning/wills-survey; Victoria Lurie, "2024 Wills and Estate Planning Study," Caring, October 25, 2024, https://www.caring.com/caregivers/estate-planning/wills-survey.
2. "2023 Life Insurance Fact Sheet," LIMRA, 2023, https://www.limra.com/siteassets/newsroom/fact-tank/fact-sheets/0859-2023-liam-fact-sheet-2023_final.pdf.
3. "Five Reasons to Discuss Long-Term Care Insurance Options with Your Clients," LIMRA, November 7, 2024, https://www.limra.com/en/newsroom/industry-trends/2024/limra-five-reasons-to-discuss-long-term-care-insurance-options-with-your-clients.
4. "2020 Census Will Help Policymakers Prepare for the Incoming Wave of Aging Boomers," United States Census Bureau, October 3, 2024, https://www.census.gov/library/stories/2019/12/by-2030-all-baby-boomers-will-be-age-65-or-older.html.
5. Tyler Bond and Frank Porell, "Examining the Nest Egg: The Sources of Retirement Income for Older Americans," National Institute on Retirement Security, January 2020, https://www.nirsonline.org/wp-content/uploads/2020/01/Examining-the-Nest-Egg-Final-2.pdf.
6. *The 2024 Annual Report of the Board of Trustees of the Federal Old-Age and Survivors Insurance and Federal Disability Insurance Trust Funds,* Social Security Administration, https://www.ssa.gov/OACT/TR/2024.
7. "Cerulli Anticipates $84 Trillion in Wealth Transfers Through 2045," Cerulli, January 20, 2022, https://www.cerulli.com/press-releases/cerulli-anticipates-84-trillion-in-wealth-transfers-through-2045.
8. Sanford Pinsker and Ann Pinsker, *Understanding* The Catcher in the Rye: *A Student Casebook to Issues, Sources, and Historical Documents* (Greenwood, 2002).

Chapter 1

1. William J. Scanlon, "A Perspective on Long-Term Care for the Elderly," *Health Care Financing Review,* December 1988 (suppl.), https://www.ncbi.nlm.nih.gov/pmc/articles/PMC4195126.

2. "Common Causes of Long-Term Care Insurance Claims," Darras Law, https://www .longtermdisabilitylawyer.com/2017/10/common-causes-of-long-term-care -insurance-claims.

3. "The Top 10 Most Common Chronic Conditions in Older Adults," National Council on Aging, May 30, 2024, https://www.ncoa.org/article/the-top-10-most-common -chronic-conditions-in-older-adults.

4. Paul Hemez and Chanell Washington, "Living Arrangements Varied Across Age Groups," United States Census Bureau, May 30, 2024, https://www.census.gov/ library/stories/2024/05/living-arrangements.html.

5. Joy Loverde, *The Complete Eldercare Planner, Revised and Updated 4th Edition: Where to Start, Which Questions to Ask, and How to Find Help* (Rodale Press, 2023).

6. Joy Loverde, *Who Will Take Care of Me When I'm Old?: Plan Now to Safeguard Your Health and Happiness in Old Age* (Thorndike Press, 2018).

Chapter 2

1. Tara Siegel Bernard, "As Cognition Slips, Financial Skills Are Often the First to Go," *New York Times,* April 24, 2015, https://www.nytimes.com/2015/04/25/your-money/ as-cognitivity-slips-financial-skills-are-often-the-first-to-go.html.

2. "Senior Scam Alert," Elder Justice Initiative, U.S. Department of Justice, https://www .justice.gov/elderjustice/senior-scam-alert.

3. "Is Your Financial Firm Asking You for a Trusted Contact?," FINRA, https://www .finra.org/sites/default/files/2021-09/trusted-contact-infographic.pdf.

4. "Investor Bulletin: Please Consider Adding a Trusted Contact to Your Account," U.S. Securities and Exchange Commission, March 4, 2020, https://www.investor.gov/ introduction-investing/general-resources/news-alerts/alerts-bulletins/investor -bulletins-trusted-contact.

5. Annalee Kruger, *The Invisible Patient: The Emotional, Financial, and Physical Toll on Family Caregivers* (Kruger, 2021).

6. Bob Mauterstock, *Caring for Your Elderly Parents: Timely Advice for Baby Boomers* (CreateSpace, 2017).

7. Susan C. Reinhard et al., "Supporting Family Caregivers in Providing Care," in *Patient Safety and Quality: An Evidence-Based Handbook for Nurses,* ed. R. G. Hughes (Agency for Healthcare Research and Quality, 2008), chap. 14, https://www .ncbi.nlm.nih.gov/books/NBK2665.

Chapter 3

1. Warren Kozak, *Waving Goodbye: Life After Loss* (Post Hill Press, 2024).

2. "Understanding Cemetery and Burial Plots," Perfect Memorials, https:// perfectmemorials.com/guides/cemeteries-and-burial-plots-understanding-your -options.

3. "Become a Diamond or Get Launched into Space—7 Alternatives to Burial or Cremation," *Los Angeles Times,* May 19, 2023, https://www.latimes.com/lifestyle/ story/2023-05-19/of-alternatives-for-traditional-burial-and-cremation.

4.   "6 Burial and Cremation Alternatives," Funeralocity, November 3, 2024, https://
     www.funeralocity.com/blog/6-burial-and-cremation-alternatives.

Chapter 4

1.   Beth Pinsker, "My Mom Gave Me These Cheat Sheets Before She Had Surgery
     Recently and They Saved Me Tons of Anxiety," MarketWatch, November 19, 2022,
     https://www.marketwatch.com/story/fear-or-love-let-actions-speak-louder-than
     -words-when-it-comes-to-emergency-documents-11668623148.
2.   "Advance Care Planning: Advance Directives for Health Care," National Institute on
     Aging, October 31, 2022, https://www.nia.nih.gov/health/advance-care-planning/
     advance-care-planning-advance-directives-health-care.
3.   "Prepare Your Health: Paperwork," U.S. Centers for Disease Control and Prevention,
     April 18, 2024, https://www.cdc.gov/prepare-your-health/take-action/paperwork
     .html.
4.   "Individuals' Right Under HIPAA to Access Their Health Information," U.S.
     Department of Health and Human Services, https://www.hhs.gov/hipaa/for
     -professionals/privacy/guidance/access/index.html.

Chapter 5

1.   "Financial Institution Employee's Guide to Deposit Insurance: Joint Accounts,"
     Federal Deposit Insurance Corporation, last updated May 29, 2024, https://www
     .fdic.gov/financial-institution-employees-guide-deposit-insurance/joint-accounts.
2.   "What Happens If I Have a Joint Bank Account with Someone Who Died?," Consumer
     Financial Protection Bureau, May 15, 2024, https://www.consumerfinance.gov/ask
     -cfpb/what-happens-if-i-have-a-joint-bank-account-with-someone-who-died
     -en-1101.

Chapter 6

1.   "Caregiving in the US: Research Report," AARP, July 2025, https://www.aarp.org/
     content/dam/aarp/ppi/topics/ltss/family-caregiving/caregiving-in-us-2025.doi.10
     .26419-2fppi.00373.001.pdf.
2.   Steven May, Jr., "Caregiving in the US 2020," The National Alliance for Caregiving,
     January 10, 2014, https://www.caregiving.org/research/caregiving-in-the-us.
3.   "Celebrating National Family Caregivers Month with BLS Data," U.S. Bureau of
     Labor Statistics, November 30, 2023, https://www.bls.gov/blog/2023/celebrating
     -national-family-caregivers-month-with-bls-data.htm.

Chapter 7

1. "Federal Bureau of Investigation Elder Fraud Report 2022," Federal Bureau of
    Investigation, https://www.ic3.gov/Media/PDF/AnnualReport/2022_IC3
    ElderFraudReport.pdf.
2. Pamela Teaster, Georgia J. Anetzberger, and Elizabeth Podnieks, *The Worldwide Face
    of Elder Abuse* (Springer International, 2023).

Chapter 8

1. "Financial Caregiving: Power of Attorney," American Bankers Association, https://
    www.aba.com/advocacy/community-programs/consumer-resources/financial
    -caregiving/power-of-attorney.
2. "Power of Attorney," American Bar Association, https://www.americanbar.org/
    groups/real_property_trust_estate/resources/estate-planning/power-of-attorney.
3. "5 Types of Power of Attorney, Explained," FreeWill, June 11, 2021, https://www
    .freewill.com/learn/5-types-of-power-of-attorney.
4. Jenny Rozelle, "I Just Replied to a Financial Advisor Who Tweeted About a Bank/
    Banker Who Was Failing to Honor a Power of Attorney," Twitter, April 15, 2023,
    https://x.com/jennyrozelle/status/1647214704903835650.
5. Beth Pinsker, " 'It Broke Me': Everyone Says You Need Power of Attorney, but
    Nobody Tells You How Hard It Is to Use," MarketWatch, March 2, 2023, https://www
    .marketwatch.com/story/it-broke-me-everyone-says-you-need-a-power-of-attorney
    -but-nobody-tells-you-how-hard-it-is-to-use-1c861600.
6. NNA Staff, " 'Medallion Signatures' Explained," National Notary Association, July 5,
    2023, https://www.nationalnotary.org/notary-bulletin/blog/2011/04/medallion
    -signatures-explained.

Chapter 9

1. "Form SSA-1696, Claimant's Appointment of a Representative," Social Security
    Administration, https://www.ssa.gov/forms/ssa-1696.html.
2. Michael Picón, *The Power of Attorney's Notebook: Everything You Need for Managing
    Your Loved One's Estate* (Pen&Paper Books, 2023).
3. Michael Picón, *The Caregiver's Notebook: Everything You Need for Managing Your
    Loved One's Long-Term Care* (Pen&Paper Books, 2023).
4. "About Form 56, Notice Concerning Fiduciary Relationship," Internal Revenue
    Service, September 11, 2024, https://www.irs.gov/forms-pubs/about-form-56.
5. "About Form 1310, Statement of Person Claiming Refund Due a Deceased Taxpayer,"
    Internal Revenue Service, last updated December 3, 2024, https://www.irs.gov/
    forms-pubs/about-form-1310.
6. "About VA Form 21-22," U.S. Department of Veterans Affairs, last updated
    February 2, 2025, https://www.va.gov/find-forms/about-form-21-22.

Chapter 10

1. Jim Berchtold, "Guardianship Data Reform," Justice in Aging, October 25, 2024, https://justiceinaging.org/guardianship-data-reform.
2. Nardine Saad and Meg James, "Jay Leno Clarifies Why He Set Up Conservatorship amid Wife Mavis' Dementia Battle," *Los Angeles Times,* January 30, 2024, https://www.latimes.com/entertainment-arts/tv/story/2024-01-30/jay-leno-conservatorship-mavis-leno-dementia-will.
3. Sally Balch Hurme, *Checklist for My Family: A Guide to My History, Financial Plans, and Final Wishes* (American Bar Association, 2022).
4. Elizabeth A. Moran, "Legal & Legislative Review 2023," National Conference on Guardianship, Orlando, Florida, October 14–17, 2023.

Chapter 11

1. Peter F. Edemekong et al., "Activities of Daily Living," in *StatPearls* (StatPearls Publishing, 2023), https://www.ncbi.nlm.nih.gov/books/NBK470404.
2. "Cost of Long Term Care by State: Cost of Care Report," CareScout, https://www.genworth.com/aging-and-you/finances/cost-of-care.
3. Beth Pinsker, "$3,000 a Week? The Enormous Cost of Care for Elderly Loved Ones That Nobody Warns You About," MarketWatch, February 3, 2023, https://www.marketwatch.com/story/3-000-a-week-the-enormous-cost-of-one-on-one-care-for-sick-loved-ones-that-nobody-warns-you-about-11675382348.
4. Dan Gray, "Life Expectancy Gap: Women in U.S. Now Outlive Men by Nearly 6 Years," Medical News Today, November 15, 2023, https://www.medicalnewstoday.com/articles/why-women-in-the-us-now-have-life-expectancy-nearly-6-years-longer-than-men.

Chapter 12

1. "Facts & Figures," American Health Care Association and National Center for Assisted Living, https://www.ahcancal.org/Assisted-Living/Facts-and-Figures/Pages/default.aspx.
2. "Investing in Seniors Housing & Care Properties: Executive Summary," National Investment Center for Seniors Housing & Care, 2020, https://info.nic.org/hubfs/Investment_Guide/NIC_InvestmentGuide-ExecSumm_INTR.pdf.
3. Kathleen M. Rehl, *Moving Forward on Your Own: A Financial Guidebook for Widows* (Rehl Financial Advisors, 2015).
4. Celli Horstman, Evan Gumas, and Gretchen Jacobson, "U.S. and Global Approaches to Financing Long-Term Care: Understanding the Patchwork," The Commonwealth Fund, February 16, 2023, https://www.commonwealthfund.org/publications/issue-briefs/2023/feb/us-global-financing-long-term-care-patchwork.
5. Beth Pinsker, "You Don't Have to Be Dead to Use Life Insurance. It Can Also Fund Long-Term Care," MarketWatch, May 28, 2024, https://www.marketwatch.com/

story/you-dont-have-to-be-dead-to-use-life-insurance-it-can-also-fund-long-term
-care-2a6b63db.

6.   Christopher Rowland, "Seniors on Medicaid Are Getting Evicted from Assisted-
Living Homes," *Washington Post,* April 6, 2023, https://www.washingtonpost.com/
business/2023/04/06/seniors-assisted-living-medicaid-eviction.

7.   "What to Do When an Assisted Living Facility Refuses to Accept Medicaid," Justice
in Aging, October 11, 2023, https://justiceinaging.org/assisted-living-what-to-do
-when-facility-refuses-accept-medicaid-attempts-evict.

Chapter 13

1.   "Medicare Basics: Parts of Medicare," Medicare.gov, https://www.medicare.gov/
basics/get-started-with-medicare/medicare-basics/parts-of-medicare.

2.   Marcia Mantell, *Creating Your Medicare Recipe: Your Guide to Enrolling on Time and
Without Penalties* (Mantell Retirement Consulting, 2024).

3.   "Using Medicare: Helpful Tools," Medicare.gov, https://www.medicare.gov/basics/
get-started-with-medicare/using-medicare/helpful-tools.

4.   Brandy Bauer, "The Medicare Part D Donut Hole: What You Need to Know,"
National Council on Aging, January 8, 2025, https://www.ncoa.org/article/the
-medicare-part-d-donut-hole-what-you-need-to-know.

5.   Beth Pinsker, "MarketWatch—Answering Your Medicare Open Enrollment
Questions," *Barron's Live* (podcast), October 11, 2023, https://www.marketwatch
.com/podcasts/barrons-live/marketwatch-answering-your-medicare-open
-enrollment-questions/833b9389-d619-47d2-80c6-cc9e551fb946.

6.   Cameron Huddleston, *Mom and Dad, We Need to Talk: How to Have Essential
Conversations with Your Parents About Their Finances* (John Wiley & Sons, 2019).

Chapter 14

1.   "Inpatient Hospital Care," Medicare.gov, https://www.medicare.gov/coverage/
inpatient-hospital-care.

2.   Beth Pinsker, "My Mother Has to Go into a Nursing Home. How Do I Get Her the
Care She Needs?," MarketWatch, February 9, 2023, https://www.marketwatch.com/
story/i-just-got-the-dreaded-list-of-nursing-homes-from-my-moms-hospital-how
-do-i-stand-up-for-my-senior-to-get-the-care-she-needs-11675910674.

Chapter 15

1.   Beth Pinsker, "Medicare Wanted to Stop Paying for My Mom's Stay in Rehab. I
Successfully Appealed—Twice—and You Can, Too," MarketWatch, May 25, 2023,
https://www.marketwatch.com/story/i-won-2-medicare-discharge-appeals-by
-working-the-system-heres-how-you-can-too-6ba30bab.

2.   "Make an Appeal," Quality Improvement Organization, https://qioprogram.org/
appeals.

3. Susan Jaffe, "Nursing Home Surprise: Advantage Plans May Shorten Stays to Less Time than Medicare Covers," KFF Health News, October 4, 2022, https://kffhealthnews.org/news/article/nursing-home-surprise-medicare-advantage-plans-shorten-stays.

Chapter 16

1. Robin Rudowitz et al., "10 Things to Know About Medicaid," KFF, July 11, 2024, https://www.kff.org/medicaid/issue-brief/10-things-to-know-about-medicaid.
2. Celli Horstman, Evan Gumas, and Gretchen Jacobson, "U.S. and Global Approaches to Financing Long-Term Care: Understanding the Patchwork," The Commonwealth Fund, February 16, 2023, https://www.commonwealthfund.org/publications/issue-briefs/2023/feb/us-global-financing-long-term-care-patchwork.
3. "Eligibility Policy," Medicaid.gov, https://www.medicaid.gov/medicaid/eligibility-policy/index.html.
4. "Executive Order on Increasing Access to High-Quality Care and Supporting Caregivers," The White House, April 18, 2023, https://www.whitehouse.gov/briefing-room/presidential-actions/2023/04/18/executive-order-on-increasing-access-to-high-quality-care-and-supporting-caregivers.

Chapter 17

1. "Request Your Military Service Records (Including DD214)," U.S. Department of Veterans Affairs, last updated February 7, 2024, https://www.va.gov/records/get-military-service-records.
2. "The Program of Comprehensive Assistance for Family Caregivers," U.S. Department of Veterans Affairs, last updated February 24, 2025, https://www.va.gov/family-and-caregiver-benefits/health-and-disability/comprehensive-assistance-for-family-caregivers.

Chapter 18

1. "Five Reasons to Discuss Long-Term Care Insurance Options with Your Clients," LIMRA, November 7, 2024, https://www.limra.com/en/newsroom/industry-trends/2024/limra-five-reasons-to-discuss-long-term-care-insurance-options-with-your-clients.
2. Celli Horstman, Evan Gumas, and Gretchen Jacobson, "U.S. and Global Approaches to Financing Long-Term Care: Understanding the Patchwork," The Commonwealth Fund, February 16, 2023, https://www.commonwealthfund.org/publications/issue-briefs/2023/feb/us-global-financing-long-term-care-patchwork; George Wehby, Benjamin W. Domingue, and Fredric D. Wolinsky, "Genetic Risks for Chronic Conditions: Implications for Long-Term Wellbeing," *Journals of Gerontology Series A: Biological Sciences and Medical Sciences* 73, no. 4 (August 2017): 477–83, https://pmc.ncbi.nlm.nih.gov/articles/PMC5861924.

3. "Long-Term Care Insurance Health Qualifications. Are You Even Insurable?," American Association for Long-Term Care Insurance, https://www.aaltci.org/long-term-care-insurance/learning-center/are-you-even-insurable.php.

4. *Long Term Care Insurance Underwriting Guide,* Genworth Financial, May 2007, https://www.resourcebrokerage.com/pdfs/ltci/underwriting/genworth.pdf.

5. Beth Pinsker, "'Mom and Dad, How Much Money Do You Have?': The Question You Need to Ask Your Parents Now," MarketWatch, December 24, 2024, https://www.marketwatch.com/story/mom-and-dad-how-much-money-do-you-have-the-question-you-need-to-ask-your-parents-now-11669209716.

6. Beth Pinsker, "I've Been Paying for 20 Years and Now Can't Afford My Insurance Premium Hike. Is There Anything I Can Do to Save My Long-Term Care Coverage?," MarketWatch, February 27, 2023, https://www.marketwatch.com/story/ive-been-paying-for-20-years-and-now-cant-afford-my-insurance-premium-hike-is-there-anything-i-can-do-to-save-my-long-term-care-coverage-465a6caf.

7. Beth Pinsker, "You Don't Have to Be Dead to Use Life Insurance. It Can Also Fund Long-Term Care," MarketWatch, May 28, 2024, https://www.marketwatch.com/story/you-dont-have-to-be-dead-to-use-life-insurance-it-can-also-fund-long-term-care-2a6b63db.

8. "2023 Life Insurance Fact Sheet," LIMRA, https://www.limra.com/siteassets/newsroom/liam/2023/0859-2023-liam-fact-sheet-2023_final.pdf.

9. Beth Pinsker, "Should I Sign Up for Long-Term-Care Insurance Through Work?," MarketWatch, September 18, 2023, https://www.marketwatch.com/story/should-i-sign-up-for-a-hybrid-life-insurance-and-long-term-care-policy-through-work-4d5af466.

Chapter 19

1. "NHPCO Facts and Figures: 2023 Edition," National Hospice and Palliative Care Organization, December 2023, https://www.nhpco.org/wp-content/uploads/NHPCO-Facts-Figures-2023.pdf.

2. Pamela Harris et al., "Can Hospices Predict Which Patients Will Die Within Six Months?," *Journal of Palliative Medicine* 17, no. 8 (August 2014): 894–98, https://pmc.ncbi.nlm.nih.gov/articles/PMC4118712.

3. Austin Godfrey, "What Is Hospice?," Hospice Foundation of America, September 24, 2024, https://hospicefoundation.org/Hospice-Care/Hospice-Services.

Chapter 20

1. Beth Pinsker, "I Took Over My Mom's Finances and Now I'm Worried I'm Screwing Things Up," MarketWatch, May 10, 2023, https://www.marketwatch.com/story/my-mothers-day-money-confession-im-worried-im-screwing-up-my-moms-finances-df397cca.

2. Beth Pinsker, "My Mom Has $550,000 and Dementia, and I'm Worried What Happens When Her Money Runs Out," MarketWatch, October 5, 2023, https://www

.marketwatch.com/story/my-mom-has-550-000-and-dementia-and-im-worried
-what-happens-when-her-money-runs-out-bef37ec1.

3. Susan L. Hirshman, *Does This Make My Assets Look Fat?: A Woman's Guide to Finding Financial Empowerment and Success* (St. Martin's Press, 2013).

4. Chad Holmes, *The Inheritance Playbook: Helping Your Parents Pass the Torch, Not the Tax* (Chad Holmes, 2023).

5. "2022 Survey of Consumer Finances (SCF)," Board of Governors of the Federal Reserve System, 2023, https://www.federalreserve.gov/econres/scfindex.htm.

6. Cameron Huddleston, *Mom and Dad, We Need to Talk: How to Have Essential Conversations with Your Parents About Their Finances* (John Wiley & Sons, 2019).

7. Beth Pinsker, "Reverse Mortgages Can Offer Senior Homeowners a Financial Lifeline with Both Stocks and Bonds Sinking," MarketWatch, September 30, 2022, https://www.marketwatch.com/story/reverse-mortgages-are-mostly-misunderstood
-they-can-offer-seniors-a-lifeline-as-markets-sink-11664544715.

8. "Reverse Mortgages: A Discussion Guide," Consumer Financial Protection Bureau, August 2021, https://files.consumerfinance.gov/f/documents/cfpb_reverse
-mortgage-discussion-guide.pdf.

9. Pam Krueger and Les Abromovitz, *The MoneyTrack Method: The Real Person's Guide to Successful Investing* (John Wiley & Sons, 2008).

10. "Savings Distribution Calculator," KJE Computer Solutions, https://www.dinkytown
.net/java/savings-distribution-calculator.html.

Chapter 21

1. "Retirement Topics—Required Minimum Distributions (RMDs)," Internal Revenue Service, last revised December 10, 2024, https://www.irs.gov/retirement-plans/plan
-participant-employee/retirement-topics-required-minimum-distributions-rmds.

2. John Waggoner, "Estimate Your RMD Using Our Required Minimum Distribution Calculator," AARP, October 16, 2024, https://www.aarp.org/retirement/required
-minimum-distribution-calculator.

3. Beth Pinsker, "The Days of IRS Forgiveness for RMD Mistakes May Soon Be Over," MarketWatch, January 13, 2023, https://www.marketwatch.com/story/did-you
-forget-to-take-your-rmd-you-can-beg-forgivenessbut-maybe-not-for-much
-longer-11673564219.

4. Beth Pinsker, "Back-to-School Financial Lessons for Teachers," Reuters, September 6, 2018, https://www.reuters.com/article/business/back-to-school-financial-lessons
-for-teachers-idUSKCN1LM1B9.

Chapter 22

1. "Family and Medical Leave (FMLA)," U.S. Department of Labor, https://www.dol
.gov/general/topic/benefits-leave/fmla.

2. Beth Pinsker, "I Thought My Mom Had Done All the Right Estate Planning Before She Died, but I Missed Some Important Things," MarketWatch, July 25, 2023, https://

www.marketwatch.com/story/i-thought-my-mom-had-done-all-the-right-estate
-planning-before-she-died-but-i-missed-some-important-things-90970501.

3. Beth Pinsker, "My Father Is Leaving Me and My Brother $20,000 'Hidden' Checks to Find After He Dies. Is This a Good Idea? Will We Owe Taxes?," MarketWatch, April 9, 2024, https://www.marketwatch.com/story/my-father-is-leaving-me-and-my -brother-20-000-hidden-checks-to-find-after-he-dies-is-this-a-good-idea-will-we -owe-taxes-1376d0b6.

Chapter 23

1. Joan Didion, *The Year of Magical Thinking* (4th Estate, 2021).
2. Beth Pinsker, "What Should Be in Your 'Death' File," Reuters, August 4, 2014, https:// www.reuters.com/article/markets/wealth/what-should-be-in-your-death-file -idUSKBN0FK1RV.
3. "How Many Americans Have a Will?," Gallup, June 23, 2021, https://news.gallup .com/poll/351500/how-many-americans-have-will.aspx.
4. "Pet Industry Market Size, Trends & Pet Industry Statistics," American Pet Products Association, 2024, https://americanpetproducts.org/industry-trends-and-stats.
5. "Census Bureau Releases New Estimates on America's Families and Living Arrangements," United States Census Bureau, November 17, 2022, https://www .census.gov/newsroom/press-releases/2022/americas-families-and-living -arrangements.html.
6. Ben Sisario and Ryan Patrick Hooper, "Four Pages Found in a Couch Are Ruled Aretha Franklin's True Will," *New York Times,* July 11, 2023, https://www.nytimes .com/2023/07/11/arts/music/aretha-franklin-will-couch.html.
7. Jean-Pierre Aubry, Alicia H. Munnell, and Gal Wettstein, "Can Incentives Increase the Writing of Wills?," Center for Retirement Research at Boston College, April 23, 2024, https://crr.bc.edu/can-incentives-increase-the-writing-of-wills.
8. Gary Belsky and Thomas Gilovich, *Why Smart People Make Big Money Mistakes* (Simon & Schuster, 1999).
9. Beth Pinsker, "Dearly Beloved: Prince's Death Prompts Uptick in Wills," Reuters, May 19, 2016, https://www.reuters.com/article/markets/wealth/dearly-beloved -princes-death-prompts-uptick-in-wills-idUSKCN0YA2QD.

Chapter 24

1. "Charitable Remainder Trusts," Internal Revenue Service, August 26, 2024, https:// www.irs.gov/charities-non-profits/charitable-remainder-trusts.
2. Justin Miller, "Estate Tax Planning: Act Now, Before It's Too Late," *Independent Thinking* 43 (2021), https://evercorewealthandtrust.com/wp-content/uploads/2024/ 04/Independent-Thinking-Volume-43_Lo-Res.pdf.
3. Michael Ettinger, *Ettinger Law Firm's Guide to Protecting Your Future* (Independently published, October 2023).
4. Ruth Sara Lee, "Over My Dead Body: A New Approach to Testamentary Restraints

on Marriage," *Marquette Elder's Advisor* 14, no. 1 (Fall 2012): article 5, https://scholarship.law.marquette.edu/elders/vol14/iss1/5.

Chapter 25

1. Leanne Potts, "What to Do When a Loved One Dies," AARP, June 11, 2020, https://www.aarp.org/home-family/friends-family/info-2020/when-loved-one-dies-checklist.html.
2. "Standard Forward Mail & Change of Address," USPS, https://www.usps.com/manage/forward.htm.
3. "2023 NFDA General Price List Study Shows Inflation Increasing Faster than the Cost of a Funeral," National Funeral Directors Association, December 8, 2023, https://nfda.org/news/media-center/nfda-news-releases/id/8134/2023-nfda-general-price-list-study-shows-inflation-increasing-faster-than-the-cost-of-a-funeral.
4. Beth Pinsker, "Can Dementia Be Funny? How About Elder Scams? 'The Conners' Mines Difficult Aging Topics for Laughs," MarketWatch, April 17, 2024, https://www.marketwatch.com/story/the-conners-tries-to-find-the-funny-in-dementia-elder-scams-and-difficult-parents-9953ce2c.
5. Beth Pinsker, "Will You Be 'Cheated' Out of Your Last Social Security Check?," MarketWatch, August 31, 2023, https://www.marketwatch.com/story/will-you-be-cheated-out-of-your-last-social-security-check-136c8502.
6. "Social Security Benefits Are Not Paid for the Month of Death," Congressional Research Service, updated July 5, 2011, https://crsreports.congress.gov/product/pdf/RS/93-792.
7. "Form SSA-1724 | Claim for Amounts Due in the Case of Deceased Beneficiary," Social Security Administration, https://www.ssa.gov/forms/ssa-1724.html.

Chapter 26

1. "Final Expense Insurance Quotes Calculator," Choice Mutual, https://choicemutual.com/get-quote-now.
2. "Survivor's Benefits," Social Security Administration, January 2024, https://www.ssa.gov/pubs/EN-05-10084.pdf.
3. "2023 Life Insurance Fact Sheet," LIMRA, https://www.limra.com/siteassets/newsroom/liam/2023/0859-2023-liam-fact-sheet-2023_final.pdf.

Chapter 27

1. "The State of Probate in America," Trust & Will, 2024, https://trustandwill.com/documents/probate-study-2024.
2. Beth Pinsker, "My Mom Had a Trust, So Why Do We Still Need Probate to Settle Her Estate?," MarketWatch, August 16, 2023, https://www.marketwatch.com/story/my-mom-had-a-trust-so-why-do-we-still-need-to-go-probate-to-settle-her-estate-6c2bef9c.

3.   Warren Kozak, *Waving Goodbye: Life After Loss* (Post Hill Press, 2024), chap. 23.

4.   Lynnette Khalfani-Cox, *Zero Debt: The Ultimate Guide to Financial Freedom* (Advantage World Press, 2017).

5.   Lynnette Khalfani-Cox, *Bounce Back: The Ultimate Guide to Financial Resilience* (John Wiley & Sons), 2024.

6.   Daniel Kreps, "Prince Estate Battle Rages On as Judge Declines to Dismiss Lawsuit Against Heirs," *Rolling Stone,* July 6, 2024, https://www.rollingstone.com/music/music-news/prince-estate-lawsuit-heirs-llc-1235054438.

7.   John M. Goralka, "Tony Bennett's Daughters Share Thoughts on How to Prevent Inheritance Disputes," Kiplinger, December 30, 2024, https://www.kiplinger.com/retirement/tony-bennett-daughters-on-preventing-inheritance-disputes.

Chapter 28

1.   *The Summer I Turned Pretty,* Netflix, season 2, June 2022.

2.   "Topic no. 703, Basis of Assets," Internal Revenue Service, https://www.irs.gov/taxtopics/tc703.

Chapter 29

1.   George Carlin, *George Carlin: All My Stuff,* MPI Home Entertainment, September 2007.

2.   "How to Add a Legacy Contact for your Apple Account," Apple Support, 2004, https://support.apple.com/en-us/102631.

3.   "About Inactive Account Manager," Google Support, 2024, https://support.google.com/accounts/answer/3036546.

Chapter 30

1.   Susan Meyer, "Pet Adoption Statistics," The Zebra, updated July 10, 2024, https://www.thezebra.com/resources/research/pet-adoption-statistics.

2.   Beth Pinsker, "Your Money: How to Protect Your Prized Pet with a Trust," Reuters, December 13, 2016, https://www.reuters.com/article/us-money-retirement-pettrust/your-money-how-to-protect-your-prized-pet-with-a-trust-idUSKBN1422AV.

3.   Robert Schapiro, *Secrets from the Cockpit: Pilots Behaving Badly and Other Flying Stories* (Jonathan Ball, 2021).

4.   "Transfers of National Firearms Act Firearms in Decedents' Estates," Bureau of Alcohol, Tobacco and Firearms, September 5, 1999, https://www.atf.gov/file/97596/download.

5.   Behi66, "How to put bitcoin in your will, so your loved ones can inherit it?," R/bitcoin, Reddit, 2022, https://www.reddit.com/r/Bitcoin/comments/r244l3/how_to_put_bitcoin_in_your_will_so_your_loved.

Chapter 31

1. Sara Wollner (@sarawollner), "Confessions to Our Dead Mom," TikTok, November 3, 2023, https://www.tiktok.com/@sarawollner/video/7297349595846315310.
2. "Survivors, Executors, and Administrators," Publication 559, Internal Revenue Service, 2024, https://www.irs.gov/pub/irs-pdf/p559.pdf.
3. Beth Pinsker, "Doing My Mother's Final Tax Return Is the Hardest Financial Task I've Ever Had," MarketWatch, February 29, 2024, https://www.marketwatch.com/story/doing-my-mothers-last-tax-return-is-the-hardest-financial-task-ive-ever-had-61dc5b56.

Chapter 32

1. Jesse Bricker et al., "Wealth and Income Concentration in the SCF: 1989–2019," Board of Governors of the Federal Reserve System, September 28, 2020, https://doi.org/10.17016/2380-7172.2795.
2. Eric Reed, "What Is the Average Inheritance?," SmartAsset, June 29, 2023, https://smartasset.com/estate-planning/average-inheritance.
3. Melanie Wadell, "Ed Slott: Big Moves Clients Should Not Make Before Year-End," ThinkAdvisor, December 4, 2024, https://www.thinkadvisor.com/2024/12/04/ed-slott-big-moves-clients-should-not-make-before-year-end.
4. Beth Pinsker, "How to Invest Your Annual IRA Contribution: 3 Strategies for Your Last-Minute Tax Deduction," MarketWatch, March 26, 2023, https://www.marketwatch.com/story/how-to-invest-your-ira-contribution-3-strategies-to-fit-your-mind-set-in-a-turbulent-market-1ca62749.

Index

About the Author

Beth Pinsker is an award-winning journalist with more than thirty years of experience. She is a financial-planning columnist at MarketWatch and has been a CFP® professional since 2018. She won a SABEW Best in Business award in 2023 for commentary for a series of columns about caring for her mother that she turned into this book.

Previously, Pinsker was a personal finance columnist and editor at Reuters, where she was part of a team that won a 2018 Front Page award for Live Online Video from the Newswomen's Club of New York. She also was editor of Walletpop.com, a personal finance website owned by AOL. Pinsker spent the first part of her career as a film critic and entertainment business reporter, writing for many publications, such as *Entertainment Weekly, The Dallas Morning News, The Independent Film and Video Monthly, Variety,* and *The New York Times.* She had brief stints at *Who Wants to Be a Millionaire* and was an intern for *Late Night with David Letterman.* She has a B.A. in English from Harvard University. She is the mother of two humans and one dog and lives in Brooklyn.

You can get more of Pinsker's financial caregiving advice and ask questions on her website, bethpinsker.com, or follow her on social media.